The Low Countries

D1540393

Cover:
Still from *Antwerpen Centraal*,
a film by Peter Krüger.© Sophimages, 2011.

TLC

2012 The Low Countries

ARTS AND SOCIETY IN FLANDERS AND THE NETHERLANDS

Tenacious

Worldwide

Enchanting

Notable

Tempting

Yearbook

20

**Published by
the Flemish-Netherlands
Association**
Ons Erfdeel vzw

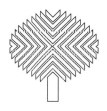

4

Contents

The Seriousness of Play

Chronicle

___

Next page:
Burst, Flanders, Belgium, 2000. Photo by Hans van der Meer.

'About suffering they were never wrong, / The Old Masters': so W.H. Auden writes of Bruegel's painting of the fall of Icarus in his poem Musée des Beaux Arts. The real suffering always happens in a remote corner of the image, of reality. Meanwhile life goes on, people do their thing. It's the same in this moving photo: a football match at the low level of some rural league, way out in the country. The invisible game continues. The goalkeeper watches and waits. The sheep just lie there indifferently, pensively. The local middle class plugs a brand of doors. A savings bank which disappeared long ago (having turned itself into a bank, then a big bank, an excessively big bank and finally a failed bank) blows its own trumpet. And outside the line, and thus no longer part of the game, non-existent as far as the other players are concerned – the felled player. What is he thinking about? What is wrong with him? Or is he shamming? Playing games? Taking a breather? How did the player come to be there? Is he a hit striker? A back? How long has he been lying there? Will he ever get up again?

It looks to be a winter morning. Sunday, probably. There are no spectators. Only us.

This is to tell you that the theme of this twentieth edition is sport and play. The national sports of the Netherlands (skating!) and Flanders (cycling!) are hymned in it. But also on parade are Belgium's racing pigeons, rated the best in the world, and the Dutch footballers who are constantly labelled as, if not the best, certainly the most attractive to watch. But we would also draw your attention to Huizinga's Homo Ludens, one of his most profound books, and to the Olympic Games which are to be held this summer in London.

As well as the themed pieces this volume offers the usual choice of essays on writers and artists past and present, on history that survives to the present day and society that has evolved from its past.

This yearbook marks a whole twenty years that we have been playing in the global competition of cultural areas that put themselves on the map and demand attention. The editors of this yearbook are concerned above all with information, presentation and opinion-forming. Because we believe that the Low Countries have a great deal to offer, to show and to say. Because we want to make contact with other people. Because we believe in exchanging ideas.

Hundreds of artists, thinkers, writers, social trends and phenomena of former times and today are represented in the columns of the twenty editions of this yearbook. Together, they provide an interesting sampler of that low-lying delta area in Western Europe which through its strategic situation, the density of its population, its economic strength and cultural brilliance has an unassailable place in the history and the present of European culture. In the past the Low Countries extended over an area that now forms part of four European states: Belgium, the Netherlands, France and Germany. Nowadays it is mainly taken to mean the area where Dutch is spoken: in other words the Netherlands and Flanders, part of the Belgian federation. This area's age-old relations with the rest of Europe and the world remains central to our thinking.

One final point: the editors have put together a selection of the finest and most idiosyncratic pieces from these twenty years, something like 'the best of', which you can find on our website www.onserfdeel.be / www.onserfdeel.nl. They speak for themselves.

11

LUC DEVOLDERE | Chief Editor

The Dutch Thaw Out When It Freezes

Skating as a National Sport

[MAX DOHLE]

The Dutch like to skate, and they do it a lot. When there is safe natural ice, on any weekend three million Dutch people will be out on it. Throughout the country there are artificial ice rinks and every village has one with natural ice. Skating is popular, and it's also part of the image of the Netherlands as a country of water, windmills, tulips and bicycles. How did this image come about and why is skating so popular in the Netherlands?

Skating on iron blades began in the 13th century in the Low Countries: Holland and Flanders. The oldest skates were discovered in Holland, the low-lying area on the west coast of the Netherlands. They date from 1225 and were found in Dordrecht. The oldest picture of a skater we find as a marginal illustration on the calendar page for February in a Flemish psalter of 1325, which is now in Oxford. In the Middle Ages skating was reserved for the upper class.

Skating only became a popular sport in the 17th century, the so-called Golden Age when Dutch commerce, art and science led the world. And in Flanders, during that century and later, skating was just as popular as it was in the Netherlands. On several of Pieter Brueghel's paintings we see expanses of ice, dotted with skaters and pall-mall players. When the Scheldt froze over, the river would be black with people on skates. But in Flanders skating's popularity has largely faded away. Skaters in Flanders need harder frosts than those in the Netherlands, since rivers take much longer to freeze over than stagnant water in canals.

Such hard frosts were common during the Little Ice Age, which lasted roughly from 1450 until 1850. In the Little Ice Age winters were significantly longer and more severe than they are now. The winter of 1740, in particular, was renowned: it had 13 weeks of severe frost. By our standards, winters were harsh indeed. People died from the cold or from starvation. And when the ice broke up after the frost, it would damage the dikes. But in spite of all these difficulties thousands of people would take to the ice. The Dutch thaw out when it freezes. Even the dourest Calvinist became a bon vivant. And the Catholics celebrated carnival on the ice. The ice regularly turned into a great fairground where almost everything that wasn't allowed on land was permitted: gambling, whoring and such heavy drinking that many a skater could no longer stand up.

Hendrick Avercamp,
Ice skating in a Village,
c. 1610. Oil on panel,
36 x 71 cm.
©Mauritshuis,
The Hague. Detail.

Fen skating

During the Little Ice Age the Thames too regularly froze over. There were `frost fairs' and people skated on the river. The Dutch brought skating to England at the end of the 17th century. The first to write about it was Samuel Pepys in 1662. `...*over to the Parke (where I first in my life, it being great frost, did see people sliding with their skeats which is a very pretty art)...*' Especially in the area of the Fens skating became just as popular as in Holland.

If you leave Cambridge on a fine summer's day and head downstream along the River Cam, just outside the city you will see a field with a few old, rusted street-lamps in it. Most Brits would wonder what its function was, but Dutch people will immediately recognize it as a skating rink deserted for the summer. In the second half of the Little Ice Age skating actually migrated from Holland to the Fens, a former marshy delta that was drained by the Dutchman Cornelis Vermuyden on the orders of King Charles I of England. To enable the draining to take place an extensive system of ditches (which the locals call dykes) and canals was constructed, creating unprecedented possibilities for skating. The Dutch workers had brought their skates to the Fens, so that when frost prevented them working they could enjoy the ice. Skating then became wildly popular in the Fens. In the second half of the 19th century Fen skating reached its peak. The fastest skaters in the world came from the Fens. The availability of long straight stretches of ice, as in Holland and the Fens, is one of the best explanations for the popularity of skating.

Holland mania

At the height of Fen-skating a curious movement began in the United States, sparked by the celebrations of the country's centenary. Quite a few Americans claimed that not England but the Dutch Republic was the mother of the U.S. Americans fondly called the Netherlands 'Holland', though Holland is only one part of the country. American artists traveled to Volendam, Edam and Zeeland to paint the last remnants of a bygone world. American tourists wanted to know where Hans Brinker had lived. They had to look hard to find the stereotypes. The pancakes, windmills, wooden shoes, skates and traditional costumes were mainly to be found in America itself: in children's books. Mary Mapes Dodge had written *Hans Brinker and the Silver Skates,* although she had never set foot in the Netherlands. Hans Brinker skated his way through the provinces of North and South Holland in search of a doctor who could treat his father. The beguiling story about the son of a Haarlem lockmaster who puts his finger in the dike to prevent a flooding disaster appeals to the imagination of the whole world, from Japan and Siberia to South Africa. Everybody has heard of Hans Brinker.

This period of American history has become known as 'Holland mania'. The Americans created this image of the Netherlands, and the Netherlands is still profiting from it. Every year hundreds of thousands of foreigners come looking for tulip fields, wooden shoes, windmills and quaint traditional dress. In a limited number of villages they can find exactly that. But many Dutch people find this image pathetic; the only aspect they can relate to is the skating. It is the national sport and we derive a part of our identity from it. As we do from our fight against the water.

Luctor et emergo: I struggle and emerge

The Netherlands very largely has itself to thank for this fight against the water . The Dutch dug holes in their peat deposits and cultivated them. An extensive system of ditches and canals became necessary, so the water could drain away. In order to keep its feet dry the Netherlands is regularly pumped out through these waterways, and at the same time we store enormous amounts of fresh water in lakes. However, the ground compacted, down to below the level of groundwater. Part of the Netherlands now lies below sea level: if the sea were left to its own devices many polders would flood in no time at all. That is why, besides the dunes, we have fourteen thousand kilometres of dike to protect us against the water of the sea and the big rivers.

The big rivers do not freeze over quickly, but ditches, canals, lakes and waterways are regularly covered with ice. On these frozen watercourses and reservoirs a Dutchman could skate a distance equal to several times around the world. Many historians see skating as the ultimate victory in the battle against the water. But is that true?

The problem with a scientific explanation like this is that it's not an answer you'd be likely to get if you asked a skater why he skates. So on a conscious level this argument doesn't hold good. As for what might be going on at a subconscious level, I gladly leave that to the experts. I personally have a problem with this theory. It doesn't appeal to me as a skater. And that goes for many skaters.

Elfstedentocht
(11 Town Tour)
passing through Sloten,
Friesland, 1985.
Photo by Vincent Mentzel.

Why do we skate?

The first answer to this question has already been implicitly given: we skate because we can. That's not only so in the Netherlands, but also in the Fens, as it was in London on the Thames in the 18th century. In Norway and Russia skating has also been very popular. In the first half of the last century the Norwegians always outclassed the Dutch on skates. But the problem in Scandinavia and Russia is that the ice is often covered with a thick layer of snow. In the Netherlands this is hardly ever the case: when we have ice in the winter, an east wind from Siberia brings a dry cold to the Netherlands. It seldom snows when it's freezing. And that's a necessary condition for skating long distances. The Dutch are crazy about long-distance skating. So geography and climate are ideal in the Netherlands. Still, our fight against the water, the resulting geography and the climate are not the reasons why we skate, but they do provide the conditions that make skating possible. The fight against the water is something most Dutch people are oblivious of. Like many other of the world's citizens we go to the office, the store, the factory, to earn a living and our knowledge of this daily `battle' is small. And it is actually fought in silence by the district water boards. With great reluctance the Dutch pay their yearly taxes to them and only 20% of the eligible voters turn out for their elections. And that while this is one of the oldest forms of democracy in Western Europe: district water boards have been around since the 12th century. Counts of Holland, townspeople and farmers were forced to fight the water together. For anything done to the water system could have big consequences for the neighbours. But though the fight against the water is still going on in the Netherlands, that's something you don't talk about. So it's not a conclusive answer to the question of why we skate.

The competition skater

In the cold winter of 1740, mentioned earlier, we find the first descriptions of skating competitions. The contestants competed on a straight track about 150 metres long and the one who crossed the finish line first went on to the next round. These contests were organized by innkeepers and were a great success, for they drew thousands of spectators. It was during this winter, too, that Frisian skaters tried to skate round all eleven Frisian cities in one day. As proof that they had done so, they asked the local innkeeper for his signature. Both traditions still exist. The modern competition skater skates laps on a 400-metre oval track. This oval is a Norwegian invention that allows the skater to take in curves. For it is there that he builds up speed.

Top skaters can make a lot of money. The first skating millionaire was Rintje Ritsma in the 1990s. Several American speed skaters have accepted sponsorship from Dutch companies. This does not mean that talented young skaters are intent on becoming rich through their sport. Nor is winning competitions a daily preoccupation. Research shows that along with social factors – the friendly contact with other skaters –their main motivation is the desire to improve their technique. Skating is after all a technically complicated sport, which you only really master after four seasons. `One day I want to skate a perfect curve,' a young skater said: a telling example of why he and his like are on the ice every day. Complete mastery of the technique, then, as far as that's ever possible in skating.

The recreational skater

Among recreational skaters you also find people who like to notch up as many kilometres as possible, biking in summer, skating in winter. Technically speaking, these are quite different sports. Skating is much more complicated than cycling, which is perhaps the reason why skaters cycle, but cyclists rarely take up skating. The high point of the season for the dedicated recreational skater is the Elfstedentocht, the 11 Town Tour mentioned earlier. A monster ride of 200 kilometres, only open to members. On this tour, which could be held only fifteen times during the last century, the skaters pass by all the Frisian cities. It is partly a competition and partly a non-competitive ride. Winners of the race are certainly the greatest sporting heroes of the Netherlands. Everyone knows the names and faces of the skaters who have won since the Second World War. The 16,000 non-competitive participants are also heroes for a day, cheered on by hundreds of thousands of onlookers along the route. Crown Prince Willem Alexander completed the tour in 1986. Because this somehow reduced the heroic status of the others, some of them still maintain that the prince skated only half the course. But if you have trained for it and can start early, you can certainly complete it in 15 hours. Even a prince.

Why does the recreational skater skate?

Most recreational skaters think that a distance of 30 kilometres is more than enough. When there are 8 centimetres of ice, tours are organized at many places in the country. They lead to places the skaters normally don't get to or can't get to otherwise. Beautiful, quiet pockets of nature where you only hear the swishing of your skates. All nature is hushed. The hoar-frost on the trees and bushes makes the Netherlands look like a Christmas card. Many skaters seek the silence, others the hustle and bustle. Although the Netherlands is already a fairly egalitarian society, all class differences vanish totally on the ice. The ice not only thaws out the Dutch, it also creates a sense of community. Making contact with others is never easier than when you're on skates. People are helpful and many skaters have found the love of their life on the ice. Not too long ago it was a gentleman's moral duty to `take on' a lady who was alone on the ice. It meant that the gentleman skated in front of the lady to keep her out of the wind. She would lay her right hand on one of the hands he had put on his back. They would skate a fair distance like that. Today the Dutch are no longer that gallant. And besides, nowadays the ladies are quite capable of managing by themselves on the ice.

Why do I skate?

In this article we have looked at the motivation for skating from different perspectives: spatial (the geographical possibility), economic (money), social (the atmosphere), natural (the hushed landscape). There remains the personal perspective, or rather the question: `why do I skate?'

I skate because it feels almost like flying. On skates there is only 1.1 millimetres of steel connecting you to the earth. You give a little push with your left leg and already the right skate has glided several metres across the smooth surface of the ice. Top skaters can reach a speed of 60 kilometres per hour, recreational ones about 30. Skating is a form of floating, it is flying without wings. Skating sets you free. ∎

Translated by Pleuke Boyce

Flanders Is Racing, Racing Is Flanders

Cycle Racing as a National Sport

[PATRICK CORNILLIE]

It was hardly more than thirty-five years ago, but what seems perfectly normal today was still a rarity back then. In the small village of Erpe-Mere, somewhere in East Flanders, an American appeared at the registration table for a junior cycle race. He was a lad of seventeen from Washoe Valley, Nevada. As soon as the starting pistol was fired, he moved to the head of the peloton. The spectators watched, amused, and shrugged: 'Ach, another foreigner who thinks he can race. And from the United States, too, where cycling means nothing at all to people...' But in the second lap the Yankee was still in the lead; at a later stage none of the other competitors could keep up with him and, after a solo of sixty kilometres, he won the race by six minutes. In the weeks that followed, the lad proved his skill in a succession of Flemish villages, with the same scenario each time.

The young American was extremely fast – that was a fact. All he now needed to do was refine his brute strength, hone his tactical skills, and familiarize himself with the traditions and culture of cycle racing. He learned fast. The next summer, as a junior, he became world champion, an achievement that he repeated as a professional – at the age of 22 and as the first non-European to do so. His name: Greg LeMond. In 1986 he was also the first non-European to win the Tour de France.

In the late 1970s and early 1980s LeMond was not the only American to leave family and friends behind, cross the ocean and throw himself into adventure. Australians and Canadians followed in his footsteps – and one or two cyclists from New Zealand and South Africa. They were Phil Anderson and Alan Peiper, Davis Phinney and Jonathan Boyer, Steve Bauer and Frankie Andreu, and they descended on host families in Flemish villages such as Marke, Nevele and Gullegem. Later, after the fall of the Berlin Wall, it was Russian, Lithuanian and Ukrainian riders who chose to make Flanders their second home. They had hardly any money, but they did have a bicycle. And a dream – a boy's dream of becoming a champion! They wanted to learn the ropes. And what better place to do that than Flanders, where there is always a race going on somewhere, and where there are good clubs, soigneurs and mechanics. When it comes to cycle racing, Flanders has a rich history, a great tradition.

Albéric 'Briek' Schotte.
Photo by Stephan
Vanfleteren.

Born in France

Among non-Europeans, Flanders is regarded as the birthplace of cycle racing. But that is not actually the case. Even in the invention and development of the bicycle – an essential part of the sport's history – the region played no part whatsoever. That history begins when the 'running machine' (or 'draisine') invented by the German Karl von Drais became a pedal cycle, with pedals on the front wheel, the brainchild of a Frenchman called Michaux. In the mid-19th century the bicycle became a very important status symbol. The first 'sporting demonstrations' took place in 1868 in Parisian parks, as an entertainment for 'le beau monde'.

Nor did Flanders play any part in the chapter in the bicycle's history in which, with the further development of spoked wheels, the heavy and uncomfortable Michaux-type cycles – which still had thick wooden spokes – were replaced by lighter bicycles. It was cycle builders from France (the true birthplace of the bicycle) and England (the country where, at the time, the industrial revolution was most advanced) which brought about this remarkable innovation. The same is true of the bicycle chain (invented by a Frenchman called Guimet and a Briton called Lawson), the inflatable tyre (invented by Dunlop, an Irishman), the easily removable tyre (developed by Michelin, a Frenchman) and, later, the first experiments with gear mechanisms (refined by Campagnolo, an Italian).

New inventions always generate competition, and this is no less true of the evolution of the bicycle. There were the first 'cycling competitions' with the Michaux, and from 1880 penny-farthing races over short distances were held, often amounting to recklessness. The taste for cycling as a sport blew over from England to Belgium, where it was a phenomenon found only in the cities. Between 1885 and 1890, the 'safety' – or low, safe bicycle – displaced the penny-farthing, and races in parks and along boulevards made way for long-distance races, which were feasible with the new low bicycles. Although the first *Liège-Bastogne-Liège* race was held in 1890, in its early days it was beset by confusion and it did not become an annual race for professionals until 1908. The same was true of the Paris-Brussels race. This first took place in 1893, but it was a whole thirteen years before the second such race was held.

France had progressed much further when it came to organising major cycle races. Before 1900, it was certainly the country where cycle racing enjoyed the greatest popularity. The newspapers saw cyclists as a source of revenue and challenged them to ever greater efforts over ever longer distances. In 1891 they came up with a race that was held every year until 1988, from Bordeaux to Paris: a distance of no less than 600 km. *Paris-Roubaix,* held for the first time in 1896, was initially 'only' a preparatory race for Bordeaux-Paris.

The Lion of Flanders

How far can a person go, how great is his endurance on a bicycle? In 1903, the newspaper *L'Auto* came up with the idea of sending a peloton of daredevils out onto the road for a genuine *Tour de France,* in six stages, over a distance of 2,428 km – a task that was considered impossible. Not only the press, but also the bicycle manufacturers bid strongly against each other. They wanted riders under contract to their companies and were willing to pay up to 3,000 French francs per month – more than a government minister's salary – for the top riders.

At this time, cycle racing still meant very little in Flanders, although a *Fédération Vélocipédique Belge* was founded in 1892, and in 1900 Emile de Beukelaer of Antwerp was elected the first president of the recently established *Union Cycliste Internationale* (UCI). But after a brief resurgence at the end of the 19th century, Belgian cycle racing appears to have slipped into a downward spiral. For a long time the bicycle remained a rich man's toy and, notably, the first Belgian cycling clubs were established mainly in the university cities.

The tide did not turn until after 1900. From a diversion for rich men's sons the bicycle gradually metamorphosed into the symbol of the lower classes' social mobility . At the same time it ceased to be an exclusively urban phenomenon. But this evolution was slow, and the bicycle was far from becoming generally popular. In Flanders, racing was often no more than a fairground attraction. For real cycle racing you had to go to France, where the major races were held and where there was money to be won. A certain Cyriel van Hauwaert, a simple country lad from Moorslede, understood this only too well. In 1906, from just over the border, he watched the finish of the *Paris-Roubaix* race, and saw the frenzied spectators and the hero worship. He wanted to take part in a race like this, no matter what it took. The following year, in spite of French protectionism and chauvinism, he made it to the starting line of the *Paris-Roubaix* race.

Eddy Merckx
Photo by Stephan Vanfleteren.

And promptly finished in second place. When two weeks later he did even better and actually won the *Bordeaux Paris* race, there was no stopping him.

The sport of cycle racing thus took root relatively late and slowly in 'poor Flanders', but as soon as the bicycle became affordable for the man in the street, it became the Flemings' top sport. Before long Flanders had more races and better practitioners of the sport than anywhere else. In that respect, 1907 was the year everything changed. Cyriel van Hauwaert was the first Fleming to win an international classic, an achievement that met with an enormous response. Moreover, the following year he added *Milan-San Remo* and *Paris-Roubaix* to his victories. The modest farm hand immediately found himself thousands of francs richer. This appealed to people's imagination, since the daily wage of a farm worker at that time was no more than 1 franc for 15 hours' hard work.

In France, Van Hauwaert was nicknamed 'the Lion of Flanders'. In his own region he became a role model for many others who hoped that the sport would help them, literally, to crawl out of the mud. At the beginning of the 20th century, there were few opportunities to do so. Young men were doomed to a life of 'hard labour' – unless they tried their luck as cyclists. They sought hero status on their metal steeds. A few made it straightaway. They left for the cycle tracks or the Tour de France and came back rich and famous.

The realization that it was possible to cycle one's way to a small fortune, and hence greater esteem, prompted many a factory hand and farm worker to reach for their bicycles. Following in the footsteps of Van Hauwaert, they went to take part in the major French and Italian races. And they were successful. In 1912, Odiel Defraye of Rumbeke won the first Belgian Tour. This was an enormous boost for the sport in Flanders. What was previously seen as a pastime soon became a professional occupation.

As a result the number of races increased just as quickly. In 1908, inspired by the 'Flemish Lion' Van Hauwaert, a Flemish Championship was held in Koolskamp. This, in turn, inspired an actual *Tour of Flanders,* established by Karel Van Wijnendaele and held for the first time in 1913. At this time, too, many cycle tracks were built. At one point there were more than 50 in use in Belgium. Well before the Second World War, therefore, track racing was very popular.

There is no conclusive scientific answer to the question of what cycle racing awakened in broad swathes of the Flemish population. But it appears clear that it had a powerful influence on thinking and lifestyles in those days. It was a new topic of conversation for the man in the street, it aroused people's curiosity and it encourged them to read. Karel Van Wijnendaele founded not only the Tour of Flanders but also *Sportwereld,* which between the wars was the top newspaper for sports fans. In his contributions Van Wijnendaele reinforced and glorified the feeling that racing cyclists are 'gods'. Not infrequently, he would paraphrase the 19th-century writer Hendrik Conscience and let fly with sentences along the lines of: 'If anyone should dare to speak disparagingly of Flanders, tell them of its cyclists, whose achievements leave the world speechless!' He made ordinary men into stars, and that appealed to ordinary people. Someone just like them, a boy from their village or area, became a sporting cyclist and part of a fairytale. On Mondays, when the sports results were published, and during the Tour de France in particular, *Sportwereld* sold like hot cakes – often as many as 120,000 copies per day, phenomenal figures for that time.

Bruno Risi.
Six-day race (Ghent).
Photo by
Stephan Vanfleteren.

A nation enraptured

Interest in a sport grows by grace of its stars, and since that celebrated year of 1907 there has never been any shortage of these in Flanders. Supporters look up to champions. This explains why, although skating is popular in the Netherlands and cross-country skiing in Norway, these disciplines will never be popular in Flanders. There isn't a single Fleming who has achieved anything of note in these sports. But cycle racing is a very different matter. Flanders may not – historically speaking – be 'the birthplace of cycle racing', but with its rapid succession of champions, its many races and enormous public interest, it has become *the* land of cycling.

With Philippe Thys (1913, 1914, 1920), Firmin Lambot (1919, 1922) and Leon Scieur (1921), initially it was the French-speaking Belgians who triumphed in the Tour de France, but thereafter West and East Flanders took command. Lucien Buysse won the Tour in 1926, Maurice De Waele in 1929, Romain Maes in 1935 and Sylvère Maes in 1936 and 1939. Georges Ronsse won the world title two years running (1928, 1929). Before the Second World War Karel Kaers, Jean Aerts, Eloi Meulenberg and Marcel Kint also won the rainbow jersey. They also excelled in the classic races, along with Jules Van Hevel, Gerard Debaets, René Vermandel and Gaston Rebry among others. On the track, too, Flanders has produced top cyclists: Jef Scherens sprinted to the world title every year from 1932 to 1937.

After the German invasion in May 1940, the sport recovered as quickly as it

Nico Verhoeven
(Roubaix). Photo by
Stephan Vanfleteren.

had been disrupted. Rarely has it attracted so many fans as during the Occupation. Cycle racing flourished as never before. Indoor and outdoor cycling tracks attracted mass audiences, thousands sprang to their feet at the spectacular sprints of Poeske Scherens. With the exception of the *Tour of Flanders*, there were no major classics, but all the more town-fair races and criteriums – often with potatoes, butter or bacon as prizes. De 'Witte' Van den Meerschaut, Staf Van Overloop, Georges Claes and Robert Van Eenaeme were the 'big names' in these races.

After the Liberation, when the international cycling calendar returned to normal, the sport remained extraordinarily popular. Although Flemish riders were no longer among the winners of the major races, the likes of Briek Schotte and Rik Van Steenbergen, and later Raymond Impanis, Fred De Bruyne, Germain Derycke and Rik Van Looy were successful in the one-day races. Alberic Schotte became world champion in 1948 in Valkenburg and again in 1950 in Moorslede. Rik Van Steenbergen was a dominant figure for almost 20 years, notching up 3 world titles, a whole series of classics, stages and track-cycling victories. Rik I was succeeded by Rik II (Rik van Looy), the 'Emperor of Herentals'. He won all the great classic races at least once, along with two world titles.

The late 1960s and the 1970s were the heyday of Belgian cycle racing. Walter Godefroot, Herman Vanspringel, Roger De Vlaeminck and Freddy Maertens were among the world leaders in the classics, and Lucien Van Impe shone in the Tour de France. At the same time Patrick Sercu became the undisputed king of the track. Erik de Vlaeminck rode to victory seven times in the world cyclo-cross championship. But the champion of this generation was of course Eddy Merckx, the finest road racer of all time. He became world

champion three times, won the *Tour de France* five times, the *Tour of Italy* five times and the *Tour of Spain* once, as well as a record number of classics: *Milan-San Remo* (7x), *Liège-Bastogne-Liège* (5x), *Paris-Roubaix* (3x), *Ghent-Wevelgem* (3x), *La Flèche Wallonne* (3x), the *Tour of Flanders* (2x), the *Tour of Lombardy* (2x) and the *Amstel Gold Race* (2x). In 1972 in Mexico he set a new world record for the hour with 49.431 km. Merckx's achievements held the whole nation entranced.

As far as successes are concerned, Flemish cycle racing had to yield quite some ground after the period of Merckx and Maertens. At the end of the 1990s Johan Museeuw was the only Fleming who could compete with top international cyclists in one-day races. But the supporters continued to enjoy the sport. The number of spectators for the Tour of Flanders and other spring races such as the *E3-Prijs Harelbeke* and *Ghent-Wevelgem* grew year after year. At the same time, cyclo-cross in particular enjoyed an enormous 'boom'. The level of public interest was phenomenal, and with Mario De Clercq, Erwin Vervecken, Bart Wellens and Sven Nys our country produced one world champion after another. Cyclo-cross is even more of a purely Flemish affair than road racing. In 2009 no fewer than 1.2 million Flemings watched the Belgian cyclo-cross championships on their public broadcasting channel. The Walloon channel *La Deux* attracted only 47,000 viewers. No other sport highlights the differences between Belgium's two communities as strongly as cyclo-cross.

Following in the tracks of cyclo-cross, since 2000 road racing has also enjoyed a renaissance. This has everything to do with the successes of Tom Boonen and, recently, Philippe Gilbert. Their popularity takes us back to the great days of Van Looy and Merckx. Boonen became the icon of a trendy generation and has attracted thousands of female supporters to the sport. Gilbert is currently the strongest one-day rider and the Flemish have taken him to their hearts, despite the fact that he is a Walloon. Cycling is still very popular. Politicians, businessmen and professors take to the saddle during weekends and holidays to compete against each other. They are only too keen to ride in the team vehicles during the *Tour de France*. The doggedness of the poor country boy who looked to racing to make a living and a future may have largely disappeared; the people's sport of times gone by may have become commercialised, doping may now be commonplace, but all this has done nothing to diminish the fascination: the sport's accessibility and epic character endure. In Flanders, cycle racing is and will remain a sport for all people from all walks of life. The riders aren't stars you watch from a distance in a stadium or across the width of a court. Cycle racing takes place in the streets. You can get up close to the cyclists, so to speak, even before the start, and ask for an autograph. And as a Fleming you have the advantage that even if the peloton doesn't go past your front door, at least it will regularly pass through your area. Moreover, cycle racing still represents the often lonely and always unequal struggle between the athlete and the elements: the rain and wind, dust and mud, cobbles and hills.

It is difficult to gauge what cycling means to social, socio-economic, sporting and cultural life in Flanders, but during the past century it has undeniably had a great influence on every sphere of existence. The major races have become red-letter days in the calendar, 'festivals' as it were. For a Fleming, the year begins on the day that the first race results are published in the newspapers, and spring is associated with the restless excitement that heralds the start of a new cycle-racing season – the 'resurrection' of the road racer – rather than with the awakening of nature. For a Fleming, Easter no longer means Easter, but the *Tour of Flanders* – it isn't called the 'High Mass of cycling' for nothing. Flanders is racing and racing is Flanders; it seems to have become a 'national religion', full of emotion and devotion, popular adoration and the annual 'pilgrimage' to the sacred places along the route.

Every rider dreams of being adorned with the title of 'Flandrien' in the 'Ronde'. He wants to be identified with the dogged, gruff, resilient worker and warrior from a distant, eroded past.

Time and again, every Fleming becomes passionately intoxicated by the images of Cancellara and Boonen juddering over the cobbles of the Steenbeekdries in the rain. He willingly surrenders to the bacchanal of sweat and snot and spattering mud, becomes intoxicated by the penetrating smell of oiled calves, the thundering mass of the peloton. The Tour of Flanders brings us close to delirium. An estimated 1.5 million people follow the race on television, and almost the same number line the route, cheering the riders on to the finish. This means at least one out of every two Flemings is gripped with cycling fever. Cycle racing remains a heroic activity, a sport that is tailor-made for the Flemings. ∎

Translated by Yvette Mead

Let's Play

Portfolio

[LUC DEVOLDERE]

How have painters captured play in paint? There is of course the inevitable Brueghel (c.1525-30 – 1569), who portrays dozens of children's games as one swirling round dance which leaves one wondering whether it is light-hearted or agitated.

Fernand Khnopff (1858-1921) does the opposite: tennis may have been an elegant pastime and a badge of distinction for the upper classes of the fin de siècle, but it does nothing to bring these women together. They remain isolated in their boredom.

Then the luminist Emile Claus (1849-1924) shows us a half-frozen boy on the ice in the warm winter light: here the play seems to be an innocent pleasure that has just ended. Jozef Israëls (1824-1911) does something different again: children gazing in fascination at a little sailing-boat floating in a pool on the beach. On the horizon a sailing-boat floats on the real sea. What is play? What is reality? But the play may be more real than it looks.

In his cockfight in Flanders Rémy Cogghe (1854-1935) bluntly confronts us with the passion of the spectator: bourgeois and working man are united around the arena where the duel to the death is taking place.

Gustave De Smet (1877-1945) portrays in angular outlines card and darts players, two very different forms of play which met in the Flemish café and decided to stay together. We have come a very long way now from the elegant pastime casually demonstrated by ladies and gentlemen in their fine interiors, as in the card-game set down by Eglon Hendrick van der Neer (1634?-1703) almost three centuries before.

Raoul De Keyser (1930) is fascinated by the lines that ritually separate the field of play from the outside world, and Carel Willink (1900-1983) tries to capture the essence of the young girl posing proudly with her ball: she is one with her game, which is just beginning.

Pieter Bruegel,
Children's Games, 1560.
Oil on oak panel,
118 x 161 cm.
Detail. Kunsthistorisches
Museum, Vienna.

Fernand Khnopff, *Memories (Lawn Tennis)*, 1889.
Pastel on paper marouflé on canvas, 127 x 200 cm.
Royal Museum of Fine Arts, Brussels.

Emile Claus, *Kingfishers (The Skaters)*, 1891.
Oil on canvas, 148 x 205 cm.
MSK Ghent © Lukas - Art in Flanders vzw.

Jozef Israëls, *Children of the Sea,* 1872. Oil on canvas,
48.5 x 93.5 cm. Rijksmuseum, Amsterdam.

Eglon Hendrick van der Neer,
An Interior with Ladies and Gentlemen at Cards, ca. 1665.
Oil on canvas, 65.9 x 73.4 cm. Ferens Art Gallery,
Hull Museums, UK. © The Bridgeman Art Library.

Rémy Cogghe,
Cock Fight in Flanders,
ca. 1889. Oil on canvas,
206 x 129 cm.
© Musée La Piscine,
Roubaix. Dist. RMN /
Alain Leprince.

Gustave De Smet, *The Café* (Vogelpik, Darts), *1925*.
Oil on canvas, 140 x 110 cm. Private collection, Ostend.

Raoul De Keyser, *Soccer Field*, 1971. Pencil, watercolour and acrylic on paper,
21 x 29.7 cm. MSK Ghent © Lukas - Art in Flanders vzw.

Carel Willink, *Girl with Ball*,
1925. Oil on unprepared
linen, 135 x 91 cm.
Museum voor Moderne
Kunst, Arnhem. ©
Mrs. Sylvia Willink.

The People's Bird

On Belgians and Their Pigeons

Pigeon!
Winged cloak of grey,
In the city's hellish maw,
One glance and you fly away,
Your grace holds me in awe.
Ben, in: Man Bites Dog, 1992
(C'est arrivé près de chez vous)

In 1878 Sylvain Wittouck, a town clerk in West Flanders, published a comprehensive handbook for pigeon fanciers complete with advice on hygiene and allopathic and homeopathic medications. Wittouck's intention was that this monograph should offer 'scientific knowledge' to everyone involved in pigeon racing. And it was aimed at a large readership. Whilst the success of dog and cock fights or song contests with 'blind finches' had drastically declined (partly because of new laws on the protection of animals), pigeon racing flourished as never before in the late nineteenth century. In 1878 it ought to have been clear, according to Wittouck, that the sport dedicated to these 'graceful air travellers' 'is no humbug but, on the contrary, a respectable game.' Furthermore, it was a game with a national flavour. After all, there was no other country where pigeon racing was as widespread as in Belgium.

The carriers are waiting

The fact that until recently there were programmes devoted to the pigeon fancy on both French- and Dutch-language public-service radio in Belgium should be an indication of the position it held in the national culture. The programmes in question always listed the places where pigeons were to be released. It was a virtual network of towns and villages, most of which any particular listener would never have visited: Arras, Bierset, Quiévrain, Elsenborn, Kleine Brogel or Le Touquet. The review included fashionable French seaside resorts, but also outlying villages in the Kempen and small Walloon industrial towns. Listeners were told what the temperature was in these places and which direction the wind was coming from there. They learned

whether visibility was good, moderate or bad and whether the carriers were waiting or not. These radio reports had an important place in pigeon fanciers' lives and the place-names referred to still play an important role in their collective memory. In the preface to a heritage book about pigeon racing published in 2006, Yves Leterme (Prime Minister of Belgium 2008-2011), who at the time was Minister-President of Flanders, remembers: 'Clermont, Jourdan, Arras, Quiévrain, Limoges, Bordeaux, and occasionally Barcelona - they were names that radiated heroism.'

In 2004 the Dutch-language 'Information for Pigeon Fanciers' was banished from Radio 1 to the medium wave. Soon afterwards they did away with it in French-speaking Belgium too. Until then the two programmes had been regular listening in the living rooms of thousands of families – like the shipping forecast, which had already been abolished. In Flanders, certainly, it had always been very static radio: a list read in a disciplined fashion by the same presenter for nearly thirty years. From the 1960s onwards the programme was unfailingly announced by the same signature tune, based on *I do so love my pigeon loft* (Ik zie zo gere mijn duivenkot) by Bobbejaan Schoepen. 'Information for Pigeon Fanciers' seemed changeless, and therefore a remnant of times gone by. That is probably why its disappearance provoked a feeling of unease in many people. A point of reference had disappeared. It was the radiophonic equivalent of the abolition of the Belgian franc or the bankruptcy of the national airline, Sabena.

Photo by Stephan Vanfleteren.

Photo by E. Bonte.

Not only the 'Information for Pigeon Fanciers', but also the actual practice of keeping pigeons has since become a subject of nostalgia. Since 1950 the number of pigeon fanciers in Belgium has steadily declined and nowadays it is mainly the preserve of older people. Probably because of this, pigeon racing features increasingly often in books devoted to times gone by or lost youth. Pigeon fanciers belong to a universe in which village policemen, poachers and café landlords figure. It is a nostalgic universe, often with a national flavour. In *My Belgium* (Mijn België, 2004), published on the occasion of the country's one hundred and seventy-fifth anniversary, Leen Huet says: 'Breeding pigeons is as much a part of the Belgian people's soul as the inclined plane of Ronquières and news reports about raised stop logs.' Dimitri Verhulst comes to a similar conclusion in *Tuesday Land. Sketches of Belgium* (Dinsdagland. Schetsen van België), which was published on the same national birthday. The opening story in the book is called 'Komkomkomkom' and is dedicated to a pigeon fancier. In an interview about the book Verhulst said: 'Maybe pigeon racing is an atavistic Belgian characteristic. After all, what do you do with a pigeon? You send it away but actually you want it to come back again as fast as possible. That is a typically Belgian thing to want.' Leterme would certainly *not* agree with this. Indeed, in the above-mentioned preface he stated categorically: 'Pigeon racing is Flemish. And therefore it is also popular.'

The field of associations that Leterme evokes differs from that of Huet and Verhulst. For the former Minister-President, pigeon racing is mainly important for creating communities. It is a 'popular sport that brings people together and which, along with so many other types of association and organisation, ensures that society stays together'. Here Leterme is repeating an old argument. As long ago as 1878 Sylvain Wittouck said that 'this splendid hobby brings all the classes and levels of society [...] together as brothers'. 'Yes,' he continued, 'apart from the enjoyment and benefit that it provides this hobby is also conducive to developing friendly relations.' Authors like

Huet and Verhulst, on the other hand, find the pigeon fancier appealing as a rather surrealistic character – an icon of a rather surrealistic country. For them pigeons returning from Quiévrain are as much part of Belgium as Holy Blood processions and cycle racing, or Captain Haddock, the Atomium, Belgian chip stalls and rustic farm-style houses.

A somewhat sadder variation of this same universe is the focus of *The Carriers Are Waiting (Les convoyeurs attendent)*, a Belgian film from 1999 with Benoît Poelvoorde in the leading role. In it the waiting carriers are a metaphor for 'bad weather' and the dead-end situations in which ordinary people endeavour to survive in the suburbs of post-industrial Walloon Charleroi. Here absurdity is combined with sadness. The pigeon breeder plays a secondary role in the film, along with majorettes and schoolmasters. The main character is a man who wants to get his son into the *Guinness Book of Records*. He can't think of anything better than to train the boy to open and close a door as often as possible in 24 hours. In this film, waiting for the carriers is the sad Belgian variant of waiting for Godot.

The atmosphere of *The Carriers are Waiting* is very different from the jubilant national pride that pigeon racing evoked in previous decades. In 1911 Wittouck argued: 'We can [...] state with pride, that Belgium, our dear fatherland, is the cradle of the science of pigeon keeping and that in addition to the well-deserved honour and fame, Belgium can also claim to be the father of it.' Wittouck was referring here to the fact that Belgians had been the first in the world to organise pigeon races. As early as 1806, pigeons were released in Paris that flew back to Liège, and in 1816 a flight from London to Antwerp was arranged. In the 1820s races were organised from Ghent and Brussels. Cities such as Verviers, Namur and Lier followed.

Initially, pigeon keeping was anything but a popular sport; it was a rather expensive hobby for the urban elite. Over time the sport became cheaper and around the middle of the nineteenth century workers increasingly became involved in it. The expansion of the railway network round 1840 was of crucial importance here, as in previous years pigeons had had to be transported by horse and cart or carried on the backs of walkers. Mineworkers, in particular, developed into passionate pigeon fanciers during this period. 'Managers of coal mines,' wrote Wittouck, 'know from experience that the best workers can be found amongst those who have pigeon binoculars in their homes.' At the end of the nineteenth century the hobby spread from the industrial centres to the countryside. In the same period the first pigeon magazines began to appear with the results of the races, advice on care and advertisements for 'pigeon elixirs'. In subsequent decades the number of pigeon fanciers continued to rise. In 1951 the Belgian Pigeon Association, the *Belgische Duivenbond*, had no fewer than 237,965 members.

Photo by E. Bonte.

Not only pigeon racing but the homing pigeon itself was a Belgian creation. According to many pigeon handbooks, the type of pigeon that is used worldwide for pigeon racing is a cross between the Antwerp breed (which is big and slender) and the Liège breed (which has a sturdier appearance and a short beak). So both the Walloon and the Flemish parts of the country can claim their place in the history of the origins of the homing pigeon. In 1975 the successful pigeon fancier and diplomat, Henry Landercy, warned against the dangers of 'the imagined superiority of the Walloon or the Flemish pigeon'. Pigeon racing has a Belgian soul. Furthermore, the homing pigeon became an important export product. Indeed the breed spread with the sport, first to Northern France, later to the Netherlands, England and Germany, and most recently to the Middle East, China and Taiwan. In these latter countries, especially, very high prices are paid for Belgian pigeons. When the renowned pigeon breeder Pros Roosen died in 2010, his pigeons were auctioned for a total of 1.38 million euros. 156,000 euros were paid out for his most sought-after pigeon, De Blauwe Prins (The Blue Prince). The buyers were Chinese.

The people and their feathered friends

In 1981 a major study was carried out into the sociological profile of the Belgian pigeon fancier. The results were hardly surprising. The majority of them, according to the study, were older, married men over fifty. They preferred to compete over 'medium distances', for example Orléans, and in 'speed' (or 'short distances', for example Quiévrain). The sport's geographical heart lay in Flanders, where around 80% of pigeon fanciers were active. They lived in the towns (51%) and urbanised municipalities (44%). The majority of them were working class (51%) or white-collar workers (18%).

The image of pigeon racing is that of a 'popular sport' pure and simple – an image that combines amazingly well with the idea that this hobby brings together *all* levels and classes. Or, as Jozef Henin put it in *To Become a Champion* (Om kampioen te worden, 1926): 'One finds pigeon fanciers at every level of society. From king to simple workman, you can find people fond of Venus's beloved bird everywhere; but the pigeon fancy is still the *popular sport par excellence.*'

Photo by E. Bonte.

In its capacity as a 'popular sport' pigeon racing is sung about by 'popular' singers, written about by 'popular' writers and performed in 'popular' theatre. We have already mentioned the song 'I do so love my pigeon loft', by the cowboy of the Kempen, Bobbejaan Schoepen – a number that made him one of the most popular artists in Flanders. Twenty-five years later the Antwerp *Strangers* had their own hit with '*Oh, my blue-bar*' ['Oh, mijne blauwe geschelpte',], adapted from 'Paloma Blanca' from the Dutch *George Baker Collection*. With this song about pigeon racing, the *Strangers* became part of a long Belgian (mainly Flemish) literary tradition. Pigeon fanciers had already featured in literary work by Jan van Rijswijck (*The Pigeon Fancier's Household*/ Het duivenmelkershuishouden, 1886), Pieter Geiregat (*Stories of the People*/ Volksverhalen, 1888), Leo Meert (*The Pigeon Fanciers*/De duivenmelkers, 1906) and Jef de Pillecijn (*The Champion*/De Kampioen, 1934. The 'people's poet' Guido Gezelle dealt with the subject in his poems: ('*Clap-clap-clap / my thirteen pigeons / beat their wings / one on top of the other*' / 'Klap-klap-klap / m'n dertien duiven / slaan hun vlerken, de eene op de aâr'). And from the middle of the nineteenth century pigeon breeders were very prominent in popular theatre too. In the 1850s Emmanuel Rosseels' *The Pigeon Fancier* (De duivenmelker) was performed over a thousand times in Antwerp. In Liege Henri Simons's *Li Bleû-Bîhe* (1886), played in Walloon dialect, was a great success and in Tournai Arthur Hespel's Picardian *Les Noces d'ein Coulonneux* (1912) was also greeted with acclaim. Pigeon fanciers turned up in popular dramas as well as in sitcoms and farces. There is no doubt that the unusually popular Flemish TV programme *FC De Kampioenen*, which not coincidentally has a pigeon fancier amongst its characters, is part of this latest tradition.

In popular literature pigeon fanciers are often not very nice figures. They neglect their families, spend their time gambling and in cafés, and brag and curse. In Rosseel's moralising play the ill-mannered main character is so caught up in pigeon racing that his young son dies of neglect. This makes the pigeon fancier repent and at the end of the play he promises to better his life ('Hurrah! After rain comes sunshine; all's well that ends well'). According to the literati, however, pigeon fanciers neglected more than their families. In *Before Flanders is Lost* (Eer Vlaanderen vergaat, 1927) the Flemish militant Jozef Simons links it, in particular, to the neglect of the Flemish cause. One of his characters claims dogmatically: 'Your average Fleming drinks and plays around with pigeons – the Flemish militant votes on motions. As long as the average Fleming can drink his Sunday pint in peace and win a prize in the race from Arras or Bordeaux, the Flemish militant will not get him near his stall'. According to Simons, Flemings were just *Lamme Goedzaks* – mild-mannered *bon-vivants* – and pigeon racing symbolised that cast of mind.

Even outside moralistic literature the image of the pigeon fancier is often negative. He poisons cats, forbids the neighbours to hang out their washing, complains about boys playing football and denies his wife her holiday every year. It is no different in Verhulst's *Tuesday Land*. The pigeon fancier is included, it is true, in a nostalgic 'declaration of love for the 'little' Belgian', but then principally as a favourite enemy. Verhulst: 'Our neighbour was a pigeon fancier, a *duivensjapper*, as they say, and that fact alone was sufficient reason to mount one vendetta after the other against him. *Duivensjappers* are troublesome people, they impose their will on the whole neighbourhood. [...] If we were playing in the garden when his pigeons had to dive into their loft, he was up like a shot, and all we got in return was that our backyard was always covered in pigeon shit. The result could only be war.' Finally, when the pigeons of the neighbour in question came back from Quiévrain, Dimitri's uncle Potrel shot down 'the whole damned lot'. That, too, is nostalgia.

Nostalgia of a very different kind overcomes politicians when they speak of pigeon racing. Yves Leterme is not the only one to consider himself a defender of the pigeon fancy. In 2004, when Belgian Railways decided they would no longer transport pigeons by rail to the places where they were to be released, several representatives of the people made a fuss in the Chamber. The Socialist Phillipe de Coene pointed out that the rail company's decision would mainly affect 'very ordinary people'. The Liberal Guido de Padt talked of a 'man-in-the-street' sport and 'an important social fabric' that was under threat. He added that 'transporting the pigeons by rail is really in our genes'. The Christian Democrat, Pieter De Crem, immediately suggested bringing in a 'pigeon cheque' to preserve the transport of pigeons by rail for posterity.

The abolition of the pigeon transports in the same year that the 'Information for Pigeon Fanciers' disappeared was the writing on the wall. In recent years it has been generally acknowledged that Belgian pigeon racing is in trouble. In the press there are articles about drug use and falling membership of the Belgian Pigeon Association. A recent poll of pigeon fanciers themselves indicates that there is considerable discontent amongst them too. Many apparently harbour a 'nostalgic longing for a past when pigeon racing still meant something'. Responses to the poll show a deep cultural pessimism. The pigeon breeders complain of the Association's 'profiteering mentality', the rising cost of their hobby, increasing regulation and interference by 'the greens'. There is an idea that there used to be more social contact in the pigeon fanciers' clubs years ago, whereas now everyone goes straight home. And there are references to the 'big money' that has destroyed much of the old ways.

Parallel to (and perhaps because of) this decline, pigeon racing is also being turned into heritage. Lavishly illustrated books sponsored by the heritage sector are being brought out, pigeon-racing clubhouses are being put on the architectural heritage list, and on heritage days attention is paid to 'the racehorse of the working classes'. Pigeon racing has become a subject of nostalgia. Dissatisfaction with the current situation has led to the past being cherished – a past in which pigeon racing was still said to be a real people's sport. ∎

Translated by Lindsay Edwards

Winning or Playing Nicely

Dilemmas in Dutch Football

Dutch footballers used not to need to be told they were the best, and, officially, they were not. The teams of Johan Cruyff, Ruud Gullit and Dennis Bergkamp never topped the world rankings, but were universally recognised as being magnificent.

Now, everything is reversed. Despite the embarrassingly violent "anti-football" played by less gifted Dutchmen at the last World Cup, the Netherlands stands at the very pinnacle of the world game.

In August 2011, when FIFA, the sport's governing body, issued its monthly rankings, a new name topped the list. The pragmatic new *Oranje*, were, for the very first time, statistically the supreme nation in the most important sport of all.

Oddly, the last few steps to the summit involved no physical exertion. Holland went top because their match against England was cancelled while Spain, previous top-dogs and reigning world champions, lost in Italy.

Celebrations in Amsterdam were, naturally, a little muted: you can't wave a FIFA computer printout to fans on a triumphal canal trip. Nevertheless, national coach Bert van Marwijk, architect of the triumph, was quietly satisfied. He said: "this team has learned to win no matter the circumstances, whether they feel motivated or not".

Indeed. His team had won every one of its World Cup and Euro qualifying matches over the last three years, and only lost in the dying minutes of the World Cup Final.

Historically speaking, this is an unprecedented achievement and Van Marwijk has wrought a cultural and psychological revolution. No previous national coach, not protean Rinus Michels, father of the Dutch style, nor brilliant Guus Hiddink or even legendary Louis van Gaal, can begin to match Van Marwijk's figures.

The FIFA rankings only began in 1993, but earlier generations of Dutch players would never have done so well.

Old Dutch teams were built around freewheeling, opinionated geniuses. Men like Cruyff, Van Hanegem, Van Basten, Rijkaard and Seedorf didn't make their orange shirts famous by winning trophies. (If you wanted that sort of thing you could follow Germany or Italy). Instead, the Dutch used football as a vehicle for artistry and moral superiority.

De Hoef, The Netherlands.
Photo by Hans
van der Meer.

In terms of trophy-winning, these 'total footballers' never missed an opportunity to miss an opportunity. They dazzled opponents with the skill and daring
of their clever attacking style, then suffered peculiar meltdowns in the biggest
matches. They practised unique forms of football democracy and teamwork,
yet were prone to bitter squabbling and destructive rivalries.

Van Marwijk has done away with all that. He is not particularly interested
in football as art and has instilled in his team a mentality closer to that of the
unloved but indomitable West Germans of the mid-1980s. The consequences
of this cultural change for the Dutch nation are not yet clear.

Total Football emerged under coach Rinus Michels and the young Johan
Cruyff at the Ajax club in Amsterdam in the late 1960s and early 70s and was
rooted in a unique and daring Netherlandish conception of how to use and
control space.

Over hundreds of years, the Dutch had developed clever ways of creating
and using their small spaces. This tradition was deeply embedded in everything from landscape painting to town planning, and now it found its way into
football too.

Other nations saw football differently. For the English, football was always
an energetic manly and martial contest, a series of duels all over the field
settled by strength, courage and hard work. The Brazilians valued individual
skill and creativity. Italians traditionally aimed to not lose: if you couldn't score
against them you'd never beat them.

Thanks to Michels and Cruyff, the Dutch came to see football more as physical chess, where the object was to manipulate and manage space. Technique

Oudega, The Netherlands.
Photo by Hans van der Meer.

was essential but position, passing, and movement off the ball were the most important arts. The key attributes were intelligence and speed of thought.

'Don't run around so much,' said Cruyff, 'football is a game you play with your brain'. The purpose of having supreme ball skills was not to perform tricks or go on mazy dribbles but to control and direct the flow of movement around the field. The most revered players were the ones like Cruyff and Bergkamp, who saw and understood space most profoundly.

The Dutch writer Arthur van den Boogaard argues that Cruyff discovered the 'metaphysical solution' to football. If you play his way to the max, using the best players, it's almost impossible to lose. Today's supreme Barcelona and Spain 'tiki-taka' teams seem to bear this out.

This is because the reigning world and European champions may be Spanish by passport and language, but they are Dutch by philosophy and history. Spain's team is mainly made up of Barcelona men, and Barca's philosophy, tactics and sensibilities were shaped by almost 40 years of Dutch influence, first under Rinus Michels, later because of Cruyff who played and coached there. 20 years ago Cruyff built Barcelona's 'dream team' and created the club's youth development system as a perfect copy of the one at Ajax. Later Dutch coaches Louis van Gaal and Frank Rijkaard continued this work. Current Barcelona coach Pep Guardiola is a Cruyff disciple. As he says: "Cruyff built our cathedral and we just maintain it".

But we are getting a little ahead of ourselves.
Before we can understand the current situation, we must return to the best and most important Dutch team of all, the majestic Michels/Cruyff'

total football' side of the 1974 World Cup. In that tournament the Dutch played the most graceful, intelligent and irresistible football ever seen, entranced fans everywhere and even took the lead in the first minute of the final against West Germany in Munich. And then ... disaster struck.

Instead of closing out the game as they should, the Dutch relaxed. As Brian Glanville, the great British football journalist writes, the Dutch took the lead against the Germans but were then 'moved to play cat and mouse with an opponent which, for historical reasons, they longed to humiliate. For twenty-five minutes the Dutch did as they pleased against a stunned German team, rolling the ball about, making pretty patterns, but creating no real opportunities.' The Germans recovered their nerve, fought back and won 2-1. The Netherlands was stunned. Many Dutch men remember July 7th 1974 as the first and only time they saw their fathers cry.

Even now, the Dutch have never quite recovered from this trauma and the Lost Final warped all future developments. Perhaps most damagingly of all, Cruyff justified the failure. He said that although the Dutch had lost the match they had won a great moral victory. As he put it: 'there is no greater medal than being recognised for your style'. Thus was established the justification for nearly four decades of romantic underachievement.

In fact, this founding moment of 'beautiful losing' was an accident, an aberration. The total footballers were tough and ruthless as well as beautiful and were accustomed to winning. After all, in the early 70s Dutch club teams Ajax and Feyenoord had won the European Cup four years in a row.

Two other near-misses followed over the next four years. In 1976 internal rivalries wrecked Holland's chances of winning the European championship. In 1978 they were unfortunate enough to face Argentina in Buenos Aires in the final of a World Cup manipulated by the host nation's fascist ruling junta. Nevertheless a pattern had been established.

In the decades which followed, the Dutch usually had the players to win pretty much every tournament they entered. But sticking both to their style and their excuses, they found it easier to lose. (Euro 1988 which they actually won is the exception which proves the rule).

Endlessly, unconsciously repeating the psychodrama of 1974 came somehow to be an expression of Dutchness. The Dutch strategy was: charm everyone with what Ruud Gullit called 'sexy football', then lose in tragic crazy circumstances.

These failures were invariably self-inflicted. Arrogant Dutch superstars squabbled over money, tactics or had 'artistic differences' with each other. Sometimes their best players refused to play. Alternatively, they collapsed psychologically when the going got tough or failed to take the opponents seriously. During the 1990s, *Oranje* developed the ridiculous habit of losing crucial matches on penalties, which they rarely bothered to practice. The team of such luminous talents as Dennis Bergkamp, Patrick Kluivert, Edgar Davids and the De Boer brothers which should have won both the '98 World Cup and Euro 2000 in fact won so few matches they were 22nd on the FIFA list in 1997.

'Taking the easy way out and being overly confident are classic Dutch traits,' said Van Marwijk recently, 'That was the first thing I had to battle against ... The opponent that this team needs to fear is itself.' Exactly right.

But there was at least one great advantage to all this neurosis: Holland's footballers were profoundly loved all over the world. Like Byron, Jimi Hendrix,

Kurt Cobain, Heath Ledger or Marilyn Monroe, the men in orange shirts were romantic heroes precisely because they were both beautiful and doomed never to fulfil their enormous potential.

The importance of all this for the Netherlands' international image and reputation can hardly be overstated.

Holland has a population of sixteen and a half million: roughly the same size as the average Chinese mega-city. The world profile of the Netherlands is commensurately tiny. Few ordinary folk around the globe know the names of Dutch artists, novelists, politicians, royal family members. From Guangdong to Guatemala, however, Dutch footballers are known and, until recently, adored.

Dutch footballers defined the nation to the outside world, and they've been important for the Netherlands' notion of itself too.

This is partly because football is now the biggest cultural form on the planet. Thanks to its strategic alliance with satellite TV, the game grows ever more powerful, eclipsing pop music and even Hollywood movies to be a kind of global language. The game of football cuts across barriers of language, religion, climate and culture and is followed with equal passion almost everywhere.

In few places, though, is it as important as in the Netherlands. The country has about a million registered players, roughly the same number as giant Germany whose population is five times bigger. Membership of a football club is an important part of the social fabric of many Dutch lives.

Professional club teams excite relatively minor devotions. But the national team provides a national sense of community and identity to replace crumbled old political and religious allegiances. The famous old 'pillars' of Dutch society have disappeared. But every two years the Netherlands gets together for a month-long orange festival, decorating their streets, painting their faces and staging a vast orange carnival in front of their TV screens as their team competes in world or European championships.

Just how important this ritual had become was illustrated by the curious crisis of late 2001, when the Dutch were suddenly overwhelmed by anxiety and populist politician Pim Fortuyn emerged, lurching Dutch politics to the right. None of the usual cultural or economic indicators quite explain the suddenness of this transformation – but Fortuyn's ascent began the same month the Dutch had shockingly lost to Ireland and failed to qualify for the 2002 World Cup: a genuine national trauma. As Sir Colin Budd, the highly-respected British ambassador in The Hague, reported to London: '[The Dutch] used to think they had a country where things worked ... In 2001 however they worried about the shortcomings of their railways/schools/hospitals; their failure to shrink their massive list of claimants for disability benefit; foot and mouth; growing public untidiness; the behaviour of immigrants; and - not least - the national football team's failure to qualify for the World Cup.'

In Fortuyn's wake (he was assassinated by an animal rights activist) Dutch football also began to shift towards conservativism. Cruyff, previously the nation's favourite guru, began to be viewed as out of touch. On TV and in his newspaper columns, he demanded fealty to the old ways, with 4-3-3 formations and wingers. Other coaches, however, were moving towards a more cautious, fearful pragmatic style.

A brief revival occurred at Euro 2008, when Holland, now coached by Cruyff's protégé, Marco van Basten, thrashed once-mighty Italy and France, before falling feebly to Russia. This, as the Financial Times columnist Simon Kuper argues, was a turning point: 'I think the KNVB [the Dutch football association] decided: 'this beautiful losing is just no fun anymore'.'

They turned to Van Marwijk, the steel-haired, unsentimental former Feyenoord man. Previously, national coaches were contractually obliged to play traditional attacking football. This was now quietly ditched. Winning had become the overriding objective, 4-5-1 the new preferred formation. Marwijk promptly raised morale and achieved an ever-lengthening sequence of wins, albeit against weak opponents. Only when his team arrived in South Africa for the World Cup proper did the world realise that something more fundamental had shifted.

The first clue was when Nike, the sportswear company with close ties to the Dutch players and the KNVB, aired a commercial on the eve of the tournament. Nike had picked up something others had missed: Van Marwijk's *oranje* was going to be different. The so-called 'Blood Orange' commercial features team captain Giovanni van Bronckhorst and others training with the inten-

sity of soldiers preparing for war. Drums beat in a military manner. As grim-visaged stars sweat and suffer, captions spell out a radically new philosophy: 'tears of joy are made of sweat'... 'destroy egos, starting with your own'. The Cruyff legacy is explicitly rejected: 'football isn't total without victory' and 'a beautiful defeat is still a defeat'. Old individualism, fun and artistry are out; discipline, loyalty and strength are in. The players embrace as comrades and march together down a corridor like reservoir dogs. The orange-clad masses exult. Short of seeing a three-engined plane in the clouds bearing a great leader, the message could hardly be more alarming.

The rest is now history. In South Africa, *Oranje* appeared to have undergone some kind of *Manchurian Candidate*-style personality-alteration. Holland

Marle, The Netherlands.
Photo by Hans van
der Meer.

deployed their famous footballing intelligence and understanding of space now to shut down games and do only what was necessary for victory. In the quarter final, Holland, displaying formidable willpower, came from behind to beat a technically superior Brazil. Only the semi-final against Uruguay seemed in keeping with the old spirit: Holland were more adventurous, took a 3-1 lead then almost collapsed at the end.

And then came the final against - of all people! - Spain.

Back in the 70s, admiring South Americans had dubbed the Dutch *La Naranja Mecanica,* The Clockwork Orange, like the Kubrick film. Now, faced with a side playing Dutch football, Holland resorted to genuine ultraviolence, cynically attempting to kick the Spanish into submission. At one point Spanish midfielder Xavi protested to his old friend and Barcelona team-mate Mark van Bommel (who happened to be Van Marwijk's son-in-law and was the Dutch team's principal destroyer). 'What the hell are you all doing?' said Xavi. Van Bommel gave him a cold stare, refused to answer and ran off.

A total of five Dutch players - and a couple of Spaniards - could or should have been sent off instead of just the one, Johnny Heitinga, who was. Holland played for penalties and defended in depth. Spain won with a late goal. The enduring image of the most widely seen TV event in history was of Dutch hatchet man Nigel de Jong apparently attempting to perform open heart surgery on Spaniard Xabi Alonso with a kung fu kick to the chest.

Van Marwijk, the coach obsessed by the idea of righting the wrong of 1974, had ended up presiding over the biggest PR disaster in Dutch history. The watching world was appalled. Cruyff denounced the Dutch tactics as 'anti-football'. Many Dutch fans were ashamed. A couple of journalists called for Van Marwijk to resign.

But many Dutch people were proud. Queen Beatrix, Prime Minister Balkenende and Royal Dutch Air Force F-16s painted orange joined 700,000 orange-clad fans in welcoming their heroes back to Amsterdam. At a time of political, cultural and economic uncertainty, Balkenende praised the team for demonstrating *eenheid* (unity). "They were a strong team, mentally and physically," he said. 'It was a disciplined collective with a mission, with full resilience, fighting spirit and confidence. Look how far that attitude brought us... *Oranje* was one, and the Netherlands stood as one behind *Oranje*.'

As total football had reflected and exemplified the spirit of its time (the freewheeling optimism of the 70s), so it was natural that Van Marwijk's hard-nosed approach reflected the straightened circumstances of a more uncertain and economically frightening era. But the supreme irony was that it didn't have to be this way.

The dichotomy between football beauty or ugliness, between winning or losing was historically false.

Total football had been originally created as a system for winning. Rinus Michels wanted his teams to dominate. Players like Johan Neeskens, Ruud Krol and Wim Suurbier played dirty when required. By the same token, modern stars such as Arjen Robben, Robin van Persie, Wesley Sneijder and Rafael van der Vaart are perfectly capable of playing the beautiful Dutch style almost as well as most of their predecessors.

The Dutch will be among the favourites for next year's Euro 2012 Championships in Poland and Ukraine. If Bert van Marwijk can finally find a way to integrate the two aspects of Dutch history – to win and play nicely - then perhaps he will be forgiven the horrors of Johannesburg 2010. Maybe he might even begin to exorcise the ghosts of the more distant past. ■

Man the Player

Huizinga's 'Homo Ludens' Revisited

In 1972, in a lecture at the big Huizinga congress in Groningen, Ernest Gombrich made the suggestion that Huizinga's biography of Erasmus was a form of self-criticism. 'Somehow the great humanist aroused in him all the ambivalent feelings that sprang from a life-long fight against the temptations of cultured aestheticism.' Gombrich's polite suggestion was to compare *The Praise of Folly* with *Homo ludens*, because one could discover a lot about Huizinga from the similarity between the two books.

Huizinga himself denied any possible identification with Erasmus. In 'My path to History', the autobiographical notes that he put down on paper at the start of the Second World War, he wrote: 'With regard to my biography of Erasmus, some people have thought: the writer has indeed put himself into this. Personally I have always rejected that opinion as completely incorrect. Great as is my admiration for Erasmus, my fellow-feeling is just as limited.' That does not prevent Erasmus playing the role of a witness in *Homo ludens*. 'Erasmus, how he radiates the spirit of play from his whole being!'

In his 1933 rectoral oration , 'On the limits of play and seriousness in culture', in which he reflected on the theme for the first time, Huizinga calls play 'a category that devours everything, just as Folly, once she had taken shape in Erasmus's mind, had to become the queen of the whole world.' And he returns to this comparison in *Homo ludens*. Here, too, he associates play with folly, in this case to specify that the concept is separate from the antithesis wisdom – folly. 'Nonetheless, the concept folly also had to serve to express a great divergence of sentiments. In the linguistic usage of the late Middle Ages the collocation *folie et sens* more or less covered the distinction between play and seriousness', 'until,' he added in the English translation, 'Erasmus in his *Laus Stultitiae* showed the inadequacy of the contrast.'

In his biography of Erasmus, too, Huizinga emphasises that *The Praise of Folly* embodies the passion for play to perfection. 'Anyone who tears off the masks from the game of life is thrown out. [...] Those who do not conform to what currently exists and demand that the game should no longer be a game do wrong.' Huizinga particularly admires the virtuosity with which Erasmus intertwined his two themes, 'that of salutary folly, which is the true wisdom, and that of deluded wisdom, which is pure folly. As both are proclaimed by Folly, one

Chess game on the roof of the
Groothandelsgebouw next to
Rotterdam Central Station, 2007.
Photo by Vincent Mentzel.

would have to invert them both to get to the truth, if Folly ... were not wisdom. It is clear that the first is the main theme. That is Erasmus's starting point and that is what he comes back to. Only in the middle section, the review of human skills and values in their general foolishness, does the second theme take the upper hand, and the work becomes an ordinary satire, like so many others, although few are as fine as this one. In the other sections *The Praise* is something much more profound than such a satire.'

Virtually the same can be said of *Homo ludens.* Here, too, there is the same dichotomy. As Huizinga sees it, Play has its antithesis at its core. It is even defined as a contrast, as non-seriousness. At the same time there is mention

Girl with games computer, 2001. Photo by Vincent Mentzel.

of 'far-reaching contamination of the spiritual values' of play and seriousness. Play and seriousness constantly turn into each other. Play loses its quality of independence and lack of inhibition and wants to pass for seriousness. At the same time one finds serious technical and economic activities involved in the realm of play. 'Play,' says Huizinga, 'is a category that devours everything, just as Folly, once she had taken shape in Erasmus's mind, had to become the queen of the whole world.'

Children, animals, primitive people and visionaries

It is this element of devouring that makes the two books, *The Praise of Folly* and *Homo ludens*, so comparable. Not only are the main principles of both books constructed around the paradoxical dichotomies of folly-wisdom and playfulness-seriousness, but in both books this leads to a division into three parts. Erasmus divides his book into description, criticism and wisdom; in other words, first the fact of the everyday practice that turns folly into wisdom and vice versa, then the satire on intellectuals and especially the church, and finally the higher folly that links religion and philosophy. In Huizinga's book it is the explanation of play as the border between seriousness and non-seriousness and the ability of archaic cultures to formalise it in sacred acts and festive contests. Then come the increasing complexity and seriousness of culture and the submersion of play in forms like the administration of justice, war, poetry, philosophy and art. And finally the total victory of seriousness, personified by Huizinga in the figure of the political philosopher Carl Schmitt. His redefinition of war as 'der Ernstfall' (Emergency) is, for Huizinga, the most horrifying example of what he now calls 'the demonic, enchanted shackles of play'.

Another, at least equally important, similarity is the fact that in both books the argument is not rational but associative, not historical but literary, that it rests not on causality or development but on metamorphosis. Folly refers to the transformation of foolishness into wisdom and back again literally as metamorphosis. 'Compare now, if you please, this generosity of mine with the metamorphoses that other gods bestow.' 'That is why I can never praise that one cockerel, Pythagoras, enough,' she says. 'After he had been everything all by himself: philosopher, man, woman, king, citizen, fish, horse, frog and I believe even sponge, he decided no creature was more disastrous than man, because all the rest are content with the limits nature sets, only man wants to exceed the limits of his lot.'

In *Homo ludens* we see the same metamorphoses occurring. In this book, and indeed elsewhere in Huizinga's work too, sensitivity to the ludic is reserved for a specific capacity that is peculiar to children and primitive peoples, poets and visionaries. Only those who can project themselves into play can understand what it is. In *Homo ludens*, for example, play goes hand in hand with poetry. 'If one interprets seriousness as that which can be reasonably expressed in terms of waking life, then poetry will never be completely serious. It stands on the far side of seriousness, on that original side where children, animals, primitive people and visionaries belong, in the realm of dreams, of ecstacy, intoxication and laughter.' The whole of *Homo ludens* seems aimed at eradicating the difference between children and adults. The child becomes one with its play, just as primitive man in his magic dance *is* the kangaroo . 'It is a mystical identity. The one has become the other.' It is the realm of the sacred game, where children and poets are at home, along with the primitive folk.'

A third similarity is the particular importance attached to Plato in both books. Not only does Erasmus model his differentiation of the two sorts of folly on Plato's differentiation between the two sorts of love but, more importantly, in several places he uses the myth of the cave, the difference between the changeable world on the one hand and the enduring realm of the true and the beautiful on the other. Eventually this leads to the identification of Platonism with Christianity, to a rejection of material reality and a 'soaring upwards to the eternal, the invisible, the spiritual reality.'

Plato fulfils the same function in *Homo ludens*. With Plato's help Huizinga elevates play to a sacred act, reversing the economy of play and seriousness in exactly the same way Erasmus does. It is not war that is serious – that is more of a folly – but ordinary everyday life, and one should take it seriously through playing because that is what God wanted. God has created man as a toy, his play is our seriousness, our seriousness his play. 'If play, then, is the most serious thing,' says Huizinga at the end of his book, and he quotes Plato, '"then people must spend their lives playing certain games, making sacrifices, singing and dancing, to gain the favour of the gods and win the battle." In this way "they will live life according to their nature, because in most respects they are puppets, but share a small part of the truth".'

Perhaps the most important overlap between *The Praise of Folly* and *Homo ludens* concerns the function of the rules of the game. Both Erasmus and Huizinga want to make it clear that those who break the rules spoil more than a game. Either you join in the game or you politely allow yourself to be deceived. 'Is that then not proof of folly?' Stultitia asks herself. 'I shall not deny that,' is her answer. Provided that one acknowledges 'that that happens to be the way the comedy of life is played.' In Huizinga's notion of play, too, the difference between belief and pretence is lost. He even goes as far as to distinguish between

Amusement park De Efteling,
Kaatsheuvel, 2007.
Photo by Vincent Mentzel.

cheating and being a spoilsport. The cheat still pretends to play the game. 'He maintains the pretence of recognising the magic circle of the game. Those involved in the game forgive his sin more easily than they do the spoilsport, because the latter shatters their very world.'

There is a difference between cheating and spoiling the game. And we can only see that difference if we reverse the relationship between play and seriousness. Again, the chief witness is Carl Schmitt, who was for a while Hitler's court theoretician. Schmitt based his political theory on the fundamental difference between friend and foe. War was just the ultimate consequence of that difference. Huizinga turned this reasoning around. It was not war that was serious – that was more like folly – but ordinary everyday life, and one should take it seriously by playing along, that is, by abiding by the rules of the game. Only in this way could one free oneself from the 'enchanted shackles' of play. It is not war that is the 'emergency situation' but peace; the point is not the game as such but the rules of the game, or rather the ethics of it.

It is with this particular point that modern criticism of the book has problems. Three of the best reactions to the *Homo ludens,* Gombrich's lecture, mentioned above, and essays written by George Steiner and Umberto Eco as prefaces to the English (1970) and Italian (1973) translations of the book respectively, agreed on one crucial point: Huizinga simply did not understand the concept of 'the rules of the game'. Whether one looks at it from the point of view of ethology like Gombrich, or the mathematics of play behaviour like Steiner, or structuralism like Eco did, their criticism came down to the same thing: that by seeking to use ethics to get away from play Huizinga remained even more in its thrall. They reproach Huizinga for having written about play but not about the rules of the game.

If he had done that, his critics believe, then he would have realised that what he, Huizinga, saw as spoiling the game, was clearly a subordinate part of the game's structure. The sensitive aesthete, says Eco – and here we hear an echo of Gombrich and many other Dutch critics – who was capable of grasping the moment of play in the cruelty of the Sphinx who sent those who failed the test to their deaths, was unable to see it also in the cruelty of the contemporary dictatorship that puts its dissidents to death. That means, writes Eco, that Huizinga has not really accepted the idea he puts forward: that as well as being serious play can also be terrible and tragic.

Order and keeping faith

It is striking that this criticism is clearly about morality. According to his critics, Huizinga invokes morality to say that the game is over. His critics look for the morality within the game itself. For it is exactly in those rules, exactly by freeing them of any specific content, that the moment lies in which culture keeps its forms in shape. It is exactly when one is free of the content that one can recognise, play and finish the game as a game. 'And therefore it is play,' concludes Eco, 'that is the moment of social wellbeing, the moment of greatest functionality, when society, if we may put it like that, lets the engine idle so as to clean the spark plugs, avoid flooding, let the cylinders warm up, allow the oil to circulate and to check everything. Play, then, is the moment of greatest and most responsible seriousness.'

Hula-Hoop, 2003.
Photo by Vincent Mentzel.

That is nicely put, and it is relevant in general terms, too. Huizinga often came surprisingly close to a number of structuralist notions, but in the end it was not the structure that interested him but man's behaviour. He did not write a book about play, but about man the player. However, Huizinga clearly tried to look for the moral criteria he was after in play itself. He begins, it is true, with what he calls 'the deep aesthetic quality of play', but he transforms it into an ethical one. Aesthetic qualities are rhythm and repetition, cadence and refrain, closed form and harmony, 'all of which are attributes of play,' he says, 'and they are also all constituents of style.' And then it comes, one of those wonderful associations on which Huizinga had the patent: 'What is called style in the aesthetic is called order and loyalty in the ethical.' When he evokes these criteria to characterise certain phenomena, such as spoiling the game, he stays within the limits of play, or at least of what he defines as play, which had chiefly formal characteristics.

With Huizinga, as with Eco, the difference lies not between playing and not playing but between playing and being played with. With Huizinga, however, it is not the 'matrix' that plays with us but God, not an anonymous structure but a last judgement, an ethical instance, whether we project it outside ourselves or carry it within us. God made toys of man, his game is our seriousness, our seriousness his game. That is how Huizinga tries to free himself from the 'enchanted shackles' of play. Huizinga clearly has a theory of play, i.e. a theory of decision. Just as he said to the ethologists that man could choose not to be a flesh-devouring animal, so he said to the structuralists that man could choose not to be a puppet with no will of its own.

But man must adapt. The balance that Huizinga sought between art and science and between aesthetics and ethics had to do with this, with the conviction that man must subordinate himself, must conform to the rules of a higher game. He did not turn his back on his time, he criticized his contemporaries. He thought they took themselves too seriously. 'Liberation lies not in the renunciation of culture but in the renunciation of the ego,' he said in 1915 when he accepted his professorship at Leiden. Culture is about rules, not about our own particular case, about keeping loyalty, not our own self-interest. ∎

Translated by Lindsay Edwards

The Podium for Holland,
The Plush Bench for Belgium

The Low Countries and the Olympic Games

Dutch Inge de Bruin wins
gold. Freestyle, 50m.
Athens, 2004.

The Netherlands is certain to win its hundredth gold medal at the London 2012 Olympics. Whether the Belgians will be able to celebrate winning gold medal number 43 remains to be seen, but that is not Belgium's core business: Belgium has the distinction of being the only country to have provided two presidents of the International Olympic Committee.

The Netherlands initially did better in the IOC membership competition, too. Baron Fritz van Tuijll van Serooskerken was the first IOC representative from the Low Countries, though he was not a member right from the start; this Dutch nobleman joined the International Olympic Committee in 1898, two years after its formation, to become the first Dutch IOC member. Baron Van Tuijll is still a great name in Dutch sporting history; in 1912 he founded a Dutch branch of the Olympic Movement and became its first president. However, it was not long before Belgium caught up. There were no Belgians among the 13 men – even today, women members are still few and far between – who made up the first International Olympic Committee in 1894, but thanks to the efforts of Count Henri de Baillet-Latour, who joined the IOC in 1903, the Olympic Movement became the key international point of reference for sport in the Catholic south.

The Belgian Olympic Committee was formed three years later – a year after Belgium, thanks to the efforts of King Leopold II, had played host to the prestigious Olympic Congress. In Belgium sport was the prerogative of the well-to-do classes– the aristocracy and the bourgeoisie – and was organised from the centre, namely Brussels. The Netherlands had a much smaller aristocracy, and virtually no bourgeoisie comparable to that in Belgium. Moreover, Baron Van Tuijll was a socially committed nobleman who devoted part of his fortune to good causes. Yet it still took some time before sport became accepted as a pastime in the Netherlands. Even today, physical exercise is regarded as a sinful activity in some strict Reformed circles.

Amsterdam 1928 more important than Antwerp 1920

Initially, Belgium was noticeably stronger than the Netherlands in the Olympic arena, at least in the first seven Games. Up to 1924 Belgium had won 72 medals, half of them at its own Games, held in Antwerp in 1920. This was another first for Belgium, which had been awarded the first post war Games in recognition of its heroic resistance during the First World War.

In the event, Antwerp 1920 proved to be a cesspool of corruption and nepotism, and badly organised to boot. And one way or another it ushered in the decline of Belgian sport, while by contrast it was in Antwerp that the Dutch discovered themselves and rapidly developed into a true sporting nation.

The Dutch had long campaigned for the Games to be brought to the Netherlands, but during the selection of the venue for the next Olympic Games Baron Pierre de Coubertin, the French founder of the International Olympic Committee, uttered the legendary words: 'I am going to die; give me one more Paris.' And so Paris became the venue for the 1924 Olympic Games; but with no trouble at all it was agreed that the other candidate, Amsterdam, would host the next Games four years later. And so it came to pass.

In contrast to Antwerp, where virtually nothing remains of the 1920 Games apart from a few walls in Beerschot AC's football stadium at Het Kiel, the site of the 1920 Games, the Olympic Stadium built by the Netherlands in the southern suburbs of Amsterdam was a monument which can still be visited today, albeit in much restored form.

Belgian Ulla Werbrouck wins gold. Judo (under 72 kg.). Atlanta, 1996.

A feature of the Amsterdam Games was the presence of Coca-Cola; the company had just become an Olympic sponsor and for the first – and last – time had drinks stalls in the stadium. These were also the first Games with no significant political riots, whereas at all previous Games some group or other had sought to take advantage of the Olympic stage to convey its message to the world.

Breakthrough for women's sport

There were many reasons why Amsterdam 1928 was symbolic, and more important than Antwerp 1920. Not only was the Olympic flame lit for the first time – by an employee of the gas company – but the parade of competing nations was also led for the first time by Greece, the country where the Games had begun. The host country brought up the rear of the parade, thereby establishing two traditions which persist to this day. The closing ceremony took place on a Sunday, to the frustration of the Dutch Reformed Political Party (Staatkundig Gereformeerde Partij). The best-known athlete was Johnny Weissmuller, who later achieved world cinematic fame as Tarzan. Weissmuller won two swimming gold medals. The Finn Paavo Nurmi won his ninth gold medal in the 10,000 metres.

Germany took part in the Games for the first time since the First World War, with a team of no fewer than 223 competitors who between them won 31 medals. A total of 46 countries took part, but the number of competitors was less than in Paris in 1924.

Despite protests, women's athletics and gymnastics were on the programme for the first time. The Pole Halina Konopacka became the first female Olympic athletics champion. After the women's 800 metres several of the participants collapsed from total exhaustion. This prompted a heated debate within the IOC about women's events in the Olympic Games. The new president of the IOC, the extremely conservative Belgian Count Henri de Baillet-Latour, argued that women should only be allowed to take part in gymnastics, swimming, tennis and skating events, but in fact only the 800 metres was scrapped. Not until the 1960 Games would women again be allowed to compete over distances longer than 200 metres.

In Amsterdam the Netherlands had discovered sport, and especially women's sport. Belgium was left standing. In six successive Olympic Games, Belgium won 33 medals and the Netherlands 47. Followed by a big fat zero for Melbourne 1956, because the Netherlands had had the courage to ban all its athletes from taking part in protest against the Russian seizing of Budapest earlier that year.

The tallest younger generation in the world

It is well-known today, but it was apparent as long ago as 1937 that the Netherlands was a nation of swimmers, thanks to its robust, strong women competitors. In 1937 half the 26 world records were held by Dutch swimmers. A year earlier, Dutch women won four of the five medals that were up for grabs at the Berlin Games.

Dutch women's hockey team wins gold with a 2-0 win over China. Beijing, 2008.

Ma Braun and her daughter Marie (known as Zus Braun) (from 1928) and Willy den Ouden and Rie Mastenbroek from the mid-1930s are household names in Dutch sport. The latter pair were part of the Dutch relay team who beat the - already rather detested and feared - Germans at the Berlin Olympics in 1936.

If the Netherlands is better at sport than Belgium – and Olympic medals are the ideal benchmark for measuring this – then as well as organisational and motivational factors, there is also a physical reason for it. The Dutch have always been tall, and after World War II they simply continued to grow. Today, the native Dutch younger generation are the tallest in the world.

Being tall has almost always been a decisive factor in sport, except in sports where centrifugal force plays a part, such as short-track skating or gymnastics. Oddly enough, though, the Dutch system has recently been producing some excellent performers in this latter sport, too.

Up to and including the recent Winter Games in Vancouver, the Netherlands has won a grand total of 98 gold medals. Belgium has stood on the central podium 42 times. We should not delude ourselves that this is all about the Winter Games, in which the Netherlands, as a well-known skating nation, naturally performs well. Leaving aside the Winter Games, the gold medal ranking is still 73-42 in favour of the Netherlands, and 254-154 for medals in total. It is also worth noting that half the Belgian medals were won in the period up to and including 1924.

Montreal 1976

There are two yardsticks for benchmarking modern and post-modern sport: the Olympic Games in Montreal in 1976 and the Seoul Games in 1988. Belgium did reasonably well in Montreal, with six medals, partly due to its strong athletics team. Two comparable countries – the Netherlands has a population

Belgian Tia Hellebaut
wins gold. High jump.
Beijing, 2008.

one and a half times as big as Belgium's, while Australia's is roughly twice the size – did no better. Each secured a place on the podium five times and, like Belgium, failed to win a single gold.

Australia decided to do something about it and began developing the Australian Institute of Sports, and with it an unequalled sporting model. At first sight the Netherlands did not take any specific action, but in reality Dutch society changed visibly in the 1960s and 70s. In no time at all this flat, dull country with its conservative, dour population was transformed into a sort of guideland which sought to show the way to itself and the rest of Europe. Secularisation was just one aspect of this process, but it did lay the foundations for a leisure-time culture within which sport came to play an ever-increasing role.

And what of Belgium? Belgium was too busy splitting up its sporting apparatus which, since it was part of the cultural system, had become a regional matter as a result of the first major state reform. That conflicted with the central authority of the Belgian Olympic and Interfederal Committee, where a monolingual (Francophone) colonel ruled with an iron hand and a Francophone Brussels fixer carved a path for himself to the plush benches of the International Olympic Committee.

Jacques Rogge, President of
the International Olympic
Committee (IOC).

Belgium lost its way after Montreal 1976, despite a number of fantastic private projects initiated by passionately committed athletes such as the judoka Robert Vandewalle. It was striking that the Netherlands was able to profit from the Eastern Bloc's boycott of Los Angeles and win 13 medals there, whereas Belgium had to make do with four.

After 1976, the Netherlands won gold on no fewer than 29 occasions; Belgium managed five. The biggest difference was in Sydney in 2000, when the Netherlands won 12 golds out of a total haul of 25 medals. For half its medal tally to be gold was out of proportion in qualitative terms, but it did demonstrate how the Netherlands had evolved from a reserved sporting country to a sporting nation which regarded winning as normal. At that time, there was as yet no established Dutch sporting model. Pieter van den Hoogenband and Inge de Bruijn (swimming), Anky van Grunsven (dressage) and Leontien van Moorsel (cycling) all owed their victories to private projects sponsored by trainers, athletes and parents who saw the sky as the limit.

Four years earlier, when the Netherlands had produced its sporting performance of the century by winning gold in volleyball, Belgium had also scored, though not in the Olympic arena. In the mid-1990s Belgium had seven members on the IOC; the Netherlands had just one, the former judo gold med-allist Anton Geesink. In 1996 the Dutch Hein Verbruggen also became an IOC member, as did Crown Prince Willem-Alexander in 1998.

In the dying years of the 20th century Belgium lost much of its Olympic ad-ministrative status, as one IOC member after another either stepped down or died; but Count Jacques Rogge, an ex-sailor, powered on to the highest level, becoming president of the IOC in Moscow on 16 July 2001, thanks in part to the personal support of the Dutch Crown Prince.

Prince Willem Alexander and Mark Tuitert (Skating gold medal, 1500m.). Vancouver, 2010.

With Rogge (2001-2013) and De Baillet-Latour (1925-1942), Belgium is the only country which can boast having produced two IOC presidents, and when Rogge steps down in 2013 a Belgian will have been at the pinnacle of the Olympic Movement for 30 of its 120 years. Partly because of this, the Nether-lands looks at its southern neighbours with admiration – 'you have to hand it to the Belgians; they're good at lobbying' – while the Belgians look at their north-ern neighbours just as admiringly – 'you have to hand it to the Dutch; they're good at sport'.

The current reality is more nuanced. Both nations have lost their places on the plush benches. For a time, the Netherlands had four IOC members in the persons of Geesink, Willem-Alexander, Verbruggen and International Hockey Federation president Els van Breda-Vriesman. The latter was not re-elected, Verbruggen resigned and Geesink died in 2010. That leaves the Crown Prince, who in reality is no more than a lame duck as regards his Olympic function.

Belgium, in particular, has lost much of its Olympic administrative status: Jacques Rogge will remain in post until 2013, but after London 2012 he will in reality be the outgoing president. Both the Netherlands and Belgium need new IOC members, but one thing must always be remembered: it is the IOC which co-opts new members, rather than them being selected by individual countries.

The power of numbers

Belgium is holding its own on the Olympian fields. What that means in reality is: hardly any medals since 1976. It is a precarious business, because in Beijing Belgium flirted for a long time with 'nul points'. London 2012 again promises to be a difficult Olympic Games for Belgium, given the dismal results of individual Belgian athletes at the European and World Championships during the latest Olympiad. Belgium has never performed worse than in the period between 2009 and 2011, and that is an indicator of its medal prospects at the forthcom-ing Olympic Games.

The sporting achievements of the Netherlands have also declined compared with ten years ago. Following the 25 medals collected at Sydney, the Neth-erlands set up a sporting model based on innovation and aimed at securing a permanent position among the top ten countries in Europe. The resources ploughed into elite sport increased by 60 percent in the space of ten years; the medal haul fell by 36 percent over the same period.

Belgium is a structural underperformer when it comes to sport, but for the Netherlands the current results would appear to be a reflection of the intrinsic level of its elite sport. The Netherlands is experiencing the power of numbers.

The geopolitical trend is clear: sporting success is consolidating around a few major power blocs. This trend has continued since the collapse of the Eastern Bloc in the late 1980s and early 1990s. The first relevant Olympic Games which are comparable with Beijing in this geo-sport perspective were the Atlanta games in 1996, when the three best-performing countries – the US, Russia and Germany – garnered 229 medals between them.

In Beijing, the top three countries – China, the US and Russia – ended the Games with an unprecedented 283 medals between them, 30 percent of the total number of medals awarded. The harvest of gold was almost hallucinatory: 110 out of a total of 302 gold medals. Number four in the medals table was Great Britain, the host country in 2012.

For a small country like the Netherlands (and an even smaller country like Belgium), the competition is becoming ever more fierce. The position of the Netherlands as the smallest major sporting nation is consequently under attack from all sides, and it is very debatable whether throwing even more money at it is the solution, not least because any such action would be socially irresponsible.

Belgium has expressed its ambition of one day winning ten medals at the Olympic Games. The Netherlands is not satisfied with such a target; the former guide-land would so much like to become the Australia of the northern hemisphere. Against that backdrop, great efforts are being invested in an attempt to bring the Olympic Games to the Netherlands in 2028. The last time Brussels had that ambition was when Tokyo was selected for the 1964 Games. Since then the Belgians have learned better, partly because they are much more familiar with the Olympian corridors of power. The Dutch have no such inhibitions: they dream of the Games, just as they dreamed of World Cup glory and of securing a place among the top ten sporting nations. Dreaming is not forbidden. Sometimes the journey towards an unattainable goal is just as rewarding as actually attaining it. ■

Translated by Julian Ross

Fanny Blankers-Koen (The Flying Dutchmam) wins gold on 100 m, 200 m, 80 m hurdles and 4 x 100 m relay. London, 1948. She was 30 at the time and mother of two children.

'Writing Poetry's Cycling Up Mont Ventoux'

Ten Poems on Sport

Cycle 'Boxers'
Armando

neil got a glass jaw, has he?

well nail him right in the throat
cut his fucking breath off

, a feint one or two little jabs
I come from the left he comes from the right
I go inside I catch him
down he goes on his arse for three grand,

isays: undo my gloves. water.
esays: control yourself.
isays: undo my gloves. water.
esays: control yourself.
isays: take your fucking self-control and
                              stuff it. water.]

Cyclus 'Boksers'

heeft nelis een glazen kin?

priem hem precies op z'n strot
godverdomme geen asem meer

, een schijnstootje een paar plaagstootjes
ik kom van links hij komt van rechts
ik ga binnendoor ik pak'm,
hij gaat op z'n kont voor 3 rojen,

zeg: maak m'n handschoenen los. water.
zegt: toon zelfbeheersing.
zeg: maak m'n handschoenen los. water
zegt: toon zelfbeheersing.
zeg: krijg de kelere-kanker met je zelfbeheersing. water.

Cyclus 'Boksers' from *Verzamelde gedichten*,
De Bezige Bij, Amsterdam, 1999.

Arrival of the 100 meter, Racing Club of Brussels, 1933.
Photo by Germaine Van Parys

Anti-Freezeland

Driek van Wissen

In Holland when winter is all about
and we shiver in hibernation,
Friesland, we find, has a huge population
of freaks who in wintertime really freak out.

Taut, tanned, dumb faces no longer pout,
but suddenly show more relaxation
while their macho chops with animation
produce what is a smile, no doubt.

Impenetrable conversation
spreads rumours all round and about,
and wakens vain anticipation,

till the gods, by putting the ice to rout,
thwart the poor dumbos' expectation.
This year's twelve-town skatathon's up the
spout!]

Anti-Fries

Als Holland winters is getooid
en wij van kou welhaast verrekken,
blijkt Friesland dichtbevolkt met gekken,
die 's winters gekker zijn dan ooit.

De maffe koppen, strak gelooid,
ontspannen plots in losser trekken,
terwijl zich rond de stuurse bekken
een soortement van glimlach plooit.

In onverstaanbare gesprekken
worden dan praatjes rondgestrooid,
die ijdele verwachting wekken,

totdat de goden, als het dooit,
de hoop der dwaze halzen nekken
Nee, de elfstedentocht komt nooit!

Driek van Wissen, *De badman heeft gelijk*, Bert Bakker,
Amsterdam, 1982.

World Champions

Nico Scheepmaker

Hockey's a game in which sticks are used
and everyone watching is bored and bemused –
that fact is, I think, abundantly clear,
although It's hard to accept the idea.

We don't want to know, because it's a sport
that not only has games that are far too short, but
has fans that are now few and far between: club
members and families, unnaturally keen.

Only when our women's eleven competes
– in skirts with quite amazingly short pleats –
and with the Krauts they contest the World Cup,
will the public at large support its own side
and gaze at the girls and go dreamy-eyed,
though their ball-handling skills at times trip
them up!]

Wereldkampioen

Dat hockey met een stokkie wordt gespeeld
en iedereen zich daarbij dood verveelt
is, dacht ik, nu wel algemeen bekend,
al is het een gedachte die nooit went.

Wij willen het niet weten, want zo'n sport
komt niet alleen in speelduur al te kort,
maar kampt ook met een uitgedund publiek
dat clublid is dan wel familieziek.

Alleen als onze meisjes moeten knokken
- in overigens verrassend korte rokken –
voor 't wereldkampioenschap met de mof,
is het publiek nog wel bereid te komen
om even bij die meisjes weg te dromen,
al nemen zij de bal nooit op hun slof!

Nico Scheepmaker, *De Gedichten*,
Bert Bakker, Amsterdam, 1991.

A football match

Roland Jooris

not the beautifully worked out
attack ending in a
sudden galvanising flash,
but the little boy on a
patch of grass behind
the spectators playing his
own game, the dog
among those nameless backs
snuffling around the waste
ground, the torn
trampled tickets in the
well-combed grass and above
the rock-hard winter sky: only
here and there the odd wing's flap, only
now and then a faint drone
drowned out
by the cheers.

Een voetbalwedstrijd

Niet die prachtig opgezette
aanval uitlopend op een
flitsend rechtverend moment,
doch het jongetje op een
stukje weide achter de
toeschouwers zijn eigen
wedstrijd spelend, de hond
tussen die naamloze ruggen
snuffelend langs de brakke
grond, de gescheurde
vertrappelde kaartjes in het
uitgekamde gras en daarboven
de keiharde winterlucht: slechts
hier en daar wat gewiek, slechts
nu en dan een zacht geronk
in het gejuich
verdwijnend.

Roland Jooris, *Gedichten 1958-1978*,
Lotus, Antwerp, 1978.

1974

Anna Enquist

A year like no other, orange flames
crackled unstoppably across the field, high
above the grass the bullet hit the net.

We too were winners, a daughter
with thighs like bread rolls squealed with joy
at being there, in our bed, for good.

Their defeat, those football soldiers, foes' fire
flying round their ears – meant nothing
to us, scarcely touched us, bypassed

our brain. How stupid, how cocky,
offhand we were. In that festive year
our severest loss was set in train.

1974

Een jaar als geen ander, oranje vlammen
knetterden onstuitbaar over het veld, hoog
boven het gras vloog de kogel het doel in.

Ook wij waren winnaars, een dochter
met dijen als broodjes gierde van vreugde
omdat ze er was, in ons bed, voorgoed.

Dat ze verloren, die voetbalsoldaten, vijandig
vuur om hun oren floot – het betekende
niets, het raakte ons nauwelijks, we hadden

gewoon niet opgelet. Hoe dom, overmoedig,
onachtzaam wij waren In dat feestelijke jaar
werd het scherpste verlies in gang gezet.

Anna Enquist, *Hard gras*, nr. 39,
L.J. Veen, Amsterdam, 2004.

Mont Ventoux

Jan Kal

Writing poetry's cycling up Mont Ventoux,
where once Tommy Simpson died ascending.
Exhausted, here he met his tragic ending:
the world number one lacked strength to
                             continue.]

Many since have set out, intending
to make the climb, first category, now taboo.
It smells of pine trees, Sunsilk Shampoo,
which you certainly need on descending.

Unspeakable weariness keeps churning;
climbing Mont Ventoux is a painful thrill,
so: think twice before you head up there.

Yet I make it, though the heat is burning,
to the top of this high denuded hill:
mere vanity, pursuit of empty air.

Mont Ventoux

Dichten is fietsen op de Mont Ventoux,
waar Tommy Simpson toen is overleden
Onder zo tragische omstandigheden
werd hier de wereldkampioen doodmoe.

Op deze col zijn velen losgereden,
eerste categorie, sindsdien taboe
Het ruikt naar dennegeur, Sunsilk Shampoo,
die je wel nodig hebt, eenmaal beneden.

Alles is onuitsprekelijk vermoeiend;
de Mont Ventoux opfietsen wel heel erg,
waarvoor ook geldt: bezint eer gij begint.

Toch haal ik, ook al is de hitte schroeiend,
de top van deze kaalgeslagen berg:
ijdelheid en het najagen van wind.

Jan Kal, *1000 sonnetten 1966-1996*,
Nijgh & Van Ditmar, Amsterdam, 1997.

Eddy Merckx

(Winner of the Tour of Flanders, 1969-1975)
Willie Verhegghe

All hell let loose, thinks Merckx
and he thanks the cycling gods
for the strength that spurts from his trunk
and legs. Flanders bends
its trees before this unbounded force,
the churches shrink into their towers,
pigeons fall from the roof
and in unbounded pink stupor
tongues hang from the open mouths.

The Cannibal shreds the racer's flesh
that's served up to him on the Kwaremont:
every climb makes him a Gulliver
in a landscape that's descended
from Lilliput to Flanders.
Even the Wall proves a paper tiger
under the crack of his calves,
the people don't see what they see:
a new god, a lightning bolt on two wheels.

Eddy Merckx

Alle duivels los, denkt Merckx
en hij dankt de wielergoden
voor de kracht die uit zijn lijf
en benen spat. Vlaanderen buigt
zijn bomen voor dit mateloos geweld,
de kerken krimpen in hun torens,
duiven vallen van het dak
en met mateloze roze stomheid
hangen tongen uit de open monden.

De kannibaal verscheurt het rennersvlees
dat hem op de Kwaremont wordt geserveerd:
elke helling maakt hem tot Gulliver
in een landschap dat uit Lilliput
naar Vlaanderen is afgezakt.
Zelfs de Muur baart een muis
onder het knallen van zijn kuiten,
De mensen zien niet wat ze zien:
Een nieuwe god, een bliksem op twee wielen.

(Winnaar 1969-1975)
Willie Verhegghe, *De Ronde van Vlaanderen,*
PoëzieCentrum, Ghent, 1996.

Abe Lenstra (1920-1985)

Rutger Kopland

We were at the Achilles club, in the rain and
the wind, in a reek of cigars, wet grass and
                                    wet people,]

there was growling and stamping around us,
football was war, even then.

Father, remember how for a second it went
                                    quiet,]
the ball came, it came out of the grey sky
and blew across the goal,

no one had seen him standing there.

Remember he gave a slight nod of the head,
almost humble, almost embarrassed, almost
                                    apologetic.]

We'd lost before we knew it. Abe.

Abe Lenstra

We stonden bij Achilles, het regende en woei,
in een geur van sigaren, nat gras en natte mannen,

het gromde en stampvoette om ons heen,
voetbal was oorlog, toen al.

Vader, weet je nog hoe het even doodstil werd,
de bal kwam, hij kwam uit de grauwe lucht
en woei voor het doel,

niemand had gezien dat hij daar stond

Weet je nog hoe hij toen even met zijn hoofd knikte,
bijna ootmoedig, bijna verlegen, bijna verontschuldigend.

We hadden verloren voor we het wisten. Abe.

Rutger Kopland, *Verzamelde gedichten*,
G.A. van Oorschot, Amsterdam, 2006.

St Johan

Willem Wilmink

once under floodlights
when I saw footballers
weaving a goal moving
like elves across the grass,
I knew it was from here
the saviour would appear.

and lo: Johan Cruyff the dancer
the faun the eagle
of the valleys

but when we came for his sermon on the mount
he talked about paying taxes.

De heilige Johan

Eens toen ik in floodlight
voetballers een doelpunt
zag spinnen zich bewegend
als elven over het gras,
wist ik dat uit deze hoek
de verlosser ophanden was.

En zie; Johan Cruyff de danser
de faun de adelaar
der dalen

maar toen we zijn bergrede kwamen halen
had hij het over belasting betalen.

Willem Wilmink, *Verzamelde liedjes en gedichten*,
Bert Bakker, Amsterdam, 1986.

Ghent-Wevelgem

Tom Lanoye

If I could start again, I'd do things just as I
did: not for a few quid, but for that
new racing strip. That gleams and hugs
your buttocks and those of your team mates

in the peloton. I'd like to train
till I die, trailing the other guy
a fraction, I'd always bring up the rear,
enjoying the frisson. That's all

I ask. Or maybe: a send-off from Ghent
with fanfares and champagne, flag wavers
and confetti, as if for one final
ride, a festive mourning run. Then, when

we've only just left, the bloody group makes
a break, and I'm shattered, left for dead
on the straight road as if on a slack rope. Not a
supporter to be heard, not a racer's

backside to be seen. I crash a few times
as well. Perhaps starting over's still on,
but I'd do the exact same thing:
tighten the straps and pedal like mad,

who'll stop him, who'll teach him to
limit the damage, tame the id, who'll snatch
him from a brilliant triumph, the blessing of a
firm racing saddle? O Great God of Cyclists,

O Sister Brainstorm, have mercy on
your groom. Take his hand in yours and
guide his bike: he's on his way to
Wevelgem, to nowhere if you like.

Gent-Wevelgem

Mocht ik herbeginnen, ik zou net zo
doen: niet om de poen, maar om die
nieuwe pakken. Die zo glimmend spannen
om je billen, en om die van elke ploegmaat

in het peloton. Ik zou mijn hele leven
willen trainen, net iets slechter dan de
ander, dan zit ik altijd achteraan
genietend van de erotiek. Iets anders

wil ik niet. Of toch: in Gent vertrekken
met fanfares en champagne, vendelzwaaiers
en confetti, als voor een allerlaatste
rit, een feestelijke rouweditie. Dan, nog

maar pas vertrokken, springt die klotegroep
al weg, ik zit kapot en godverlaten op de
rechte baan als op het slappe koord. Geen
supporter wordt gehoord, geen achterkant

van renners nog gezien. Een paar keer
vallen bovendien. Misschien is herbeginnen
ook dan mogelijk, maar ik zou precies
hetzelfde doen: riempjes dicht en trappen

maar, wie houdt hem tegen, wie onderwijst
hem schade en fatsoen, wie haalt hem weg
van een schitterende zege, de zege van een
stevig rennerszadel? O Grote Wielergod,

o Sister Brainstorm, heb genade met
uw gade. Neem van zijn hand bezit en
leid zijn fiets: hij is op weg naar
Wevelgem, hij is op weg naar niets.

Tom Lanoye, *De meeste gedichten*,
Prometheus, Amsterdam, 2005.

All poems translated by Paul Vincent

From Our Own Correspondent

How Foreign Journalists Report the News from Brussels

[DEREK BLYTH]

You find them in the Old Hack drinking De Koninck or Leffe under large black-and-white photographs of British newsrooms in the 1930s. For several decades, this small bar near the Berlaymont building has been a favourite Brussels haunt for the foreign correspondents who cover the European Union on behalf of newspapers published in Prague, Beijing, New York and London.

The Old Hack was opened by a British journalist and is now run by a Dutch couple. It is well placed for correspondents who want to organise an informal meeting with one of the European Commission press officers. 'Do you fancy a quick one in the Old Hack?' is the perfect starting point for a confidential briefing on emerging EU policies that could eventually have an impact on the lives of some 500 million EU citizens.

The Old Hack occupies one of the last surviving 19th-century houses in a neighbourhood that over the past 60 years has become the heart (if not the soul) of the European Union. Sitting at one of the window tables tapping out a story on their laptops, the journalists have a clear view of the landmark 1960s glass and steel building built by the Belgian government as the headquarters of the European Commission.

On leaving the Old Hack, the attentive journalist can follow progress on the controversial new Council building that will one day replace the bunker-like Justus Lipsius building. A ten-minute walk through building sites and across busy roads gets the correspondent to the European Parliament, where 736 MEPs gather to debate EU legislation.

The journalists work for different audiences, in different time zones, so deadlines vary enormously. A *New York Times* journalist is six hours ahead of his editors, making it easy to meet a late afternoon newsroom deadline, whereas a Japanese reporter has to build his day around the fact that the Tokyo office is already seven hours into the working day when he turns on his computer.

When the Old Hack opened, the Brussels press corps was a modest collection of journalists who reported on the directives that came out of the European Commission. As the European Union grew larger and more important, and the stories became more gripping, the number of journalists increased dramatically.

The biggest surge came around the time of Europe's 'Big Bang' enlargement in 2004, when the EU grew from 15 to 25 members. Journalists suddenly

© David Nollet.

flooded into Brussels from Eastern European countries, dispatched to write stories for readers back home who were keen to know about the new political union they had joined. Others arrived from India and China to find out what Europe was planning that could affect their economies.

In those heady days, many people argued that the EU had become a major political and economic force on the world stage. It had the power to fine a mighty corporation like Microsoft or force Japanese car-makers to respect emission rules laid down in Brussels. The EU also had its own currency, introduced in 2002, which challenged the dollar and exercised a form of soft diplomacy that offered an alternative to the aggressive US foreign policy of the Bush administration.

Around 2006, the Brussels city authorities started to put out the boast that Brussels had the world's second-largest foreign press corps, after Washington. The exact figures are unknown, since journalists are not obliged to register with the authorities. The only figures available come from the department which issues annual press passes for the EU institutions, which accredited 1,300 journalists in 2005, not far short of the 1,500 in Washington.

It became fashionable at the time to talk of Brussels as Europe's Washington. People toyed with the concept of 'Brussels DC' and even spoke about the 'Brussels beltway'. As the city became flooded with lobbyists – another group

© David Nollet.

hard to count but estimated to number some 15,000 – it was widely agreed that Brussels was an exciting place to work as a journalist. But that was before the newspaper industry was hit by the biggest crisis in its history.

Media in crisis

The global financial crisis that broke in the autumn of 2008 hit a newspaper industry that was already battling against the rise of digital information. The internet was an infinite free resource, overflowing with news sites, bloggers and Twitter micro news. How could the old dinosaurs of print hope to compete with these smart young people on the web?

Confronted with a dramatic fall in reader numbers, as well as a decline in advertising income, many newspaper owners panicked in about 2009. They decided that the only solution was to cut staff as well as content. It was almost universally decided to focus on local news and reduce the number of foreign correspondents.

As a result, the Brussels press corps has declined dramatically in the past few years, according to the International Press Association (IPA), which represents foreign journalists in the city. It is impossible to get precise figures on the situation, but the number of journalists issued with official EU press passes has dropped from 1,300 in 2005 to just 752 in 2010.

The German press dominates Brussels these days, with 132 accredited journalists working in the city, followed by Britain with 98 and Italy and Spain each with 63. Somewhat surprisingly, France comes in fifth place, with its 56 accredited journalists. According to *Libération's* Brussels correspondent Jean Quatremer, most French newspapers have drastically cut their Brussels staff since 2008, with *Le Monde* down from five to two journalists, and *Le Figaro's* Brussels desk now manned by one person in place of two. Worse still, most Central and East European newspapers have simply closed down their Brussels offices, says Quatremer.

In his blog, the *Libération* correspondent blames the Belgian authorities for the fall in numbers. He argues that Belgium's high taxes and social contributions have forced newspapers to close their Brussels offices while keeping correspondents based in cities like London and Washington.

But Quatremer also blames the European Commission for the way it deals with journalists. Foreign correspondents traditionally gained the information they needed at weekly briefings in the Commission's press room, where they could ask difficult questions. But the Commission's press releases now go online instantly (through a service called RAPID), so a journalist sitting at a desk in Dublin or Prague can pick up the press release at exactly the same moment as someone sitting in the Brussels press room. This makes it much easier for a newspaper to cut its Brussels staff, even if it means the stories it publishes are simply based on a press release.

There is possibly one more reason why the Brussels press corps is shrinking fast – for a journalist, Brussels has become dull. 'The malaise gripping Brussels has its echo in a growing sense that the EU project is just not where the action is', *The Economist's* Brussels correspondent wrote recently.

Looking at the figures for the BBC, it's clear that the action is on the other side of the Atlantic. The British corporation employs 55 people in the United States, compared to 15 in Brussels and a further ten in other European locations. So the US (population 307 million) gets twice as many foreign correspondents as Europe (500 million).

Beyond the bubble

The Belgian authorities can hardly be blamed for everything. They have been generous to journalists over the past 10 years. In 2001, during the Belgian presidency of the European Council, the Verhofstadt government opened a smart new press centre in the Residence Palace. Facing the Berlaymont, the former 1920s apartment complex offered the press an impressive Art Deco lobby, an elegant restaurant and several rooms for hosting press conferences.

Ten years on, the government of Brussels Region went one step further and helped to fund a new Brussels Europe Press Club at 95 Froissardstraat, opposite the Justus Lipsius building where Herman van Rompuy has his office. The Region, which worked closely with the International Press Association to set up the club, hopes that it can persuade journalists to write stories on Brussels that will make it seem less boring.

But most foreign journalists based in Brussels have little inclination to seek out stories outside the 'European bubble'. 'Journalists don't move much beyond Schuman [the roundabout at the heart of the European Quarter]', one long-established journalist told me. Over the years, the international press has only taken an interest in Belgium when the story is negative. The Dutroux

© David Nollet.

child murders in 1996 were heavily reported in international newspapers under headlines such as 'Something is rotten in the state of Belgium.' The recent failure to create a coalition government has also engaged the international press. Apart from those stories, Belgium rarely appears in the international pages of foreign newspapers. 'We try to propose stories, but there isn't much interest in Belgian news back home', one journalist explained to me.

When journalists do report on Belgium, they often rely on *Le Soir* and *La Libre Belgique* for their background information, ignoring reports in *De Standaard* and *De Morgen*. The reason is simple. Journalists often have a basic command of French, but almost none (apart from those from the Netherlands) can speak any Dutch.

The Flemish government has been aware of the problem for many years, but it was finally pushed into action in 2007 when a francophone newspaper with an anti-Flemish bias started to appear in the in-boxes of EU officials. In October 2007, the Flemish foreign affairs and media minister Geert Bourgeois launched a new English-language newspaper called *Flanders Today* with the aim of providing objective news on Flanders – not a *Pravda*, insisted Bourgeois.

One of its goals was to reach the international journalists who work in Brussels, but knew very little about what went on beyond the 'Brussels beltway'. The Flemish government later launched a daily online press review in English and French which posted stories selected from the quality Flemish press on the *Flanders Today* website.

I was involved in the launch of the newspaper and served as editor for more than three years. During that time, the newspaper occasionally came into conflict with the government over content. The hardest article to bring to press involved the village of Doel. Here was a story that involved an old Flemish town that was due to be demolished because the port of Antwerp needed to expand. It was a situation that could happen in any modern industrial country, involving a difficult choice between heritage and commerce, but the government tried to stop the story being published and, when that failed, refused to cooperate with the journalist.

What does the future hold?

On 21 March 2011, a brief notice appeared in the Belgisch Staatsblad (Moniteur Belge) announcing that the Librairie de Rome had been declared bankrupt. This marked the end of the best-stocked international newsagent in Brussels, an institution that dated back to 1934. It was clear proof that the newspaper crisis was hitting Belgium hard.

Some editors go so far as to argue that the newspaper of the future will be read on screen rather than on paper. This will have profound cultural and economic consequences across the world. It will mean printing works will close down, newsagents will disappear from the streets and the old routine of press deadlines will be a thing of memory.

Not everyone, however, believes that newspapers are finished. In 2006, the Belgian Persgroep opened a brand-new printing works near Lokeren in East Flanders, the Eco Print Center (EPC). In a beautiful light-filled building *De Morgen*, *Het Laatste Nieuws* and other Flemish newspapers are printed using the latest technology of waterless offset printing.

© David Nollet.

I visited the EPC on 15 June 2011 to watch the preview edition of the *European Daily* come off the presses. The newspaper, launched by two young Swedes, aims to provide a European perspective on global news. Some 40,000 copies were printed in Lokeren and distributed the following day in Brussels, London, Paris and Berlin.

The aim of the pilot edition, edited in a borrowed apartment in Brussels, was to find out whether there was a critical mass of enthusiasm among readers, advertisers and investors for a European daily newspaper. 'The feedback has been quite overwhelming', said Christofer Berg, one of the co-founders.

The *European Daily* shows that the idea of a newspaper still remains alive, even in a generation that has grown up with Facebook and iPads. 'Reading the newspaper together with the morning coffee might seem a trivial daily routine', says Berg, 'but it is one of the pillars of a truly vibrant and democratic society.'

'Where do you plan to base the newspaper?' I asked Berg, expecting him to reply Brussels, the capital of Europe.

'Amsterdam', he said without a moment's hesitation.

'Not Brussels?'

'Brussels is too bureaucratic, too close to the institutions.'

Initially I was shocked, but it now makes perfect sense. Brussels has become a stale place to work as a journalist. It doesn't have the excitement of Washington or London.

On 18 March 2011 the International Press Association held a meeting to discuss the question, 'What does the future hold for Brussels-based journalists?'. I am not sure that the answer was very encouraging. ■

NOTE

Derek Blyth was formerly editor-in-chief of *The Bulletin* and *Flanders Today*. He edited the preview edition of *European Daily*, published on 15 June 2011. He wrote *The 500 Things You Need to Know about Brussels* and is currently working on a book about Utopia.

Literature as Resistance

Dutch Clandestine Literature (1940-1945)

[JEROEN DEWULF]

'Clandestine literature' is a general term for all literature that was published without permission from the German authorities during the occupation in the Second World War. Some of these works – which certain scholars refer to as 'illegal literature' – openly challenged the occupier and encouraged resistance, whereas other books only dealt with general themes that for specific reasons were in defiance of the regulations imposed by the Nazis. Nevertheless, in both cases the authors and printers were risking their lives in defence of freedom of the press, thought, and artistic expression. At least 700 men and women of the underground press would perish during the occupation.

Shortly after liberation, in June 1945, an exhibition about clandestine literature was inaugurated by Martinus Nijhoff at the Amsterdam City Museum. The organizers highlighted the important contribution of this literature as opposition against Nazi propaganda. They even presented it as the conscience of the Netherlands. Significantly, one of the rooms was reserved for those who had lost their lives for the sake of freedom of the press. Entering this room dedicated to the martyrs of resistance literature had almost sacral significance.

The exhibition later travelled through Europe, where clandestine literature was given a new function: it no longer served to fight German propaganda, but to promote the image of the Netherlands as a nation of heroes who had bravely resisted the German occupiers. Accordingly, Herman de la Fontaine-Verwey solemnly stated in November 1945 in *Le Monde* that this resistance had not only saved the Dutch nation, but also Dutch literature. This self-confident, patriotic perspective on the occupation characterized the early reception of clandestine literature.

DE ACHTTIEN DOODEN

Broadsheet publication of Jan Campert's poem 'De achttien dooden' (Song of the Eighteen Dead), which commemorated the first eighteen Dutchmen executed by the Germans for their involvement in resistance activities, 1943. Source: University of California Berkeley, Bancroft Library.

Een cel is maar twee meter lang
en nauw twee meter breed,
wel kleiner nog is het stuk grond
dat ik nu nog niet weet,
maar waar ik naamloos rusten zal,
mijn makkers bovendien,
wij waren achttien in getal,
geen zal den avond zien.

O lieflijkheid van lucht en land
van Hollands vrije kust -
ééns door den vijand overmand,
vond ik geen uur meer rust;
wat kan een man, oprecht en trouw,
nog doen in zulk een tijd?
Hij kust zijn kind, hij kust zijn vrouw
en strijdt den ijdelen strijd.

Ik wist de taak die ik begon
een taak van moeiten zwaar,
maar 't hart dat het niet laten kon
schuwt nimmer het gevaar;
het weet hoe eenmaal in dit land
de vrijheid werd geëerd,
voordat een vloek'bre schennershand
het anders heeft begeerd,

voordat die eeden breekt en bralt
het misselijk stuk bestond
en Hollands landen binnenvalt
en brandschat zijnen grond,
voordat die aanspraak maakt op eer
en zulk germaansch gerief,
een land dwong onder zijn beheer
en plunderde als een dief.

De rattenvanger van Berlijn
pijpt nu zijn melodie;
zoo waar als ik straks dood zal zijn,
de liefste niet meer zie
en niet meer breken zal het brood
noch slapen mag met haar -
verwerp al wat hij biedt of bood,
de sluwe vogelaar.

Gedenkt, die deze woorden leest,
mijn makkers in den nood
en die hen nastaan 't allermeest
in hunnen rampspoed groot,
zooals ook wij hebben gedacht
aan eigen land en volk,
er komt een dag na elke nacht,
voorbij trekt ied're wolk.

Ik zie hoe 't eerste morgenlicht
door 't hooge venster draalt -
mijn God, maak mij het sterven licht,
en zoo ik heb gefaald,
gelijk een elk wel falen kan,
schenk mij dan Uw genâ,
opdat ik heenga als een man
als ik voor de loopen sta.

JAN CAMPERT†

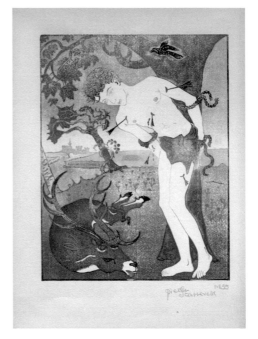

Twenty years later, the heroic image of Dutch behaviour during the Second World War was corrected. No other work had a bigger impact on this change in perspective than Jacques Presser's *Ashes in the Wind* (Ondergang, 1965). In light of the fact that some 73% of the Jewish population in the Netherlands had been transported to Nazi death camps, the largest percentage in Western Europe, Presser denounced the self-congratulatory attitude to Dutch behaviour during the war as completely inappropriate. With Presser's book in hand a new generation, too young to have experienced the war, debunked the heroic perspective of the past. Clandestine literature was also remembered in this discussion. This renewed interest was notorious in the work of journalist Adriaan Venema. In a five-volume study *Writers, Publishers & their Collaboration* (Schrijvers, uitgevers & hun collaboratie, 1988-1992), Venema saw it as his task, if not his mission, to prove how intellectuals, many of them in leading positions, had hypocritically taken advantage of the aura of resistance in order to hide their involvement in acts of collaboration. These accusations cast a dark shadow on the immaculate image of clandestine literature. What had once served as an illustration of Dutch bravery was now looked at with distrust, as if every clandestine publication was a potential fraud.

By the turn of the century, a history that traditionally had been portrayed as black and white, became increasingly seen as 'grey'. In allusion to the Dutch tendency to call members of the Resistance 'the whites' and collaborators 'the blacks' (in reference to the colour of Nazi uniforms), historian Chris van der Heijden argued in *Grey History* (Grijs verleden, 2001) that the real history of the Netherlands during the occupation should be characterized by the colour grey of accommodation. In this 'grey' perspective, there was no place for the role of the Resistance, and hence no interest in clandestine literature. This lack of interest made it possible for several of the most precious clandestine publica-

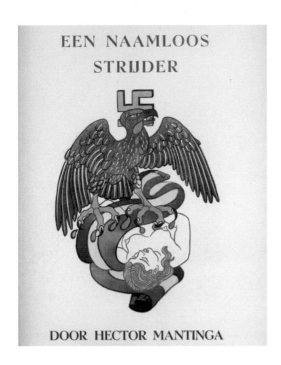

EEN NAAMLOOS
STRIJDER

DOOR HECTOR MANTINGA

It has been said that in Dutch clandestine printing, the love of freedom was inextricably linked to the love of beauty. The quality of the printing, binding, layout, and illustration of most publications is indeed impressive, especially when taking into consideration the difficult circumstances in which they were made. Because of the poor quality of the paper, printers did their utmost to make up for this deficiency by paying special attention to the typography, the use of an original font, or the preparation of an attractive title page. Famous examples are the illustrations made by Pieter Starreveld for the publication of Albert Helman's poems *De dierenriem* (The Zodiac, 1942) and Sebastiaan (Sebastian, 1944), as well as for the poem *Een naamloos strijder* (An Anonymous Fighter, 1944) by the Jewish poet Maurits Mok who lived in hiding and published his clandestine work under the pseudonym Hector Mantinga. Source: University of California Berkeley, Bancroft Library.

tions to be sold to foreign libraries such as the British Library in London, the Charles D. McCormick Library at Northwestern University (Illinois), and the Bancroft Library at the University of California, Berkeley.

This is all the more surprising considering the historical importance of this literature. In no other country under German occupation had more clandestine literature been published than in the Netherlands. In *The Free Book in an Unfree Time* (Het vrije boek in onvrije tijd, 1958), Dirk de Jong identified over a thousand titles. Perhaps even more impressive than the number of books was the unprecedented popularity of clandestine literature, poetry in particular. We know that during the Occupation no fewer than 40,000 copies of anthologies of Resistance poetry were sold. They are among the rare examples where literature unites a popular and an intellectual expression.

DE ᵢONDERGRONDSCHE ᴮPERS

Clandestine Printing "De onder-grondse pers" (The Under-ground Press). Cartoon by Karel Links making reference to the inefficacy of German measures to eradicate the illegal press, *De Moffenspiegel* (The Hun's Mir-ror, 1944), Source: University of California Berkeley, Bancroft Library.

Dutch clandestine books

The biggest and by far the most important Dutch clandestine publishing house was *De Bezige Bij*, founded by Geert Lubberhuizen. Lubberhuizen was linked to a group of students from Utrecht University who had formed a committee to help Jewish children in hiding. The group saved the lives of some 400 children. Without Lubberhuizen's financial support such success would not have been possible. In 1943 he had published an illustrated broadsheet of Jan Campert's highly dramatic poem *The Eighteen Dead* (De achttien dooden) about a group of Resistance members who were executed by the Nazis. Some 15,000 copies of the broadsheet were sold, which brought in so much money that it could secure not only the subsistence of the Jewish children, but also the financial basis for a clandestine publishing house. Unlike its French counterpart *Les Éditions de Minuit,* whose concern for saving the 'honour of French thought' was reflected in the high literary quality of its publications, *De Bezige Bij* published anything that could bring in money, from a Dutch translation of John Steinbeck's *The Moon Is Down,* poems by Edgar Allan Poe and Guy de Maupassant, to postcards with caricatures of the Nazis and calendars with pictures of Queen Wilhelmina.

Another prominent clandestine printer was Alexandre A.M. Stols, who had a network of contacts all over Europe, particularly in France. During the war Stols edited a series of beautifully printed poetry editions, entitled *Halcyon,* which he even managed to sell in Germany. To avoid problems he antedated his publications and/or indicated a non-existent place of publication. In his fertile imagination, Stols came up with names such as *The Somerset Press, Sidcot* or *Gerard Leeu, Gouda*, the latter actually being a fifteenth-century printer of incunabula.

Stols also supported the German refugee Heinz Horn, who under the pseudonym Wolfgang Cordan founded *Die Kentaurdrucke* that clandestinely published German classics. Together with Wolfgang Frommel, another German refugee, and the Hungarian K. Kollár, owner of the scholarly publishing house *Panthéon*, Cordan clandestinely published an elitist type of German literature, including authors such as Hölderin, Herder, and Stefan George. These books sold surprisingly well. Ironically, some German soldiers were among their clients and helped them to survive the war by sharing food parcels.

Until 1942, an exception to publishing regulations was made for publications that needed fewer than five pounds of paper; such publications did not need approval by the Chamber of Culture, whose task it was to push along the Nazification of Dutch literature. Bookseller A.A. Balkema took advantage of this situation by launching a series of minuscule clandestine books, which he accordingly called *De Vijf Ponden Pers*. He published mostly foreign poets for a list of trusting subscribers. One of Balkema's most dangerous clandestine publications was *Ten Little Grumblers* (Zehn kleine Meckerlein, 1943), published in German in an edition of forty copies. The satirical text by an unknown

The third edition of the Geuzenliedboek (1945), an anthology of resistance poerty, begins with an illustration representing the Dutch 'spirit of resistance' against the Spanish (on the left) and the Germans (on the right). University of California Berkeley, Bancroft Library.

Hendrik Werkman, *The Army of the Wanted*, printing-painting based on the poem 'Het leger der gezochten' by Toontje Berger about the secret activities of the Dutch resistance, 1944. Source: Francine Albach, Amsterdam.

author had been smuggled out of a concentration camp in Germany. Written and illustrated in the spirit of a children's book, the text ironically reworks the popular song *Zehn kleine Negerlein,* the German version of the old American song *Ten Little Niggers* in which the victims one by one disappear.

In terms of artistic quality, the work of printer Hendrik Werkman was truly exceptional. It was his ambition to combine graphic design with new technologies such as offset printing and photography. He therefore joined the publishing house *De Blauwe Schuit* that had been founded, in November 1940, by Ade Zuithoff, Adri Buning and August Henkels. Strictly speaking, De Blauwe Schuit was not a clandestine publisher since Werkman's name was mentioned in the colophon. Hiding his identity would have been impossible because the illustrations were so unique that they could easily have been identified. Among the most famous editions by *De Blauwe Schuit* is the beautifully illustrated *Hasidic Legends* (Chassidische Legenden, 1941), based on Martin Buber's edition of Jewish mystic tales. In March 1945 the police raided Werkman's office; he was summarily arrested and executed.

There were hundreds of similar small-scale (and often dilettantish) clandestine publishing houses all over the Netherlands. Their print numbers were usually limited; in 25% of cases, fewer than a hundred copies per book were printed. As the use of noisy printing machines implied a serious risk, most of these publishers used lithography as their printing method, often in combination with a primitive hand press, a hectograph, a platen press that had to be powered by foot or, as a last resort, a mimeograph. Another problem was paper shortage. The Chamber of Culture had a monopoly in the distribution of paper for book printing and used it as a weapon to impose its will. Consequently, clandestine books were usually thin. This also explains why most of the production of clandestine literature consisted of poetry and short stories.

Relevance of clandestine literature

Most Dutch literary histories exclude clandestine literature; they tend to focus in detail on the avant-garde literature in the 1930s and from there immediately jump to the rebellious postwar generation led by Willem F. Hermans, Gerard Reve, and Anna Blaman. The war itself, precisely the period in modern Dutch history when literature was most popular, barely receives any attention.

As a result, Dutch literary scholars have traditionally looked at 1945 as a "Year Zero," as if to say that then Dutch literature restarted from scratch. In reality, many of the "new" tendencies were already present in clandestine literature. Blaman's openly lesbian novel *Lonely Adventure* (Eenzaam avontuur, 1948), for instance, was preceded by her clandestinely published short story *Encounter with Selma* (Ontmoeting met Selma, 1943). Rein Blijstra's libertarian sexual morality, his relativistic approach to a 'hero' of the resistance, and particularly his deep-seated cynicism in *Upon Further Acquaintance* (Bij nadere kennismaking, 1944) make him, together with Blaman, a herald of changing moral values in Dutch literature that scholars traditionally — though mistakenly — date as beginning in 1947. Blijstra's other clandestinely published novel *Sharks near Nabatu* (Haaien voor Nabatoe, 1945) is also exceptional because of its anti-colonial message. With this novel, Blijstra pointed to a discussion that would flare up in Dutch society soon after the Liberation: how can a country that justified its resistance as a fight for freedom still defend the rightness of a colonial empire?

As these examples show, the prejudice that clandestine literature has little more to offer than a simplistic celebration of patriotism needs to be reconsidered. In fact, a considerable part of this literature consists of translated work. Several foreign authors were even published in their native tongues. Among these authors we find Kafka, Heine, Baudelaire, Dickinson, even Omar Khayyam and the African-American James Langston Hughes — hardly names that reflect a reactionary, nationalistic conception of literature.

Clandestine literature also contains the first Dutch ego-document on the Holocaust. Long before Anne Frank's diary was published, letters written by Etty Hillesum from Westerbork Camp were printed clandestinely in the 'Tarnschrift' *Three Letters by the Painter Johannes Baptiste van der Pluym* (Drie brieven van den Kunstschilder Johannes Baptiste van der Pluym, 1943). Another fascinating "Tarnschrift" is Albert Helman's *Thus Spoke Zarathustra* (Aldus sprak Zarathustra, 1944), an ironic portrait of Germany and the Germans composed of quotes taken from German literature.

Irony was also the weapon used by A. van Atten, who ridiculed the German propaganda in poems he published under the pseudonym Hein van Oranje. In *Wretches* (Stumpers), a caricature of one of Arthur Seyss-Inquart's speeches on the great future that awaited the Netherlands under German guidance, he writes: 'The Afsluitdijk? The work of wretches, / that was the best we Dutch could do. / Reducing Rotterdam to ruins - / that's what men of action do!'

The use of printing machines for clandestine literature implied a serious risk because the occupiers had precise information about the existing printers. Printing machines were loud, cumbersome, technically sophisticated, and used a lot of energy, which made secret printing almost impossible. It is not by chance that many more printers and graphic designers lost their lives for the sake of clandestine literature than did authors. As there was often not enough electricity to keep the machines going, it had to be tapped illegally from other lines or replaced by manpower. A typically Dutch solution was the production of electricity by bicycle. Here we see clandestine publisher Bert Bakker demonstrating after the war how a bicycle was used to produce electricity for a printing machine. Source: Francine Albach (Amsterdam).

When reading clandestine literature with an open mind, even non-believers can be impressed by the poetic expression of rock-solid faith among Christian resistance fighters. Few poems in Dutch literature contain a more radical confrontation with existential questions than those of Herman Salomonson in *School for Recruits* (Recrutenschool, 1941). Salomonson, who as a 'crusader of Christ' fought Nazism until the bitter end, openly condemns the cowardice of all those who before the invasion spoke loudly about resistance but became silent as soon as danger threatened: 'On the cold stones of the cell / truth rises from sounds of death! / O God and Father, through your stern chastisements, / the talk of idle mouths, / worn out in the usage of the day, / appears against the background of the Cross's truth.'

The assumption that critical voices about the general passiveness of the Dutch population during the occupation were only heard long after the liberation is, in fact, a myth. Those voices were to be heard loud and clear in clandestine literature by authors who not only anticipated the rebellious postwar generation in their criticism but who did so at a time when protest could have deadly consequences. This was the case of the young resistance fighter Jaap Sickenga, who shortly before his execution in May 1942 harshly condemned the general apathy in Dutch society: 'A different death / threatens us / than one from lead — / Indifference. / He who suffers from it / dies before his time.'

One of the most touching resistance poems is Martinus Nijhoff's new version of *The Children's Crusade* (De kinderkruistocht). While the previous version dealt with a topic from a vague past, *Modern Children's Crusade* (Moderne kinderkruistocht) points angrily at the passive and sometimes even collaborative attitude in Dutch society vis-à-vis the children's drama that is taking place before the public's eyes: 'People hurried on, / vengeance has no time for compassion. / They chased them, laughing at the Jew / who so loudly laments and cries out in his need.'

Perhaps more than anything else, however, the real importance of clandestine literature lies in the fact that faith in the written word could be maintained. It is remarkable that the belief in the power of literature reached its height in the Netherlands precisely at a time when German propaganda misused literature in such a way that the old perception of printing as an ally of humanism was completely corrupted. In postwar Germany, writing poetry after Auschwitz came to be seen as a barbaric act. Dutch intellectuals might have been disappointed with the sometimes poor aesthetic quality or reactionary morality of their clandestine literature, but they did not share Adorno's radical pessimism. In the occupied Netherlands, clandestine printing had been able to produce a contrast to the abuse of literature by Nazi propaganda. It was perhaps not as bright as some had hoped, but at a time of total darkness, even the smallest flame sheds a lot of light. ∎

Room for Variation

The Dance of Sidi Larbi Cherkaoui

Play, 2010.
Photo by Koen Broos.

"Le plaisir est dans l'échange, on en sort toujours plus riche."
Sidi Larbi Cherkaoui

The Flemish-Moroccan choreographer Sidi Larbi Cherkaoui (b.1976) presents himself first and foremost as a builder of bridges. Coupling frankness and modesty with unrestrained passion, he seeks out meeting grounds and blends of cultural histories, movement languages and artistic disciplines, always from a non-restrictive, non-hierarchical perspective. With him it's not so much a conscious mission as a personal inclination. Cherkaoui is known for being inquisitive and eager to learn, always bent on meeting. Just like his language of movement, his career is constantly evolving: the one flows, as if automatically, from the other. After ten years working as a choreographer he can boast a fine-mesh network of personal contacts and collaborators built on kindred spirits and mutual respect. In 2012 he won the National Dance Award for Outstanding Male Performance for *Dunas*.

Babel[WORDS] (2010), *TeZukA* (2011), his recent 'major' productions, together with *Play* (2010), a duet with the Indian kuchipudi dancer Shantala Shivalingappa, are at present the high points of his choreographic idiom.

At 35 years of age, with some thirty choreographies to his name, Cherkaoui is among the international pick of the bunch in dance. 'Breathtaking', 'genuinely global dance': thus the influential German dance magazine *Tanz* explained its decision last season to proclaim Cherkaoui as 'Best Choreographer'. From the very first it was clear that the young choreographer would scale dizzy heights. His first major creation, *Rien de Rien* (2000), toured internationally and immediately won a Special Prize at the BITEF festival in Budapest. In Flanders Cherkaoui is part of the third generation of 'Flemish Wave' choreographers, the group of innovators in theatre and dance who are now internationally renowned. At the beginning of 1980 its pioneers Anne Teresa De Keersmaeker with Rosas, Jan Fabre with Troubleyn and Wim Vandekeybus with Ultima Vez led a radical change of course, introducing post-modern dance and dance theatre in a dance scene until then dominated by ballet. Shortly afterwards their ranks were joined by Jan Lauwers/Needcompany and Alain Platel/Ballets C. de la B. From the 1990s onwards the Brussels-based American choreographer Meg Stuart with Damaged Goods provided the impetus for a second generation of innovators with her broken, abject dancing bodies.

Rêves de Babel

With Cherkaoui the need to build bridges has everything to do with making sense of his bicultural family background: his father is Moroccan, his mother Belgian. In the documentary *Rêves de Babel* (Arte, 2009) the choreographer dwells on the impact of his family background on his career. The fact that he wanted to dance, combined with his proclivities and his place in the family (with a brother four years older) all earned him equally poor marks in the eyes of his father. At school as in his social life, *second hand* was a constant part of his life: he was always being dismissed, not on account of who he was, but because of his Arabic name, or the hand-me-downs from his brother that he had to wear, and, later, because of his homosexuality. It is not without reason that the driving force in Cherkaoui's world is to demonstrate, to discuss, and to be understood. Dance

Babel^WORDS, 2010.
Photo by Koen Broos.

theatre is his medium for doing this.

It is only when his father leaves the family that Cherkaoui, in his fifteenth year, can openly opt for dance. Up to that time Larbi had to be satisfied with imitating in his own living room what he saw on television, in pop videos, Bruce Lee and ballet films. So it is logical that he should take his first steps in the professional dance world on television, as a backing dancer in a popular music programme showing Flemish hits.

1995 proves to be a key year for him. This is the year in which Cherkaoui wins a talent contest for young Belgian dancers organised by Alain Platel – leader of Les Ballets C. de la B. – and the Victoria production company in Ghent. The first prize is a trip to New York, with dance lessons on Broadway and workshops with cult choreographer Alvin Aily. That triumph gains Cherkaoui entry to P.A.R.T.S., Anne Teresa De Keersmaeker's internationally renowned school of contemporary dance in Brussels. Alain Platel has to wait until he has completed his studies there before netting Larbi for the iconic *Iets op Bach* (1998). While it is still on tour Alain Platel proposes to Larbi that he should join his Ghent-based choreographers' collective, Les Ballets C. de la B.

Frames

In 2000, with *Rien de Rien*, Cherkaoui establishes the framework for his future work: a hybrid stage environment in which cultures, ages and disciplines meet. The scenography in this first performance is reminiscent of a mosque, with oriental carpets on the ground and an inscription in Arabic on the rear wall. The imam is a cellist, the dance a prayer in which both Shiva and tango appear from time to time. The youngest female dancer is 14, the oldest 58 – and capable of seducing a young male dancer. Text and dance take turn and turn about. The female singer and the musician move with the dancers.

The choice of music for *Rien de Rien* – Edith Piaf, Kodaly, Ligeti, and old Italian songs – is typical of Cherkaoui's eclecticism. The choreographer prefers to use live music on stage, to attune the various rhythms, of dance, music and body language to each other as far as possible and then get them to resonate as powerfully as possible with the spectator. 'Rhythm is a powerful link between people', according to the choreographer, 'everyone has an intuitive understanding of rhythm and can communicate by means of rhythm.'

While preparing his first production Cherkaoui gets to know the Brussels dancer/choreographer Damien Jalet, from then on his inspiration and sounding-board. Together they are the Belgian cherry on the cake of Cherkaoui's culture-transcending mission: a French-speaking man from Brussels with French roots and a Fleming from Antwerp with Moroccan roots. In 2005 they collaborate on the choreography for the Belgian national dance event *Ik hou van u/ Je t'aime tu sais,* the wildly popular Belgian anniversary edition of Bal Moderne that was held simultaneously in twelve Belgian cities. Ten years on Jalet signs up officially as choreographer for *Babel^WORDS*.

Cherkaoui maintains his connection with the Alain Platel collective for six years in all. During this period, in addition to *Rien de Rien* he creates key productions such as *Foi* (2003), on the theme of belief and manipulation, *Tempus Fugit* (2004), a commission for the Avignon Festival, and *Zero Degrees* (2005), a duet with another kindred spirit, the British Bangladeshi choreographer Akram Khan. Their collaboration produces a first nomination for a Laurence Olivier award and for Cherkaoui a partnership of inestimable value with the leading British dance company, Sadler's Wells in London. In the same period Wim Vandekeybus writes *It* for Cherkaoui – the solo that they reprise in the Spring of 2011 as a duet. In 2002, with the Ultima Vez dancer Nienke Reehorst he creates *Ook,* a piece for mentally handicapped actors. Both Reehorst and one of the actors, Marc Wagemans, still form part of the core group around Cherkaoui.

Cherkaoui also looks for stimulus with other companies. He choreographs various works for Les Ballets de Monte Carlo, including *In Memoriam.* In this meditation on ancestral memory and personal recollection Cherkaoui lays the basis for a long-standing collaboration with the Corsican polyphonic ensemble A Filetta. Ancient folk music remains a powerful and fascinating source of collective memory for Cherkaoui as well as an answer to his need to immerse himself in time.

Antwerp

When the theatrical producer Guy Cassiers becomes manager of the Toneelhuis, the renovated municipal theatre in Antwerp, in 2006, he invites Cherkaoui to become one of the seven artists in residence. It will prove to be a golden gift. For Cherkaoui it is a dreamed-of opportunity to establish himself artistically and luxuriate in the multicultural bath of the port city that he regards as his home. On the other hand, the Toneelhuis has strong international connections and Cherkaoui can reach a new audience there through creative

TeZukA, 2011.

Photo by Hugo Glendinning.

collaboration with other disciplines – theatre, film and video art, literature, performance. The choreographer is able to contribute to *House of Sleeping Beauties,* an opera by Guy Cassiers and the contemporary composer Kris Defoort. The theatre's extensive public relations activity and regular publications ensure that his work receives comprehensive theatrical explanation. The infrastructure and technical facilities there mean that Cherkaoui's own productions can become more ambitious. At the same time he can gather around him a regular core of loyal colleagues: the dancers Damien Jalet, Darryl Woods and the music expert Christine Leboutte.

It is in this period that Cherkaoui becomes acquainted with Patrizia Bovi. She is the musical director of Micrologus, an Italian ensemble that is doing research into the musical culture of oral traditions, a continuing source of inspiration in Cherkaoui's work. Bovi advises him on music and will become a permanent influence in his productions, beginning with *Myth* (2007). In addition the highly respected Muntschouwburg in Brussels offers support as a platform for productions and as co-producer.

Man from the East

Because the production structure around Cherkaoui has become too large for the Toneelhuis and too fragmented for the choreographer himself, in January 2010 Cherkaoui sets up his own company: Eastman. It is a literal translation of his own name, Cherkaoui, the man from the East. The first new production

under this label, *Babel^WORDS*, hits the bull's-eye right away. The performance is a baroque extension of Cherkaoui's mission. The problem of Biblical language-confusion is transposed to the question of how in spite of everything we can strive towards understanding and harmony. Where is the universal beyond the differences? To reinforce their question Larbi and fellow-choreographer Damien Jalet seek out eighteen performers (dancers and musicians) from no less than thirteen different countries. Between them they speak fifteen languages and profess seven different religions. Moreover, most of the twelve dancers come from a bicultural family background, just like Cherkaoui and Jalet themselves.

Babel^WORDS is the final piece in a trilogy that marks an evolution in Cherkaoui's thinking. After *Foi* (2003), to do with the impact of belief with manipulating, invisible angels and *Myth* (2007) with archetypes and shadows from the subconscious, the characters in *Babel^WORDS* take responsibility themselves for the reality they create in the here and now.

In *Babel^WORDS* rhythm is once more a universal means of escape from the snares and pitfalls of differences in language, culture and communication. The audience is given an exposition of how as an individual spectator you can incorporate the rhythm of the performance by means of mirror neurons – showmaster Darryl E. Woods explains this with great humour and aplomb. Bodies remain the universal medium of communication *par excellence*. But there is a lot of work involved, because they have to be fine-tuned to a very high degree. 'My body's not just an object', Larbi said in an interview in 2009, 'I have to try to be every cell of that body. When you reach the point where you are one with your body, then you can transmit energy to other bodies.' The theme of conscious

TeZukA, 2011.
Photo by Hugo Glendinning.

physicality is comprehensively presented in *Babel*^WORDS in the character of avatar Ulrika Kinn Svensson. She represents hybrid worlds between man and machine, between self-determined and directed behaviour.

The British visual artist Antony Gormley makes a critical contribution in *Babel-*^WORDS. His collaboration with Sidi Larbi is a trilogy in its own right. From life-sized casts of the two dancers in *Zero Degrees* (2005), through half-open coffins for the sixteen Buddhist monks in *Sutra* (2008), his scenography has evolved to open structures with five three-dimensional aluminium frames in *Babel*^WORDS. At first sight they vary from large to very large. The ingenuity of it is that these are actually five identical volumes each of which is aligned along a different axis. In this way they demonstrate the similarities behind the differences in a very graphic manner. Gormley's volumes are deceptively simple, versatile, rectangular, extremely clear and with unlimited metaphorical potential: they are used by the performers as city, social structure, play environment, goggle box, sarcophagus, protective envelope or self-imposed limitation. At every point during the performance they present a new interpretation of what is going on at this moment. At the same time the volumes provide a counterbalance to all-too-human limitations regarding perceptive frameworks.

In 2011 *Babel*^WORDS deservedly receives a number of major prizes: two Laurence Olivier Awards in London, as well as the Benois de la Danse in Moscow.

In the same year UNESCO grants Cherkaoui the title of Young Artist for Intercultural Dialogue between Arab and Western Worlds for his research into 'the meeting between cultures and explorations of identity'.

TeZukA

Cherkaoui's latest major production, *TeZukA* (2011), is a classic example of how his creations come about. The choreography derives from his early love for graphic art. As a child he devoured comic strips and dreamed of drawing his own. Later he became fascinated by the culture of Japanese strip cartoons, his favourite being the visionary Japanese manga artist Osamu Tezuka.

Cherkaoui greatly admires the manner in which the latter handles universal themes such as human rights, ethics and tolerance in his cartoons. Moreover, through his Japanese dancers Cherkaoui had become fascinated by Japanese customs and social rituals. Cherkaoui managed to arrange for a calligrapher from Osamu Tezuka's studio to join the dancers on stage to explain the dance. Two Shaolin monks from *Sutra* also dance in *TeZukA*.

Cherkaoui carries this typical, self-organising openness through to the repertory performances that he promised the Toneelhuis in return for further logistic and productional assistance for his new company, Eastman.

In 2010 the Toneelhuis was given straightforward reprises of *Myth* (2007) and *Foi* (2003), but one season later the original version of *IT* from 2002 merely provided an excuse for further choreographic research. The original piece was a commission by Wim Vandekeybus and Cherkaoui for the Avignon Festival. On that occasion Vandekeybus decided to let his text by Paul Bowles be pondered over by a live donkey on the stage, while Cherkaoui danced the nature spirit from Bowles' tale in a continuous metamorphosis of movement. For the new *IT 3.0* the two decided to take the stage together, both using the characteristic movements of Cherkaoui's original djinn. The new version has thus become an interplay between their respective styles of movement, a confrontation with their own dancing body as it has evolved, an exercise in memory, recognition and letting go.

In 2012 Cherkaoui intends to further explore the structure of components and identities in people and objects. *Puz/zle* is the highly appropriate working title of a project in which he wonders what happens if you take away a piece of someone's identity or exchange it for a piece of someone or something else. The premiere is scheduled for the Festival of Avignon, summer 2012. Cherkaoui will not be showing a mindless reprise of earlier work in 2013 either. In that year the Muntschouwburg in Brussels also has *Three Duets*, three revised duets from earlier work by Cherkaoui in its programme: his adaptation of Nijinski's *Faun*, followed by *Rein* from the opera *Das Rheingold* under the direction of Guy Cassiers. In this Cherkaoui links the theme of obsessive cleanliness with the dancer's body. This is followed by the final duet from *Babel*WORDS with Navala Chaudari and Damien Fournier.

Meanwhile Cherkaoui continues to receive commissions from ballet companies. Last year saw the première of his *Labyrinth* (2011), a work for the Dutch National Ballet. In 2012 there are plans for a collaborative effort with the Pilobolus ballet company from Connecticut in the U.S.A..

Just as before, in Eastman Cherkaoui wants to alternate his larger scale choreographies with more intimate work and to test his own contemporary dance idiom against other dance cultures. He continues to tour with the modest *Dunas* (2009) with which he and the Flamenco dancer María Pagés walked away with the Spanish Giraldillo (the Oscar of Flamenco dancing). In the same season Cherkaoui created *Play* with the Indian Shantala Shivalingappa, a dancer who is at home in classical kuchipudi dance but who has also worked with Pina Bausch and Peter Brook. For 2013 a Tango-project is under way with a partner from Argentina. For Cherkaoui this kind of direct confrontation of movement styles invariably opens the way to inspiring research into new cross-fertilisations. ■

www.east-man.be

Translated by Sheila M. Dale

Haarlem

Wandering Through Myths

When I arrived at Haarlem station I was struck by a sense of déjà-vu. It felt almost as though I'd been there before, even though I was sure I hadn't. I sat down on a bench to allow the beautiful tiled pictures and fine woodwork of the waiting rooms – all dating back to 1900 – time to sink in. Slowly, other images began to merge with reality and it finally dawned on me. Of course I knew the station. It's a popular location for films. Whenever the filmmakers need a historic station, the advertisements are taken down and modern travellers are kept out. Paul Verhoeven's *Black Book* (Zwartboek) and Ben Verbong's *The Girl with the Red Hair* (Het meisje met het rode haar) and a number of other films owe some of their *couleur locale* to Haarlem railway station. Looking back, this first impression proved to be symbolic of my entire visit to the city. In Haarlem, you constantly move on the borders of reality, switching between past and present; when you leave, you're no longer entirely certain what is truth and what is myth.

Sitting on that bench, I also remembered that the filming for Steven Soderbergh's *Ocean's Twelve* made national news in 2004. A Thalys train had been brought to Haarlem just for the film – those international trains normally never visit the city. It became snagged on the overhead lines and rail traffic between Haarlem and Amsterdam was disrupted for days. Haarlem's station also had to stand in for the station of Amsterdam in that film; the media's reality is often at odds with actual facts. And here Amsterdam enters the picture, the city's big brother, a brother with whom Haarlem has a rather difficult relationship. Amsterdam is, of course, the capital city of the Netherlands and it eclipses neighbouring Haarlem in terms of culture, economy and tourists. But Amsterdam is in the province of Noord-Holland, of which Haarlem is in fact the capital and as such is entitled to pull rank on Amsterdam.

A good few Amsterdammers, particularly ones with children, have chosen to seek refuge in Haarlem, where it is quieter and safer and you can live closer to the beach and the dunes without having to miss out on all the advantages of the capital city. And it's only fifteen minutes by car or train between the two.

Haarlem Station.
©Fay Asselbergs.

Shattered myths

There is certainly no question of Haarlem being viewed as a suburb of Amsterdam. The city has its own rich and valued history, which can be seen in many different places. I have often wondered about the ideal way to explore a city. Do you head straight for the highlights or wander around at random? Either way, you can be sure you'll miss all kinds of things, but Haarlem really calls for the second method. Firstly, because it's not so big that you can easily get lost and, secondly, because the city constantly reveals the most marvellous secrets to the attentive traveller. You'll find *hofjes* popping up all over the city: small courtyards with almshouses around a garden, where beguines and poor men and women could spend their old age in centuries gone by. These places

Market Place
with the St. Bavo's Church.
©Fay Asselbergs.

are hidden behind small gates or impressive doors and you may need to overcome a certain reluctance to lift the latch and slip inside. But before you know it, you are surrounded by the monastic peace, order and silence that makes the busy city seem as unreal as the image before you. This isn't possible, you think, but it is possible – in Haarlem.

My decision to use the zigzag method of exploration was amply rewarded, as there are two interesting sights on either side of the station: Ripperdapark and Kenaupark. I remembered enough about the history of my homeland to realise that these parks preserved two famous names from the Eighty Years' War (1568–1648). In 1572–1573, the Spaniards laid siege to the city for seven months. Following a valiant defence, the starving city was captured: the garrison was slain and goods were looted. Kenau Simonsdochter Hasselaer is said to have played an important role during the city's defence as a leader of the women of Haarlem, who stood on the city walls and poured down boiling oil upon the enemy. Her name has become synonymous with women who can stand up for themselves. In truth, no one knows for certain that she ever actually played this role. Kenau is one of the many myths and legends that make up the history of Haarlem. But Wigbolt Ripperda was definitely one of the leaders of Haarlem's defence. He was among the 2000 leading citizens of Haarlem who met their end during the attack. Most were drowned in the River Spaarne, but Ripperda was beheaded in the marketplace.

Passing through the Hofje van Staats – where Bubb Kuyper Veilingen, the most important Dutch auction house for books, manuscripts, prints and drawings, occupies the main building – and down alleyways that took me past the old Walloon church and the neighbouring Haarlem red-light district, I made my way to the bars and restaurants of Klokhuisplein, which is surrounded by the Grote Kerk, or Large Church, also known as St. Bavo's Church, or simply the Bavo, and by the buildings where the Enschede printing house was located for over two centuries. I know my literature, so I asked the waitress if the cinnamon biscuit that came with my coffee was a *'Haarlemmer halletje'*, because I'd read about them. *The Oprechte Haerlemsche Courant* mentioned this popular treat way back in 1711, but even so the girl who brought my coffee looked at me as if I'd gone mad. When questioned further, she also proved to be unaware that our banknotes and postal stamps used to be printed only a few metres away. And she drew a complete blank when I asked her how old the Bavo was.

I soon got the answer to that question (built between 1310 and 1520; the tower was added at a later date) on the other side of the church, on the Grote Markt, the marketplace, where an elderly gentleman was enthusiastically telling an interested group about all the sights. I discreetly joined the group, as a non-paying guest, but I would more than make up for my free lecture later. Wim Vogel – that turned out to be the man's name – had written a topographical guide to literary Haarlem. I discovered that this aspect of the city's history also went back a long way. On one corner of the Grote Markt, the great Renaissance scholar and writer Dirck Volkertszoon Coornhert (1522–1590) started a printing press, while on the other corner was the printing press of Abraham de Casteleyn (1628–1681), who founded the *Uprechte Haerlemsche*

Courant in 1656, the world's oldest surviving newspaper. This square is dominated by the Bavo, which has another curious Haarlem legend attached to it. In 1218–1219, the Egyptian seaport town of Damietta was conquered during a crusade. The harbour was closed off with a heavy chain, but the Haarlemmers broke through it in a ship which had a saw attached to it. The story is apparently untrue, but every night, between nine and half past, the Damiaatjes, the bells brought back from Egypt, ring out from the Bavo's tower to commemorate this feat. The church is also the burial place of the famous poet Willem Bilderdijk (1756–1831), who spent the last years of his life in Haarlem. Bilderdijk awarded himself the noble title of 'Heer van Teisterbant', along with the authority to conduct and annul his own marriages, all through direct appeal to God, with whom he was apparently on good terms. Opposite the Bavo is the town hall of Haarlem, the former hunting lodge of the Counts of Holland, which dates back to the fourteenth century.

The Spaarne with Teylers Museum on the right.
©Fay Asselbergs.

Vogel reserved his most exuberant eloquence for the most controversial myth from Haarlem's history. We were standing at the foot of a bronze statue of a monk-like figure who, somewhat triumphantly, was holding aloft a block with the letter A on it. This was the statue of Laurens Janszoon Coster, who for centuries, particularly in the Netherlands, was believed to have invented the art of printing with movable type in around 1420, thereby, with God's help, spreading the light of knowledge across the world. When this statue was unveiled in 1856, with great festivity, the rain was pouring down. Maybe it was the Supreme Being's way of showing that he did not entirely agree. In fact, even at the time, there were Haarlemmers who doubted Coster's claim, but they didn't mention it because no one wanted to dampen the party spirit. It reflects well on the legend-loving city that it was a Haarlemmer, Adriaan van der Linde, who in the second half of the nineteenth century found arguments to prove that the figure of Coster was a composite of two people, a sexton and a candle-maker, who had this much in common: neither of them had invented printing with movable type. But the statue remained and the story continued to appear in history books until well into the twentieth century.

Bar-hopping

After Wim Vogel's audience had thanked him with a round of polite applause, I invited him for a drink, because I realised that I'd found an unexpected and inexhaustible source of information. We headed for a table outside Brinkmann, the famous café-restaurant, which has been renowned for its coffee and croquettes since 1879. Vogel talked with great enthusiasm about the buildings we could see: the Vishal, or fish hall, where the Haarlemmers used to buy the seafood brought by women from Zandvoort, and where now Haarlem's finest artists display their work; the Vleeshal, the meat hall, built for the local butchers in the early sixteenth century by city architect Lieven de Key, and now the Frans Hals Museum's modern-art annexe. Beside it, the Verweyhal, named after Haarlem painter Kees Verwey (1900–1995), about whom numerous anecdotes are still doing the rounds. If he didn't like you, he'd chase you down the stairs with his walking stick, even if you were the mayor himself.

Was it because he rarely found such an eager listener? Did he have nothing better to do? Was he bored? Whatever the reason, Vogel offered to take me on a tour of a few of the city's highlights. I gratefully accepted his offer. I paid the bill and we set off. Past the Toneelschuur, a theatre designed by Joost Swarte, the internationally renowned comic artist and graphic designer. To Teylers Museum, the oldest museum in the world, with its diverse collection of art, minerals, historical devices and other artefacts. Vogel introduced me to the Head of Exhibitions, an enthusiastic storyteller, who, gasping for air as he delivered his unstoppable torrent of words, had tales to tell about even the smallest piece of rock and tiniest prehistoric mouse tooth. He was even able to give us a fascinating lecture about the labels that were attached to the exhibits centuries ago. We visited the Frans Hals Museum, formerly a home for old men, and looked at Hals's magnificent *schuttersstukken,* his paintings of the city guard; we walked along shopping streets, gazing not at the display windows, but above them, at the impressive facades, and sampled the atmosphere of various *hofjes.* My guide was not a young man and all that talking was thirsty work, so we stopped off at every bar we passed. Our spirits rose, along with the beer bill.

On the southern side of the city, outside the original walls, I was surprised to find a beautiful square, Florapark, with monumental trees and monumental buildings. Lots of interesting facts there, too. One house, built at the end of the nineteenth century by the intellectual Johannes van Vloten (1818–1883), was made of unusual red bricks. He was an enlightened father whose offspring included three beautiful and intelligent daughters, each of whom married a prominent writer or artist – Frederik van Eeden, Willem Witsen and Albert Verwey – with the result that all three of them were unhappy in their own way. Van Vloten had his house built in the same red brick as the Rijksmuseum in Amsterdam in order to demonstrate his support for what was a controversial project. People generally use bricks in a different way when they wish to express their disapproval. The large house was guarded by a tiny, yapping dog, which was apparently called Toos, because that was the name the current owner used to call it to heel.

On the edge of Florapark is a statue of Frans Hals. It ended up in that particular location because the philanthropist who paid for it believed that it should be situated close to his home and that the artist should be gazing approvingly at his house. Nearby, we encountered Villa Welgelegen, the most beautiful neoclassical building in the Netherlands, built in around 1800 by Henry Hope, an English merchant banker, and now the seat of the provincial government. We crossed the road and came to a large field, the 'Vlooienveld', or 'flea field', where every year on 5 May a popular music festival commemorates the 1945 liberation. This expanse of grass leads to a deer park with a city farm, which then turns into a beautiful stretch of urban woodland, the centuries-old

Monument for
Laurens Janszoon Coster
in the Haarlemmerhout.
©Fay Asselbergs.

Haarlemmerhout. Vogel led me through the woodland from one curiosity to the next, including a pedestal without a statue which was unveiled in 1823 on the spot where Coster supposedly invented printing with movable type. Having cut letters from alder bark for his grandchildren, he fell asleep and woke to discover that, by divine providence, the letters had left an imprint in the sand. The Haarlemmerhout also played a part in the calculation of the year that Coster made his discovery. The trees were uprooted in 1426 during the siege of the city by Jacoba of Bavaria. According to one scholar, Coster started his experiments in 1420. Armed with these dates, the committee for the celebration to mark 400 years of printing decided to take the average, and settled on 1823.

The wood became famous in Dutch literature because of the story 'A Disagreeable Person in the Haarlemmerhout' (Een onaangenaam mens in de Haarlemmerhout') by Hildebrand (the pseudonym of Nicolaas Beets, 1814–1903). This tale expressed the hereditary animosity between Haarlem and Amsterdam in the form of a cousin from Amsterdam who comes to visit the narrator in Haarlem. The Amsterdammer is a disgruntled grouch who scoffs at all the delights of Haarlem, criticising everything as 'a poor show'. Hildebrand's grateful fellow citizens later chose to honour the writer who had fought for the city with such chivalry by erecting a monument to him in the Haarlemmerhout in 1913. A competition was held, but the winner, Jan Bronner, needed just under half a century to overcome all of the hurdles and finally have his fountain with six statues built. It was actually finished in 1962, which must be a world record.

A vision

Tired and hungry, we decided to have a bite to eat at a restaurant on Wagenweg opposite the wood, which logically also has the name 'Hout'. It turned out to be an excellent place, with good food, nice prices and very pleasant staff. During the meal, Wim Vogel had a great deal to say about the virtues of the city he loves, even though its inhabitants are sometimes described as 'houten Haarlemmers' (wooden Haarlemmers), because they have a reputation for being a little stiff. He talked about the variety of the music scene, the biennial choir festival, the organ concerts on the Müller organ in the Bavo, on which the young Mozart once played. He referred to the brewing, the damask weaving, the bleaching, the printing and the trade in flower bulbs, which had ensured the wealth of the city in the past, more so than now. He chuckled about *Haarlemmerolie,* Haarlem oil, a revolting remedy for all known ills, whose efficacy has never been proven, but which even today is still exported to distant lands and enjoys an indestructible reputation, particularly among sailors. He mentioned the baseball and the cricket that are particularly popular in this city and the football club, the HFC, which is the oldest in the Netherlands. Major names in Dutch literature also came up in the conversation, from the seventeenth-century dramatist and poet Pieter Langendijk to more recent figures such as children's author J.B. Schuil, poet Lodewijk van Deyssel ('Te Haarlem waait het zeer'), writer and media personality Godfried Bomans and poet/writer Louis Ferron. And together we also came to the conclusion that Haarlem's reputation as the place where the best Dutch is spoken should be seen as yet another of the many myths that cling to this city.

I happily paid the bill at the restaurant and then I went for a wander down Eindenhoutstraat. I looked inside the cosy, warmly lit living rooms, with their well-stocked bookcases, pianos and real art on the walls, and children and adults watching large plasma-screen televisions, glass in hand. And suddenly, in one of those living rooms, I saw a scene that struck me like a vision: a trio (piano, violin and cello) was sitting there, busily making music, just as might have happened one hundred years ago in that same living room. That's not possible, I thought; but it really was possible – in Haarlem.

Further along the street I unlocked my front door; then I quieted the dog and stroked the cat, brushed my teeth and went to bed content. ∎

Translated by Laura Watkinson

'We Can Get the Witch-Doctor but We Cannot Get God'

Witchcraft in the Low Countries

[ROBIN BRIGGS]

Witchcraft, even as a subject for historical enquiry, needs to be treated with great caution, coupled with real subtlety. Until very recently the persecution of supposed witches in early modern Europe was regularly condemned as a prime example of ignorance and superstition, which then might be used as an index to award retrospective blame or credit to particular confessions and nations. Protestant and Catholic scholars often sought to portray the 'other side' as notably guilty in this fashion, forgetting the proverbial warnings about stones and glasshouses. The Low Countries lay all too open to such facile interpretations, because the region does indeed provide some striking contrasts. Although intermittent persecution had existed since the late Middle Ages, and there were the celebrated Arras trials of 1460, the peak period (as for all of Western Europe) coincided with the Eighty Years War and the division of the 17 provinces inherited by Charles V. Three contrasting areas had emerged by the late sixteenth century. Luxembourg, whose affairs were only very loosely supervised by the Council of State in Brussels, saw an intense persecution at one of the highest levels (relative to population) anywhere in Europe, which is now reckoned to have claimed between 2,000 and 3,000 victims. This was largely a grass-roots phenomenon, often driven by special village committees appointed to organize prosecutions; the authorities in Brussels were increasingly worried about legal irregularities, which they found great difficulty in curbing. The number of trials declined after 1650, before they ended with the French occupation of 1683. Since Luxembourg would not normally be thought part of the Netherlands this tragic story will not be discussed in any detail here. By comparison the Southern Netherlands under Spanish rule had many fewer trials, but several hundred death sentences were passed and there were some more spectacular outbursts, including some cases of demonic possession attributed to witchcraft. In the Northern provinces under the States-General, with their non-inclusive minority Calvinist church, prosecutions were rarer, with perhaps 150 executions, the last at the exceptionally early date of 1608.

There has been an obvious temptation to interpret these differences in terms of a 'modernization' theory, associating persecution with rural backwardness, traditional religion, and autocratic government. Although such factors probably do all possess some marginal relevance, on closer examination none of them

comes close to accounting properly for a notably complex situation on the ground. It is far from obvious just what the numbers of trials can be taken to indicate; they are certainly not a reliable index of beliefs in witchcraft, local activity directed to countering its effects, or magical practices more generally. Apart from Luxembourg, the whole of the Low Countries really belongs with the broad sweep of Western Europe in this period, where there was an intermittent and rather inefficient attack on alleged witches by legal means, a relatively modest persecution very largely driven by local demands rather than by the rulers. Wherever the surviving documentation allows detailed investigation historians have found only contingent reasons for why one village or small region saw much greater activity than some of its neighbours. The overall conclusion is that in both rural and urban communities witchcraft beliefs were commonplace, but there was great reluctance to denounce neighbours to the authorities, coupled with a marked preference for informal methods of control. Luxembourg, on the other hand, looks to have been the north-western outlier of a zone stretching up either side of the Rhine from the Western Alps northwards. This Rhineland corridor was characterized by relatively weak states and a tendency to political and religious fragmentation, also in some cases by legal arrangements which probably made prosecutions easier. Although there were striking local divergences here too, a very high proportion of known European trials for witchcraft can be located within this relatively restricted area. The Low Countries stood on its fringe, so it is interesting that they were not drawn in to much higher levels of legal persecution.

Pieter van der Heyden's 1559 engraving after Pieter Bruegel, now in the Rijksmuseum in Amsterdam, depicts The Witch of Malleghem, a village healer who played on the gullibility of her audiences. She and her assistants were pretending to cure madness or folly by removing stones from the heads of the sufferers. This reminds us that sixteenth-century people could be well aware of the possibilities of deceit and trickery.

This is one of several illuminations in copies of a 1460s treatise on the Waldensian heresy, associated with the Arras witchcraft trials of 1460, showing a group of devil-worshippers engaged in a precursor of the witches' sabbat. This would only become a common theme for artists a century later. MS Du crime de Vauderye, Royal Library, Brussels.

Little eagerness to persecute

The Revolt itself, and the longer story of attempts to enforce religious orthodoxy, might suggest some characteristics shared by both Northern and Southern provinces. Precocious urbanization may have affected only a minority of these directly, but it implied unusual possibilities for migration from rural areas too; as in England, a relatively mobile society could defuse local tensions more readily. Power tended to be dispersed, shared out among a nexus of local oligarchies and professional groups, generally far more concerned to defend their privileges than to act as moral policemen. The ability of Anabaptists, Mennonites and other religious dissidents to survive within this milieu is striking evidence for a lack of persecuting zeal. Such reluctance can only have been powerfully reinforced by the traumatic experiences of the mid-sixteenth century, with their legacy of religious pluralism in the North and considerable tolerance even in the South. The occasional episode pointed up the danger that localism could make space for individual persecutors, but in general consensual and collegial practices look to have operated as a very effective inhibitor. This did not prevent a trickle of witchcraft cases, most of which seem to have been instigated by local officials in response to popular pressure; however these never escalated into more general campaigns, and tended to attract disapproval from central authorities if numbers of accusations increased. Hardline Calvinists in the North displayed little eagerness to persecute, being much more concerned about the ubiquity of popular superstition. If the possession cases of the early seventeenth century attracted support from some groups of Catholic zealots in the South, they found to their dismay that the political and ecclesiastical hierarchies saw matters very differently. A relatively intense early 1590s persecution inspired by two lords in Peelland was greeted with unanimous hostility by the local Catholic clergy. Like the lawyers and divines in the Republic, these priests were concerned about the abuse of process and the risks when innocent persons were accused. Such worries about the actual conduct of trials seem to have been the crucial reason why death sentences for witchcraft disappeared from the United Provinces in the first decade of the seventeenth century. Nor were similar concerns absent in the South, where the government issued several ordinances seeking to improve procedure in witchcraft trials between 1591 and 1623; these have too often been interpreted as simple encouragements to persecution, when their intention was evidently much more balanced.

Poor women or nuns

The Low Countries therefore belong to that much larger part of Europe where legal proceedings against supposed witches were commonplace but not particularly common, and the most striking feature was how soon courts in the Republic refused to pass death sentences – this also goes a long way to explain why the death rate in the South was significantly higher. Here trials continued at moderate (if very patchy) levels until the 1650s, and did not end in some places until the 1680s. The discrepancy cannot merely be ascribed to Catholic traditionalism, when one remembers the notably sceptical attitude being taken by the Roman and Spanish Inquisitors in the same period. It may well be, however, that the second phase of the Eighty Years War saw far less interchange across the frontier zones than previously, so that administrators and jurists in the South would have remained largely unaware of the changed approach in the Republic. In addition, most contemporaries probably thought witchcraft trials to be a relatively unimportant if routine phenomenon; they were far from seeing them as a touchstone of rationalism, as modern historians are prone to do, and would hardly have felt any need to worry about cases that only involved humble people. It was different when nuns at a Brigittine convent in Lille succumbed to an outbreak of demonic possession in 1612-14, and in obvious imitation of the recent Gaufridy case at Aix-en-Provence accused their convent almoner of being the witch responsible. The Dominican exorcists from Aix were brought in through the influence of a powerful nobleman, the Count of Montmorency, and started to extract astonishing claims from the nuns. These extended to the idea that exorcism could force the demons in the nuns' bodies to reveal crucial truths about religion and politics, behind which a blatant ventriloquism was all too evident to observers. Several leading Catholic clerics reacted strongly against the exorcisms, then the papal nuncio took charge of the case and with assistance from the Pope closed the whole affair down. The danger of scandal and discredit in the upper levels of the Church evidently aroused fears on a quite different scale from the executions of witches who were predominantly poor women.

Some other aspects of the persecution deserve brief mention. It is important to understand that virtually all trials took place in normal secular courts, with only minimal clerical involvement. As elsewhere in Europe, this was part of a trend towards a much more repressive judicial system, which moved from composition fines to various forms of corporal punishment. In Gelderland and other parts of the North one can discern a pattern in the spread of trials, starting around the 1470s, with ideas and practices filtering in from the nearby Electorate of Cologne where prosecutions had already begun. The relevant expertise was then gradually exported to other provinces, while executioners learned to supplement their traditional battery of tortures with what proved very effective techniques of sleep deprivation through 'watching and walking'. On the side of restraint the Northern Netherlands provide two of the very rare examples (1515 and 1553) where the law of talion was applied to accusers, who were put to death when they failed to substantiate their charges (because the accused resisted the torture). There were occasional lynchings by angry crowds, some of them in maritime communities where the loss of ships might be attributed to witches; these naturally continued into a later period, the last known case being from 1746. Something of a legend has accumulated around the weighing house at Oudewater, supposedly a place where suspects could go in the hope of clearing their names, whose role looks to have been almost entirely an eighteenth-century fable. In both North and South the authorities declared a wish to crack down on a whole range of magical and superstitious activities, but this should not lead to the conclusion that most convicted witches were practitioners of traditional healing; witchcraft was indeed very largely about sickness and healing, but in a very specific idiom that does not fit this model. Many cunning folk were prosecuted, but rarely as witches, and they continued to be punished well into the seventeenth century, often by whipping and banishment from the locality.

Witch-doctors

The greatest historical interest of Low Countries' witchcraft lies in the wealth of surviving evidence for witchcraft as a shared belief system across all social groups below the educated elites. The archives are particularly rich in material relating to the cunning folk, many of whom can properly be described as witch-doctors. What emerges is a picture of widespread therapeutic practices, plainly dating back before the witchcraft trials themselves, and continuing a vigorous life for centuries after the end of the persecution. Although these activities were anathema both to the elite among the Catholic clergy and to the Dutch Reformed Church, and were repeatedly made the subject of formal prohibitions, half-hearted repressive campaigns never seem to have achieved anything significant against them. By the eighteenth century it looks as if most hostile clerics preferred to turn a blind eye; while statistical precision is impossible, the serious decline of magical healing should probably be placed as late as the early twentieth century. This is a pattern that can be paralleled for much of Europe, with witchcraft beliefs having an immensely long history in comparison to the relatively brief period of legal action against supposed witches. Since official medicine was still largely useless, if not positively lethal, there was in truth much to be said for a style of folk medicine that relied heavily on the placebo effect, even if some of its social effects may have been unpleasant. Moreover there were real problems to be dealt with, because there is much

evidence to suggest that people who believe themselves bewitched can sicken or in some cases die as a result; it is a grave error to underestimate the power of fantasy and the imagination. There were no obvious theoretical limits to the range of misfortunes that could be attributed to witchcraft, but in practice various understandings appear to have governed suspicions. For reasons that we may never fully understand, fears of witchcraft waxed and waned, and accusations never became an automatic response to misfortune. While certain kinds of affliction were associated with the ill-will of neighbours, there was also an interpersonal element, because such a diagnosis plainly needed a plausible target, preferably in the form of someone with a reputation or with whom one had recently quarrelled. It was believed that witches could effect evil by glancing at their victim or exchanging small gifts, so it was wise to avoid any relationship and even eye contact with suspects.

In coastal areas bewitchment could be blamed for maritime accidents, elsewhere it might account for misfortunes with animals and milk churns, but everywhere human sicknesses formed the commonest basis for accusations. The surest way to lift the curse was to have the witch pronounce a blessing, so much of the activity of the witch-doctors was devoted to identifying the person(s) to be coerced – often very unwillingly – into this ritual. Some elementary counter-magic might also be employed, sometimes by priests using

David Teniers the Younger painted several pictures in the style of this Sabbat Scene from 1633, which makes witches a subject for entertainment rather than terror. Musée de la Chartreuse, Douai.

A contemporary engraving of the execution of Anne Hendricks at Amsterdam in 1571.

exorcisms or sacramentals. When the cunning-man Gillis Snouk was banished from Staats-Vlaanderen for thirty years in 1657 it was said that in some sixty cases over the last six or seven years he had used

> 'black magic, divination and blessing of people, cat-
> tle and farms in the sense that he disenchanted people
> who were already bewitched by blessing and conjuration,
> thereby using many books and documents containing
> many abominable and blasphemous conjurations, adjur-
> ing the devils, princes of evil and murderers, male and
> female witches . . .'

The official line that only recourse to God was permissible must have seemed very feeble by comparison, as it did to a farmer's wife from Gelderland, who when asked in 1647 why she did not pray to God rather than running to a witch-doctor, answered: 'We can get that man [the witch-doctor] but we cannot get God.' A remarkable analysis of these patterns was offered by the Catholic priest of Groessen in Gelderland (previously in Cleves), Jacob Vallick, in his booklet of 1559 Tooveren, wat der voor een werc is (Witchcraft, what manner of work it is), a notably shrewd and sceptical work. He was one of a number of writers from the Netherlands who expressed similar doubts, including Johan Wier, Cornelis Loos, Philippus Rovenius, and Balthasar Bekker. The most famous demonologist who took the other side was the Jesuit Martin Delrio, but the influence of his encyclopaedic 1599 work on magic on judicial practice in the South has probably been much exaggerated. There is little doubt that most of these writers were expressing an attitude common to reforming clerics of all denominations, who reacted with deep hostility to a world of popular belief that long defied all efforts at reform. They also had good reason to think that witchcraft charges might be socially disruptive, for suspects were often shunned or maltreated - one reason why they often brought slander cases against their accusers, long after they were at no risk of prosecution in the courts. ■

FURTHER READING

Marijke Gijswijt-Hofstra and Willem Frijhoff (eds), *Nederland betoverd*
(De Bataafsche Leeuw, Amsterdam, 1987).

Jos Monballyu, *Van heksereij beschuldigt:*
Hexenprocessen in Vlaaanderen tijdens de 16de en 17en eeuw (Heule, UGA, 1996).

Robin Briggs, *Heksenwaan: de sociale en culturele geschiedenis van hekserij in Europa*
(Uitgeverij Agora – Kampen, 2000). English second edition, *Witches and Neighbours:*
the Social and Cultural Context of European Witchcraft (Blackwells, Oxford, 2002).

'You Don't Know Me'

The Breakthrough of Urszula Antoniak

[KARIN WOLFS]

Safe, coquettish, caricatural, wooden and poorly balanced; the terms reviewers have used since 1993 to describe the film-maker Urszula Antoniak's early work have often been fairly harsh. So the breakthrough she achieved with her first full-length feature film *Nothing Personal* at the Locarno International Film Festival in 2009 came like a bolt from the blue. She won six prizes for it, including two prestigious 'Leopards', one for the best debut and one for the best leading actress, plus the international film critics' award. The film also won great acclaim in the Netherlands, and was awarded no less than four Golden Calves: for the best long feature film, best director, best camera and best sound design. This success meant that a year later her second feature film-in-the-making was welcomed to the Ateliers in Cannes, a networking occasion where exceptional international talent is brought in contact with financiers, co-producers and sales agents. This year, that film – *Code Blue* – which was co-produced by, among others, Lars von Trier's Zentropa production company, was given its premiere at the Quinzaine in Cannes, the antechamber for the world's best film-makers.

How is it possible for (opinions of) the quality of a film-maker's work to swing from one extreme to the other in such a short time? Antoniak would probably find the answer less interesting than the question. In interviews she has repeatedly expressed her amazement at the Dutch obsession with finding explanations and their fear of mystery. Ever since her acclaimed film debut, Antoniak has systematically ignored one of the fundamental rules of the Hollywood film tradition: that a film needs a plot-driven leading character acting in a logically explicable way to draw the viewer into the story. Humans are too complex to understand on the basis of a few simple psychological pointers. This is precisely why she uses enigmatic elements which provide the complexity to enthral her audience; they just have to think for themselves about what lies behind the character's behaviour. Antoniak doesn't give it to them on a plate. If this article had been written like one of Antoniak's films, it would not contain any analysis, only descriptions of her work.

'You don't know me' is perhaps the best summary of what Antoniak's work is all about. Although these words are actually spoken by the leading male character in *Nothing Personal,* the phrase recurs in various forms in several of her films.

Bijlmer Odyssey, 2004.

The work with which she graduated from the film academy, *Farewell* (Vaarwel, 1993) was already about the extent to which married people are able to know each other. It is a literally and figuratively dark story of an architect called Martin who suspects his wife Liz of having an affair with the lawyer Jacques. To accompany the picture of a sleeping Liz, we hear Martin in voice-over reflecting on how he is trying to see something 'that lay buried deep inside her'.

In Antoniak's first work following her graduation, the television drama *Bijlmer Odyssey* (Bijlmer Odyssee, 2004), a young man loses his new-found love when he leaves her flat in the Bijlmer estate in Amsterdam to fetch some food from a chip shop and gets lost. They have just been in bed together, but don't know each other's names. When the owner of the snack bar asks him to describe her, he doesn't get any further than 'She's special'.

In Antoniak's second television drama, *Dutch for Beginners* (Nederlands voor beginners, 2007), we see a woman teacher of Dutch trying, in a pushy and superior manner, to get the Polish woman Alina to spill the beans about her marriage to a Dutch man by saying 'I understand you'. To which Alina pulls a face and replies 'I *don't* understand *you*'.

The impossibility of knowing another person is also one of the fundamental themes of *Code Blue* (2011). This film is about a sister in a hospital who looks after terminally ill patients. If she thinks she can help them by doing so, she will even deliver her patients from their suffering on her own authority. By showing what terrible misunderstandings this can lead to, Antoniak mercilessly rebukes the arrogance of thinking one can understand another human. The truth of what Sister Marian tells others about herself cannot be checked. Her neighbour Conrad – who knows more about Marian than most – says she looks like an actress.

Nothing Personal, 2009.

A miracle in Poland

Who is Urszula Antoniak? What determines her identity as a filmmaker? Antoniak, who has lived in the Netherlands for over twenty years now, gets really worked up when she is referred to as Polish. In an interview on the Kunststof arts programme in 2009 she said: 'I am a Dutch filmmaker. I am a Dutch national but I am repeatedly confronted with my origin'. In the same interview she said: 'Migration forces you to confront who you are. You leave your environment, your culture, your language, family and friends behind and suddenly arrive in a new country where everything is alien. But it's an excellent opportunity to get to know yourself, to find out who you actually are when stripped of all those things'

It is no coincidence that in her films Antoniak makes her characters abandon their possessions and travel abroad (Anne dumps her possessions on the street when she leaves for Ireland in *Nothing Personal*; Penny throws her clothes away before flying to New York in *Bijlmer Odyssey*). Almost all of Antoniak's films feature boxes of possessions that are given away, thrown away, acquired or rediscovered: in *Farewell* and *Code Blue* there are lives hidden away in packing cases and in *Dutch for Beginners* and *Nothing Personal* we see boxes full of things that are superfluous but still not without meaning.

Antoniak's characters are always thrown onto their own resources. Loneliness and death are never far away. As a human being, can you leave your life behind and make a new start?

Urszula Antoniak was born in the town of Częstochowa in Southern Poland, the 'Polish Lourdes'. It is a place of pilgrimage that is home to the 'Black Madonna', a Byzantine icon that is credited with healing powers. She grew up there in a small flat behind the Iron Curtain with her mother, a textile worker, her father, a staunch communist who worked in a steel factory, and her five-years-older sister who is her opposite in almost every respect except their common love of books. Antoniak keeps her date of birth secret, 'because it is often used to typify a generation of filmmakers. I have very little in common with my age group, and besides, immigration takes up three to five years of your life.' When Antoniak was fourteen years old she witnessed a miracle: 'It was in the thirteenth-century baroque church with the Chapel of the Madonna: a dark place that glitters with the votive tablets of healed members of the congregation and a frightening icon of a black woman with an all-seeing angry stare. One evening there was a procession. There was a group saying the rosary. I saw a seriously spastic man rise from his wheelchair, his face absolutely terrified. Everyone went quiet. The man walked towards the icon and collapsed unconscious on the floor. The other people fell to their knees praying loudly and lying on the ground while organ music broke out. 'Wow!' I thought: 'I want this too.' I wasn't interested in the cause of the miracle but in the effect it had on people. At that moment the filmmaker in me was born.'

In the winter of 1987 Antoniak swapped the depressing, repressive climate of her homeland for the freer, capitalist Netherlands. She had just completed a course in film production at the film academy in Katowice. When she arrived in the Netherlands she did all kinds of jobs, 'I started at the bottom of the ladder as a factory worker', before enrolling at the Dutch Film Academy to study directing. She told the newspaper *Het Parool*: 'I thought it was a smart move because then I could learn the language and the profession and make contacts as well'. After graduating in 1993 she worked among other things as a screenwriter and researcher for documentaries. It was a happy time during which she lived with her great love Jacek Lenartowicz, formerly the drummer with the popular Polish rock band Tilt – 'the Polish Sex Pistols', who came to study screenplay writing and directing at the Dutch Film Academy when Antoniak was in her second year there. But in 2003, when Urszula was working on her first television drama, *Bijlmer Odyssey*, fate played a cruel trick. Jacek was diagnosed with a brain tumour and had only six months to live, during which period she cared for him at home. She revealed to *De Volkskrant* that: 'Losing your loved one, witnessing his death, experiencing the loneliness, the reflection which goes with it, changes everything. It increases the urgent need to communicate something.'

Death is part of life

Following the death of her partner, Antoniak fell into a black hole. She lost virtually all contact with other people, with the outside world. It took months before she found herself again and was able to make choices. 'I felt hardly any connection with life any more, but at the same time that gave me a great sense of freedom. I tried to stay mentally healthy by writing short stories and screenplays,' she told *Het Parool*. She developed ideas that she would later use in her films. As in the subsequent opening scene of *Nothing Personal*, she deposited her – Jacek's – things on the street to observe how passers-by picked out what appealed to them. 'For me, that was his funeral,' Antoniak said in the same interview.

Antoniak reinvented herself; perhaps she is continuously doing so. After all, what makes a human being into a person? What determines someone's individuality? And how decisive is contact with others in this? What makes someone change direction? These are the central questions in her work.

The good thing is that after Jacek's death Antoniak's work both changed and remained the same. The theme is the same but the way it is presented is bolder. The greatest difference is the extent to which, since her first feature film, Antoniak has relied on the expressive power of the image. While in *Bijlmer Odyssey* and *Dutch for Beginners* each event is still emphasised with superfluous dialogue, probably influenced by TV dramatists, in *Nothing Personal* and *Code Blue* not a single non-essential word is uttered. It is usually the silence that speaks, the landscape or body language. The scenario and editing are much more to the point; perfectly timed, pared down, tightly stylised and stripped of all unnecessary trimmings.

What remained was death, which, with the exception of *Dutch for Beginners*, always plays a role in Antoniak's work. 'Death is part of life,' Antoniak explains; death as a logical presence in films that deal with the possibility of being reborn. About surrender, loneliness, solidarity, love and letting go. The moment when the dead are laid out and disappear under a sheet is depicted with painstaking attention to detail in *Farewell, Nothing Personal* and *Code Blue.*

Kafka and Billy Wilder

Anyone who thinks that Antoniak is a purveyer of doom and gloom doesn't know her very well. Death needs a counterpart too, and in Antoniak's work this can be found in harsh, lively, black humour, whose worth in Antoniak's view can hardly be overestimated: 'I think irony is the most important thing in life. It is organically bound up with it. I find films without irony unbearable'. In an interview with *Cineuropa* she said 'For me irony is the spice of life and its greatest wisdom. I feel I belong to the tradition of Mitteleuropa that mixed Jewish, Slavic and German influences. Think Kafka, Musil, but also Billy Wilder and Ernst Lubitsch, who've spiced Hollywood movies with this typical ironic touch'.

Even *Code Blue,* Antoniak's darkest film so far, includes ludicrous situations and dialogues that appeal to a sense of the absurd. When Sister Marian notices at the supermarket till that an error has been made on the receipt, the lady at the back of the queue soon moves her trolley and goes to another till. It's only a matter of eighty cents, but for Marian it's a matter of principle. The cashier gives her a form that customers can fill in when they want their money back. Marian refuses to take it and demands to speak to the manager. 'It was a mistake,' she tells him, and then, after a silence, 'but I can live with it'. Then, with a stern, silent, superior gaze, she forces the cashier to confess her guilt.

Antoniak's visual style always was distinctive, but it has developed considerably: while her graduation film *Farewell* was already an atmospheric blend of existentialist drama in the style of Bergman and Godard, combined with romantic landscapes reminiscent of the paintings of Caspar David Friedrich and meticulously lit portrait shots evocative of Rembrandt, *Bijlmer Odyssey* was

Nothing Personal, 2009.

surprising for its playfully mobile, lively night-time camera work. In its turn, *Dutch for Beginners* was tightly stylised and carefully framed, using a fixed camera. *Nothing Personal* combined a subjectively observing camera on a tripod turning through wide-angle views of vast landscapes; a style that was maintained in *Code Blue,* but this time with rigid wide-angle shots that outline a chilly, claustrophobic environment composed of the hard, impersonal textures of glass, fabric, linoleum, metal and concrete in which there are hardly any horizons, at most a fragment of sky to provide some 'air'.

The way Antoniak uses sound to make her characters' inner lives palpable is quite striking. In *Farewell* she was already using abstract, gong-like hollow sounds and echoes, as in the scene where the woman wakes with a start when her husband announces on the voice-over that he has found out who his wife's lover is. In *Bijlmer Odyssey,* a thrillingly buzzing, effervescent mix of city sounds contributes substantially to the ominous, macho, alienating atmosphere. In *Nothing Personal,* where, apart from the music the two main characters listen to, no melodious music is played to enhance the atmosphere, the mix used for the soundtrack is, conversely, perfect as a soundscape that makes the silence audible. To achieve this, Antoniak called in the American composer Ethan Rose, who had previously created soundscapes for the skating scenes in Gus Van Sant's *Paranoid Park.* He later did the soundscapes for *Code Blue* also. In this film, Antoniak went one step further by leaving deafening silences where the image would normally demand sound. This is the case in the opening sequence, where an old face looms up out of nowhere; motionless, with glassy open eyes. Just when you start wondering whether the face is dead, its mouth opens in slow motion. To say something? The movement slowly continues into a gasp for breath, then ends in a slow, significant, silent scream.

Code Blue, 2011.

'Lula, I can't understand you!'

Finally, the way Antoniak plays with reality in surrealist or magical-realist scenes is very interesting. This had already formed the backbone of *Farewell,* in which a woman collects her husband, killed in an accident, from a mortuary. When moving house after his death, she finds the diary in which he describes his suspicions about her adultery and his plan to murder her, and thus posthumously she learns about another side of him. The extraordinary thing is that the story is told not through her eyes, but through his; eyes that see adultery while it is uncertain whether it was actually happening. And in this way the cliché of the mourning widow is also called into doubt once again.

There is a powerful scene in *Code Blue* in which Sister Marian is standing next to the door at home with a bunch of pink tulips in her hand. A couple has come to visit her, and they are admiring her new flat and chatting about the view and the traffic while a gentle wind-like murmur is heard on the soundtrack. When this is followed by a virtually identical shot of Marian with a bunch of tulips in her hand, it suddenly becomes uncertain whether she imagined the meaningless routine visit or was able to predict how it was going to be. Antoniak had previously used

Code Blue, 2011.

the same technique in a key scene in *Dutch for Beginners*, where, on a language school outing, the Polish Alina is sitting next to the African Lula on a bench by a windmill right next to its sails as they sweep by dangerously fast. In the next shot they walk into an empty field of corn stubble, speaking each in her own language, while the subtitles fade out until they become illegible. When Alina despairingly cries 'Lula, I can't understand you!', Lula has moved out of shot. Antoniak closes the scene with a shot in which the two women are back on the bench. What went before could have been an illusion, a mirage that made tangible the defective communication between the two women.

Antoniak's work cannot be captured in these few words. Clichés lurk in every sentence. Above all, readers should see Antoniak's films for themselves so as to experience their complex riches and form their own opinion of them. ■

Translated by Gregory Ball

FILMOGRAPHY:

1992: *Fietser*

1993: *Vaarwel*

2004: *Bijlmer Odyssee*

2007: *Nederlands voor beginners*

2009: *Nothing Personal*

2011: *Code Blue*

Joost van den Vondel (1587-1679) at 425

...but what is in my heart
Wells up towards my lips; the inward pressure grows:
Fermenting like new wine, it bursts and overflows
Curry-Comb, 64-66

'La langue de Vondel' – one occasionally still reads it in the French-language press as an alternative to 'Flemish' or 'Dutch'. In the nineteenth century such 'literary' language designations were commonplace, but the formulation has little substance today: the once flourishing Dutch Vondel tradition belongs to the past. Those participating in the 1987 commemoration – predominantly academics – admitted as much. Yet their attitude was not totally one of gloom and doom. Vondel was dead, so long live Vondel! By which they simply meant that what had been forgotten could be rediscovered. Freeing the poet from his own monumental shadow and the many ideological bonds by which he had for so long been shackled, would, they hoped, lead to a renewed and intensified literary-historical encounter. It seemed as if the claim that almost every Dutch political and ideological grouping had laid to Vondel, was now the exclusive right of literary historiography, the focus of whose inquiry would be on the poet as a figure from the past: what his work was like, what his intention was in writing it, what it meant and why people *found* it so wonderful. 'Vondel is a historical figure and only as such does he form part of culture,' wrote the authoritative journal *Tijdschrift voor Nederlandse Taal- en Letterkunde* in its commemorative issue.

We are now a quarter of a century and a new commemoration further on. Is the tide turning? In the current craze for historical rankings, which has not spared the Low Countries, Vondel has fared well. If in the list of the Greatest Dutchmen he ranks only (or, if you prefer, still) 53rd, in the Dutch literary canon, voted on in 2002 by the approximately 1,600 members (literary specialists, linguists and historians) of the venerable *Maatschappij der Nederlandse Letterkunde* (Society of Dutch Literature,1776!), he still occupies second place (after Multatuli). At the same time he is top of the list of unjustly forgotten writers. Productions of his plays remain rare, but when they are performed they still provoke comment. From the 1980s on they were virtually the exclusive province of Vondel's passionate advocate Hans Croiset, often with splendid results. This director was one of the co-founders of the Amsterdam company *Het toneel speelt* (Stage Play, 1996), which specialises in literary theatre and in the past few years has revived the tradition, begun in 1641 but discontinued in 1968, of performing Vondel's *Gysbreght van Aemstel* (1637) every New Year's Day. This tragedy, which dramatises the siege and fall of Amsterdam in 1304 in

Vondel aged 70 (1657), engraving by Cornelis de Visscher from his own drawing. The translation of the Latin inscription is: What Virgil's trumpet, Horace's lyre, Seneca's high buskin and Juvenal's salt wit was to the Romans, Vondel is to the Dutch, when he, vying with all in talent, opens his gifted mouth as the pinnacle of art.

'Trojan style', had, like Rembrandt's *Nightwatch,* almost become a national icon. It had all the ingredients: shocking changes of fortune for brave forefathers, emotional dialogues and blood-curdling narratives, supremely lyrical choruses and the sense of Amsterdam patriotism that was particularly intense in the Golden Age. Cultured Dutch people can still quote the Christmas and marriage choruses without stumbling. A film version announced a few years ago has still to materialise. There has also been an increase in the number of - sometimes very radical - adaptations of Vondel plays or cases of creative rewriting. On the other hand stage critics – often through laziness – continue to express their dislike of their obsolete language and themes.

The actor Willem Ruyter dressed as Bishop Goze-wijn for a performance of *Gysbreght van Aemstel*. Drawing by Rembrandt in the wings of the Amsterdam Theatre (Dresden, Staatliche Kunstsammlungen).

If older literature has been forced onto the defensive in secondary education, contemporary academic Vondel studies present a more hopeful picture. Slowly and accompanied by sometimes heated debates, interpretations are gaining ground that offer a reading of Vondel (mainly his plays) based on new approaches employed by contemporary literary studies which had rarely if ever been applied to canonical authors in Dutch literary history – such as deconstruction, discourse theory and new historicism. Vondel's work, we are now told, is not buried in his own age, but exists in the present and should be the subject of a wide variety of reading strategies. The standard-bearer of this approach is the Leiden professor Frans-Willem Korsten, who uses contemporary perspectives to demonstrate how Vondel's 'polyphonic' plays deal with 'sovereignty' and violence. He reads them as intellectual expressions of political theory that weigh the sovereignty of a natural order positively against the power-based order imposed by God. The fact that in this Korsten virtually always goes beyond the framework of interpretations based on the 'historical' Vondel and the explicit discourse with which the writer positioned his dramas in the so-called 'Berechten' (introductions) to his work, provoked much criticism. On the other hand, these extremely provocative analyses, which are now also available in English (see reading list), have reawakened interest and made the academic world at large aware that Vondel is a great and interesting poet who is still worth studying today. Korsten sees the dramas as 'politically charged, aes-

Title page print of Vondel's
Lucifer (1654), probably engraved
by S. Savry. Michael strikes down
Lucifer with a lightning bolt.
The rebel army fights in a Turkish
crescent formation.

thetically multi-faceted works of art, with their own special linguistic spar-
kle'. At the same time he has proved a passionate advocate of their consistent
translation into contemporary and lively Dutch *and* English.

Meanwhile, more traditional Vondel studies have not fallen silent. Recent
years have seen, for example, an edition of six plays in modern spelling and
with ample notes in a classic series that has since folded (*Delta*) and a new
not particularly searching biography by Piet Calis. In the as yet incomplete
large-scale eight-volume *Geschiedenis van de Nederlandse literatuur* the volume on the 17th century places great emphasis on the way in which Vondel's
work functioned in the literary life and society of his time, and the focus extends to other countries also.

Evaluating Vondel in a European context for a foreign audience, is in any
case no easy task. Vondel is in an unfavourable situation. His work originates
from a relatively small language area. Even in his own day, with the exception
of Germany his work had a low international profile. Only later did it reach
other language areas (French, English, Russian), in fragmentary form and
not always in particularly impressive versions. Other frequently heard explanations for the scant international interest in Vondel maintain that major
sections of his work present worlds that no longer strike a chord with most
people, such as that of the opulent, self-assured Catholic baroque. Another
argument is that the (mainly Biblical) tragedies, written in a brilliant classicist

style, when compared with those of Shakespeare or Racine in which compelling passion and its effects are central, often give the impression of being laborious intellectual constructs. While they treat problems of conscience with great moral and religious intensity, it is felt that they lack theatricality. Their enduring appeal, so their critics maintain, resides mainly in their lyrical content. For this monologues, descriptions of catastrophes and especially the choruses do deserve a place in the European canon. It looks as if a revival in Vondel studies will give further depth and substance to this vision. At any rate, the publishers Brill of Leiden brought out a new English-language volume of studies on Vondel's drama in 2011 (see reading list).

Living for 'Poesy'

Joost van den Vondel was born in Cologne on 17 November 1587 into an Anabaptist family that had fled from Antwerp and in 1595 was also forced to leave its new home on the Rhine. In 1597, after moving from place to place in Germany, the family settled in Amsterdam, where they ran a silk and stocking business, which from 1613 on was managed independently by the poet. His first poems date from 1605. As a devout Anabaptist Vondel is a member of the Chamber of Rhetoric for immigrants from Brabant, his own countrymen. Biblical piety and moral concern for the fatherland are the great themes of his didactic and erudite poetry.

In around the 1620s Vondel, an autodidact busily studying Latin and antiquity, fully embraces the humanist culture of the Amsterdam literary elite. Initially this volte-face is accompanied by a serious depresssion. As a moral guide for society he begins to speak out in passionate, mostly anonymous satires and invectives on the corrupt greed of church and state and the dangers of theocratic Calvinism. Central among these are works in which he takes the side of Johan van Oldenbarnevelt, the elderly chief government adviser, who in 1619 following a power-struggle with the stadholder Maurits van Nassau was sent to the scaffold by the latter under pressure from Calvinist fundamentalists. For Vondel this statesman symbolised peace and resistance to religious meddling in politics. Immediately after Maurits' death the key Senecan drama *Palamedes* (1625), which was interpreted as a political pamphlet, appeared, in which the 'martyred hero' Oldenbarneveldt appeared as a Greek commander falsely accused of treachery. Vondel avoided a potential death sentence from the Court of Holland when well-disposed Amsterdam patricians fined him and banned the play. Naturally the drama went through many editions in a very short time, and Vondel was to be eagerly read in this way on many occasions. Those combative years also see the appearance of the first great hymns, which in exalted or epic style accompany various brilliant facets of the Dutch Golden Age. One true heritage text is *In Praise of Navigation* (Het lof der zee-vaert, 1623): trade and shipping are the route to progress, provided they are employed in the service of peace in a society based on reason and mutual respect. Here Vondel is taking a stand against the violent monopolistic policies being pursued in Asia at that time by the Dutch East India Company and following the line set out by the lawyer Grotius in his treatise on the freedom of the seas.

In the 1630s Grotius, himself forced into exile as a victim of the hard-line Calvinists, becomes a literary and ideological beacon for Vondel: peace among

Vondel died on 5 February *1679* at the age of ninety-one. The drawing by Philips de Koninck dates from shortly before his death (Amsterdam, Rijksprentenbinet). The poet wrote his own epitaph: Here lies Vondel, his story's told, He has perished from the cold.

nations and restoration of the ancient universal and unified Christianity. Like a man possessed, the ambitious poet labours for a long time on a classical epic on Constantine, the first Christian emperor. The project ends in failure and the destruction of the copy. The loss of two children – one of them a son named Constantine after his hero – and his wife was commemorated in funerary poems that have become iconic in Dutch literature. He now turns his full attention on the theatre: in 1638 the Amsterdam Theatre opened with a production of *Gysbreght*, which provoked controversy because of its Roman Catholic setting.

In about 1640 the poet converts to Catholicism, which he makes no secret of. Witness the Roman Catholic martydom plays, including *Maria Stuart* – which again earned him a fine – and a didactic poem defending the Catholic eucharist (*Altaergeheimenissen/* Secrets of the Altar, 1645); Grotius is annexed as a crypto-Catholic. However, Vondel's devotion to city and fatherland remains unshakable, with as its guiding light peace and freedom, including freedom of conscience. In 1653 the Dutch painters acclaim him as their Apollo. These are years of great creativity and high points in his dramatic production and philosophical reflection. Two years after his son, who had taken over the poet's none-too-flourishing business, went bankrupt in 1656, the city regents secured for the destitute Vondel a sinecure post with the official pawnbroker's office. The poet remained extremely active well into old age, and in the 1660s produced a further eight plays (including some of his best-known works), plus a translation of four Greek tragedies and two great didactic poems – averaging over 5,000 lines of verse per year. The high-quality poem *Reflections on God and Religion* (Bespiegelingen van Godt en Godsdienst, 1662), an inspired and well-thought-out synthesis of his theological thinking in no less than 7,352 lines, represents a high point here. In the first book the poet is unmistakably taking issue with the core views of Spinoza: the unity of God and nature and its necessary mathematical basis. Thanks to his private contacts Vondel was able to do this before the philosopher, whose views had become known to an intimate circle, had published a single word. The third book has often been called a masterly interpretation of the Christian view of creation.

Master of modern Biblical tragedy

Vondel's twenty-four original tragedies form a unique contribution to European drama in the seventeenth century, the age of drama par excellence. He is one of the great creators of modern Biblical tragedy – his life's ambition. Moreover, after translating Sophocles' *Electra,* from *Brothers* (Gebroeders, 1640) onwards his aim was to construct them in the Greek style. Brothers is a richly textured and emotional play based on the revenge of the Gibeonites (2 Sam 21), in which David is obliged, because of a previous crime of their father Saul, to order the execution of seven young men. Vondel concentrates mainly on the Sophoclean motif of postponed punishment, David's inner conflict about exacting the unnatural penalty and the pathetic complexity of conflicts within a family. The play made a great impression on audiences and remained in the repertoire of the Amsterdam Theatre for a considerable time. The tormented house of David was to function in a number of plays as *the* counterpart to the Greek Atrides. As regards the application of Greek-Aristotelian dramatic theory, with the preface to his *Jeptha* (1659) the Amsterdam playwright was ahead of the French Classicists. This drive to create a 'modern' tragedy based on a contemporary cultural and philosophical dramatic grammar produced Vondel's masterpieces, which have become classics of the genre.

He begins with a number of pious plays, constructed according to the principles of multiple Biblical interpretations, in which the poet shows himself mainly as a talented innovator in the indigenous rhetorical tradition. His vocation as a 'modern' tragedian really takes off after 1620 via a number of translations of Seneca. From 1640 on this vocation becomes an obsession, certainly after he has abandoned his ambition as a writer of epics. The result is a series of well-crafted plays that are never banal and which pay less attention to the prevailing fashion for spectacle, which gradually distances him from the Amsterdam stage. The stepping stones are easy to trace. Intensely Catholic martyrdom plays which are mainly the expression of a universal idea and in which the influence of Greek concepts is increasingly clearly felt are succeeded by dualistic dramas about savage confrontations between good and evil and end with plays in which the depiction of the *peripeteia* (the sudden reversal in fortune or circumstance) forms the basic principle. The final play in the series is *Noah* (Noach, 1667), an original synthesis of the ancient Christian drama of redemption and Greek tragedy. A further point: few European tragedians have commented on and justified their evolution as explicitly in extensive introductions. These 'prose poetics' – Vondel's preferred form of self-presentation – are among the most interesting meta-texts in seventeenth-century European dramatic literature, all the more so since they relate to plays that are very much part of the collective imagination of Western baroque: rebellious sons, humiliated and triumphant fathers, the self-affirmation of the individual, the fascination of pride and violence, conflicts between reason, passion, faith, authority and justice.

First and foremost comes *Lucifer* (1654), which depicts the fall of the rebel angels. Combined with the hierarchical splendour of the verse, the daring location – 'The play is set in the heavens' – gives this typical courtly and political drama extraordinary depth. The great conflicts of seventeenth-century government are given a truly cosmic resonance: the revolt against the notion of order, the clash between absolutism and feudal allegiance, humility and self-exaltation, the dangers of the destructive power of rhetoric. When after two performances Calvinist ministers had this heavenly decor removed from the theatre as a sacriligious provocation, the play went into seven editions within the year. *Adam in Exile* (Adam in ballingschap, 1664), forms part of this same heavenly cycle that Vondel calls 'the tragedy of tragedies', not only because it deals with the fall of the first human couple, but also because peripeteia occurs in it in prototypical form. Absolute happiness is juxtaposed with utter abasement. It is Vondel's most lyrical tragedy, full of lines on marital happiness that are both ecstatic and sensual. Not until the nineteenth century did it have its first performance.

Poet of the community

A fascinating section of Vondel's poetry comprises the hundreds of poems in every conceivable genre in which, as a city laureate avant la lettre he loyally celebrated or mercilessly lampooned the life of his home town of Amsterdam and the Republic. And few poets of the time followed European history so closely and so critically: the horrors of the Thirty Years' War, the Turkish threat, the British troubles. England plays a major role in Vondel's European poetry, and a translation of these 'British' poems would make a remarkable volume. They focus mainly on England's participation in the Dutch struggle for liberation, the arguments concerning Charles I and what Vondel considered his outrageous execution – contemporaries saw the protagonist of *Lucifer* as a portrait of Cromwell – the family ties between the Stuarts and the House of Orange, the restoration of the monarchy and of course the three wars fought by the Dutch against 'seasick Albion' with the Fire of London as a well-deserved punishment. And to think Vondel once promised Charles II an epic if he would take on the Turks....

Vondel's many poems on works of art and paintings are also increasingly appreciated. He had close friendships with many artists, and apart from that his whole oeuvre is thoroughly pictorial from the outset. Religious fantasies and descriptions of nature and the human face are often consciously couched in the jargon of the artist's studio. He presents a ground-breaking play like *Brothers* at length as a fictionalised painting by Rubens, undoubtedly his favourite artist, with whose work his verse is often compared. That too makes Vondel an eminent representative of the European baroque. ■

Translated by Paul Vincent

WORKS IN ENGLISH BY AND ABOUT VONDEL

PLAYS:

Gysbreght van Aemstel. Trans. Kristiaan Aercke. Toronto: Dovehouse, 1991.
Lucifer. Trans. L.C. van Noppen. New York: Continental Publishing, 1898.
Lucifer. Trans. W. Kirkconnell. Toronto: University of Toronto Press, 1952.
Lucifer. Trans. Noel Clark. Bath: Absolute Press, 1990.
Mary Stuart. Trans. Kristiaan Aercke. Ottawa: Dovehouse, 1996.
Samson. Trans. W. Kirkconnell. Toronto: University of Toronto Press, 1964.

OTHER WORK:

Lof der Zeevaert. In Praise of Navigation. Trans. Peter Skrine, *Dutch Crossing* 8, 1979, 4-33.
Roskam. Curry-Comb. Trans. Paul Vincent and Noel Clark, *Dutch Crossing* 32, 1987, 107-15.

Survey of Vondel's work in English :

P. Vincent, 'Vondel in English. A Bibliography', *Dutch Crossing* 8, (July 1979), 87-88 and 32 (August 1987), 102-105.

FURTHER READING

Theo Hermans (Ed.), *A Literary History of* The *Low Countries*. Rochester, New York, 2009.
Frans-Willem Korsten, *Sovereignty as Inviolability.*
Vondel's Theatrical Explorations in the Dutch Republic. Hilversum: Verloren, 2009.
J. Bloemendaal and W-F. Korsten (Eds.), *Joost van den Vondel,*
Dutch Playwright in the Golden Age. Leiden: Brill, 2011.

Five Poems

By Joost van den Vondel

Beggars' Evening Prayer

Complaint against the 'money-hungry' calvinist judges
of Oldenbarnevelt. Ca. 1630, stanzas 1-4.

Geuse Vesper

Did he bear the fate of Holland
   On his heart,
To the latest breath he drew
   With bitter smart,
Thus to lave a perjured sword
   With stainless blood,
And to batten crow and raven
   On his good?

Was it well to carve that neck
   Within whose veins
Age the loyal blood had withered?
   'Mong his gains
Were not found the Spanish pistoles
   Foul with treason,
Strewn to whet the mob's wild hate,
   That knows no reason.

But the Cruelty and Greed
   Which plucked the sword
Ruthless from the sheath, now mourns
   With bitter word;
What avails for us, alas! that
   Blood and gain
Now to dull Remorse's cruel
   Gnawing pain?

Ay! content you now all preachers
   East and West,
Pray the saints of Dort to find your
   Conscience rest!
'Tis in vain! The Lord stands knocking
   At the door
And that blood will plead for vengeance
   Evermore!

Hadt hy Hollandt dan ghedragen
   Onder 't hart,
Tot sijn afgeleefde dagen,
   Met veel smart,
Om 't meyneedigh swaert te laven,
   Met sijn bloet,
En te mesten kray en raven,
   Op sijn goet?

Maer waerom den hals gekorven?
   Want sijn bloet
Was in d'aders schier verstorven.
   In sijn goet
Vont men noyt de Pistoletten
   Van 't verraet,
Wtghestroyt, om scharp te wetten
   's Vollecks haet.

Gierigheyt en wreetheyt beyde,
   Die het swaert
Grimmigh ruckten uyt der scheyde,
   Nu bedaert,
Suchten: Wat kan ons vernoegen
   Goet en bloet?
Och, hoe knaccht een eeuwigh wroegen
   Ons ghemoedt!

Weest te vreen, haelt Predikanten,
   West en Oost:
Gaet en soeckt by Dortsche santen
   Heyl en troost.
'Tis vergeefs, de Heer koomt kloppen
   Met sijn Woort.
Niemand kan de wellen stoppen
   Van die Moort.

Translated by H.J.C. Grierson

135

Dirge for a Child (1632)

Kinder-Lyck

Constantine, blessed child benign
Cherub mine, sees from on high
Pomp and show in man below,
Therefore laughs with twinkling eye.
'Mother', said. 'Lo, wherefore fret so
Why regret so by my corpse?
I'm alive here, I survive here
Angel-child in heav'nly courts:
Brightly gleaming, sprightly gleaning
All the bounteous Giver showers
And unfolds on myriad souls,
Wanton with such lavish dowers.
Turn your face then and so hasten
To this place thence from the mess
Made on earth, of little worth.
Moments yield to endlessness.

Constantijntje, 't zaligh kijntje,
Cherubijntje, van om hoogh
D' ydelheden hier beneden,
Uitlacht met een lodderoogh.
Moeder, zeit hy, waerom schreit ghy?,
Waerom greit ghy op mijn lijck?
Boven leef ick, boven zweef ick,
Engeltje van t' hemelrijck:
En ick blinck'er, en ick drinck'er,
't Geen de schincker alles goets
Schenckt de zielen, die daer krielen,
Dertel van veel overvloets.
Leer dan reizen met gepeizen
Naer pallaizen, uit het slick
Dezer werrelt, die zoo dwerrelt,
Eeuwigh gaet voor oogenblick.

Translated by Peter King

Blessed Albion

Chorus following Act III of Mary Stuart, 1646.

The antiphon that follows speaks of 'wretched Albion'.

Blessed Albion,
Concede how blessed you are
By heaven's will and grace:
You proudly rule the seas,
And from your snow white neck
Have thrown the oppressing yoke
Of foreign slavery;
The Romans nor the Danes
Exact your cows or grains;
Your sheep roam unenclosed,
Of wolves there is no trace,
And snakes you needn't fear.
Fragrant are your hedges
With rosemary fine; no reefs
Impede access to your shores;
No shallows your ports
Endanger, and ships can sail
Swiftly, undisturbed.
Oh Isle, so many envy you
And you have no idea!

Geluckigh Engelant,
Bekende ghy 't gheluck
U toegeleit van boven,
Die trots de zeekroon spant,
En hebt het uitheemsch juck
Der slaverny geschoven
Van uwen blancken neck;
't Zy Cesar, 't zy de Noor
U eischte vee en vruchten;
Ghy sluit noch koy, noch heck,
Uit angst voor wolvespoor,
Noch hoeft geen slang te duchten;
Uw heiningh geeft een geur
Van roosmarijn; geen klip
Verbiet uw strant te naecken;
Geen bancken schieten veur
Uw havens; dies geen schip
Zijn vaert behoeft te staecken.
O Eilant, waert benijt,
Ghy weet niet wat ghy zijt.

Translated by Kristiaan Aercke

Rebellion threatens,
the light's brilliance pales

Chorus of worried angels following Act II
of Lucifer (1654).

Why are the starry outposts glowing	Hoe zien de hoffelycke gevels
Red? Why shines the Holy Light	Zoo root? hoe straelt het heiligh licht
So crimson in our sight,	Zoo root op ons gezicht,
Through clouds of murky vapour flowing?	Door wolcken en bedroefde nevels?
What fog and mist obscure	Wat damp, wat mist betreckt
The silver once so pure –	Dat zuiver, noit bevleckt,
Incomparable sapphire –	Die vlam, dien glans, dat vier
The flame, the gleam, the fire	Van 't heldere Alvermogen?
Of God's serenity?	Hoe schynt ons nu de diepe gloet
Why does the Godhead's light instead	Der Godtheit toe, zoo zwart als bloet,
Now stream towards us here blood-red,	Die flus zoo klaer alle oogen
Which, until recently,	Verheughde? wie begrypt, wie kent
All eyes rejoiced? Who can explain	Deze oirzaeck, onder d'Engelsdommen,
This mystery to Angeldom,	Die, boven Adams element,
Which, far removed from Man's domain,	Noch flus op galm van keelen zwommen;
In songs and chants of praise has swum,	Op lucht van Geesten, in den glans,
In fragrant air and radiance, gilding	Die galery, en tin, en trans,
Pinnacle, battlement and building,	Gewelf van koor en hof vergulde,
Vaulted choirs and garden fair –	En met een ziel van vreucht vervulde
Joy inspiring everywhere	Al wat hier boven leeft, en zweeft?
To all that here above belong!	Wie is'er, die ons reden geeft?
Pray, who can tell us what is wrong?	

Translated by Noel Clark

Living is loving and it's unsinkable

Hedonistic chorus of court ladies from Noah (Noach),
Act III (1667).

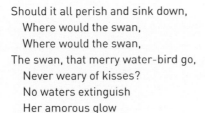

Should it all perish and sink down,
   Where would the swan,
   Where would the swan,
The swan, that merry water-bird go,
   Never weary of kisses?
   No waters extinguish
   Her amorous glow

She blithely nests on the flowing stream.
   She feeds her flame,
   She feeds her flame
In the company of her merry mate,
   As her eggs she warmes
   And heeds no alarms,
   And knows no fright.

Fluttering youngsters with her swim
   O'er sea and stream
   O'er sea and stream.
She loves the fickle element,
   And trims her feather;
   They swim together
   Till life doth end.

Dying she sings a merry song
   Mid the rushes' throng,
   Mid the rushes' throng.
And, taunting envious Death with glees
   Of mirthful singing
   With triumph ringing,
   She dies in peace.

Zou het al zinken en vergaen,
   Waer bleef de zwaen,
   Waer bleef de zwaen,
De zwaen, dat vrolijke waterdier,
   Noit zat van kussen?
   Geen wat'ren blussen
   Haer minnevier.

't Lust haer te nestlen op den vloet.
   Zy queekt den gloet,
   Zy queekt den gloet
Met hare vrolijke wederga,
   En kipt haere eiers,
   En acht geen schreiers,
   Noch vreest geen scha.

Vliegende jongen zwemmen mee,
   Door stroom en zee,
   Door stroom en zee.
Zy groeit in 't levendigh element,
   En wast de veêren
   En vaert spansseeren
   Tot 's levens endt.

Stervende zingtze een vrolijk liet
   In 't suikerriet,
   In 't suikerriet.
Zy tart de nijdige doot uit lust
   Met quinkeleeren
   En triomfeeren,
   En sterft gerust.

Translated by Theodoor Weevers

The Political Expression of Flemish Nationalism

[JOS BOUVEROUX]

The founding of an autonomous Flemish nationalist political party is inextricably linked to the First World War. Both in the German-occupied territory and in the narrow strip of land to the west of the IJzer river in the coastal province of West-Vlaanderen, where the Belgian army had dug in, a split developed between radical Flemish Nationalists and Belgium (including moderate *flamingants*). When Germany invaded Belgium in 1914, it was only a small group of Flemings in Ghent who, inspired by a Dutch parson, took an anti-Belgian stance. The vast majority of Flemish nationalists were active within the three major political movements (Christian Democrats, Socialists and Liberals) and did not question the structures of state. Yet the Flemish Movement already had a long and arduous journey behind it.

When the new Kingdom of Belgium was founded in 1830, its leaders made no secret of their desire to create a monolingual (French-speaking) state. French accordingly became the language of administration throughout the new country, including in Flanders. The only concession was that a few devotees of culture and language were allowed to use 'Flemish' – a genuine unified Dutch standard language barely existed at that time. The Antwerp writer Hendrik Conscience even received official Belgian support for his historical novel *The Lion of Flanders* (*De Leeuw van Vlaanderen*), which described the Flemish victory over the French in the Battle of the Golden Spurs (*Guldensporenslag*) at Courtrai (Kortrijk) in 1302. By an irony of fate, later Flemish nationalists would use this book to highlight the lost glory of Flanders ....

It was precisely these devotees of language who laid the foundations of the Flemish Movement. Barely ten years after Belgium achieved its independence, a petition calling for the legal right to use Dutch alongside French as the language of law, education and administration – but only in the Flemish provinces - attracted more than 100,000 signatures. However, the bourgeoisie would have no truck with this. This situation changed only slowly when the suffrage was extended and a new generation of politicians who were closer to the ordinary people took the stage,. The Flemish Movement attracted growing political support – especially within the Catholic party, though substantially less from the Socialists and Liberals. Violent mass protests by the emerging Socialist party led to the suffrage being extended further in 1893. It was no coincidence that a

Long live Belgium/Belgium burst.

few years later, in 1898, the Equality Law (*Gelijkheidswet*) was passed, theoretically according equal status to the Dutch and French languages. Although the new law had little practical effect, it did prompt the later Brussels federalist Lucien Outers to claim that: 'La Belgique Française de 1830 est morte à ce moment-là.'

This ushered in the painfully slow parliamentary process of adopting language laws, with the French-speakers frequently blocking progress towards language equality, unwilling to abandon the monolingual status of French-speaking Wallonia and the use of French by individuals in Flanders. And there was more: the French-speakers felt threatened, and there was talk of vague plans to push through an administrative division of Belgium. In 1912 the Walloon Socialist Jules Destrée penned his notorious Open Letter to the King (*Open Brief aan de Koning*) : 'Sire, permit me to tell Your Majesty a great and terrible truth: there are no Belgians, only Walloons and Flemings.' A year earlier, three Flemish members of parliament (a Christian Democrat, a Socialist and a Liberal) had tabled a bill calling for the University of Ghent to be made partially Dutch-speaking. Despite a fiercely-fought campaign in Flanders, with meetings and petitions, however, the French-speakers stood firm on this point; in their eyes the Dutch language was unsuited for delivering higher education, an assertion which caused resentment among radical Flemings.

© Johan Van Geluwe.

**SIRE,
IL N'Y A PLUS
DE PRIMITIFS
FLAMANDS**

SIRE, IL N'Y A PAS DE BELGES
JULES DESTRÉE 1912

Activism and Front Movement.

On the orders of the German Chancellor, from 1914 onwards the German Occupying Power pursued a *Flamenpolitik* ('Flemish policy'), in which privileges were bestowed on the Flemings in the hope that Belgium would fall apart. Flemish activists, whose aim was to break with Belgium, received German financial and material support. Although they did not enjoy great popular support, the Germans deployed a formidable propaganda weapon: from the new academic year beginning in 1916, Ghent University would become entirely Dutch-speaking. They went a step further, setting up a Council of Flanders (*Raad van Vlaanderen*) in which separatists formed the majority. On Berlin's initiative total administrative separation was announced; the break with Belgium was now complete.

More important for the future was the growing discontent among Flemish military men in the Belgian army behind the front regarding the inadequate implementation of the language laws. Well-educated Catholic soldiers, in particular, had formed cultural associations which levelled increasingly frequent criticism at the lack of Dutch language proficiency among the army's leadership and the officer corps. The response was a wave of fierce repression to eradicate that criticism. This led to such an escalation of the conflict that the Front Movement was forced underground. Naturally, the pro-Flemish behaviour of the Germans did not go unnoticed. Moderate Flemish leaders, who had developed a Flemish 'minimum programme' (*minimumprogramma*) in the neutral Netherlands, were astounded at the extent to which hearts and minds behind the front were becoming radicalised. It had also not escaped the notice of King Albert; in October 1916 he promised that after independence the Flemings would enjoy 'equality in law and in fact'. But French-speaking government ministers spoke a very different language. On 11 July 1917, the clandestine Front Movement published its 'Open Letter to the King' (*Open Brief aan de Koning*), in which for the first time the structure of the Belgian state was questioned: "We want a Flemish administration in Flanders." The response from the army high command was even more repression, with harsh punishments being handed down by the courts martial. A new open letter appeared in October 1917, 'Flanders' Dawn on the IJzer' (*Vlaanderens Dageraad aan de IJzer*), which is generally regarded as forming the basic programme for party-political Flemish Nationalism. Central to its demands was that Flanders must be granted the right to govern itself (*zelfbestuur*). Moderates still visualised a federal Belgium, but extremists dreamed of either total independence or linking up with the Netherlands.

The Front Party

Following the defeat of Germany in 1918, the majority of activists fled to the Netherlands or Germany. Others received severe punishments and were also subjected to the fury of the Belgian people. But the front-line soldiers, including those with Flemish nationalist sympathies, had the aura of victors about them. In November 1918 King Albert, fearing a Soviet-style revolution, even introduced universal single suffrage (for men) without revising the Constitu-

The German Governor-General von Bissing hands over Ghent University to the Academic authorities on 21 October 1916. Dutch becomes the official language of the University until the end of the war in 1918. Then the Belgian government reinstalls French until 1930.

tion, thereby meeting the most important demand of the Socialists. However, the conversion of Ghent University into a Dutch-speaking institution was immediately reversed. Leaders of the secret Front Movement founded the Front Party, which won five seats at the elections, despite the fact the party had difficulty fielding enough competent candidates and despite its open sympathy for the activists. But the party was a hotchpotch of different views, with deep internal divisions between federalists and separatists. The slogan 'Self-governance' (*Zelfbestuur*) covered a whole host of concepts - something that was to become a constant in Flemish Nationalism.

As with the Flemish Socialists, the pro-Flemish wing within the Catholic party had strengthened considerably. Its members attempted to repair the breach between the Flemish Nationalists and Belgium, though without success. In practice King Albert and the majority of Francophones did very little to implement the promised 'equality in law and fact'. Moderate Flemish

Leuven, 1968. Pupils of catholic schools support the battle for the Dutchification of the University.

nationalists did succeed in forcing the adoption of important language laws, but King Albert instructed his government to reject as a matter of principle the conversion of Ghent University to a Dutch-speaking institution and the formation of Dutch-language army units. The moderate Catholic Flemish sympathisers were therefore unable to profit from the growing differences of opinion within the Front Party. Activists resident abroad posed a greater threat: via the Catholic Front Party members in West-Vlaanderen, they succeeded in stage-managing a rejection of parliamentary democracy and allowing right-wing authoritarian views to filter through, especially after Mussolini's seizure of power in Italy in 1922. The Front Party was torn apart. For a while the liberals, especially those in Antwerp, were able to put up some resistance, and in 1928 they even caused the country to be shaken to its roots when the imprisoned activist August Borms was elected to office at a by-election in which the Catholics and Socialists had fielded no candidates. However, this would prove to be their swan song. Unlike many others, Antwerp's Front Party members supported the creation of a federal state. That did not go far enough for the radicals, however. In the following year the West Fleming Joris Van Severen, who had been defeated in the election, founded the Verdinaso party (*Verbond van Dietse Nationaal-Solidaristen*), with an explicitly authoritarian programme. In Antwerp itself, the liberal Front Party members increasingly lost ground. In 1933 Herman Vos, the leader of the parliamentary Front Party and himself an Antwerp man, tabled a bill aimed at creating a federal Belgium. However, when he was unable to secure a majority for his proposal even in his own party, Vos handed in his resignation and went over to the Socialists. The Front Party was dead and buried, especially the left wing of the Party, which preferred federalism to separatism.

The Flemish National Union

The 1932 elections turned into a rout for the Front Party. Its leader, the Brabant teacher Staf De Clercq, lost his seat, despite his continued popularity. This prompted the founding of a right-wing authoritarian movement based on the German model, the Flemish National Union (*Vlaamsch Nationaal Verbond* (VNV). De Clercq quickly succeeded in bringing the disparate groupings together. Officially the VNV advocated what was called Dietsland, a Dutch-speaking community uniting Flanders and the Netherlands. Nonetheless, the parliamentary factions also contained moderate federalists, who had no option but to accept the orders of their Leader (*den Leider*). They saw only one possible way of ending the chaos. De Clercq and his chief propagandist, Reimond Tollenaere, developed the VNV into an openly fascist party. In 1936, to their own amazement, the VNV made an enormous leap forward, doubling its parliamentary seats to 16. The fact that most of the members did not support the creation of *Dietsland* and were nothing like as extreme as the party leadership did not prevent De Clercq from accepting German financial support and establishing closer links with Nazi Germany. Despite the fact that De Clercq was portrayed by his political opponents as a 'mini-Hitler', the VNV continued to do well at elections. However, the party was politically isolated. An initial partnership with pro-Flemish Catholics was shot down in flames by the workers' wing. De Clercq was undeterred; he pinned all his hopes on a new German occupation. When the Germans did invade Belgium on 10 May 1940, De Clercq offered to co-operate in arranging the capitulation of the Belgian army.

During the four-year occupation, VNV collaboration with the Nazis was total: at the political, military and police level. Following De Clercq's sudden death, he was succeeded by Hendrik Elias, who became increasingly convinced that he was being deceived by the hard Nazis of the SS. His policy was doomed to failure, but he could not or dared not break with the Germans completely. The consequence was that the VNV collapsed ignominiously and after the Liberation was hit hard by the harsh Belgian repression; a number of death sentences were carried out after the Second World War, unusually harsh prison sentences were imposed, property was confiscated and people were declared 'politically dead' (loss of the right to vote, prohibited from working in education, administration, etc). Flemish nationalism appeared to have been removed from the political arena entirely.

The People's Union (*De Volksunie*)

Only one small group of Flemish nationalists, who had largely or completely escaped the post-war repression, dared to publish a more or less clandestine weekly newspaper from the end of 1945, which inveighed fiercely against the repression. The publication survived a bomb attack and legal action. Other publications complaining of the disadvantaged position of the Flemings also appeared sporadically. The language laws were being completely ignored, and Belgian governments in which only a quarter of the ministers were Flemish were the rule rather than the exception. Yet there were great doubts about the re-establishment of a Flemish Nationalist party. There were two favoured options: joining forces with the Flemish Christian Democrats (the CVP) – which had offered mandates to former VNV members as a way of lifting itself out of opposition – or taking the risk of forming a new party of their own. A first attempt in 1948 failed, partly because the meeting was broken up by members of the resistance. Two years earlier, Belgian soldiers, helped by a number of Liberal politicians, had expertly dynamited the IJzer Tower, the symbol of the Flemish Nationalist movement. It was the Flemish Christian Democrats who managed to channel the resultant fury and organised an IJzer pilgrimage in the hope that it would improve their electoral chances. Meanwhile, the Belgian Royal Question was raging, with the Francophones in particular opposing the return of King Leopold III, who had been carried away by the Germans. The Christian Democrats (CVP), by contrast, lined up resolutely behind the King, as did most Flemish nationalists. The latter did not even turn out to vote in 1950, enabling the CVP to secure an absolute majority and force a referendum on the King's return to the throne. The ultimate outcome of the referendum caused deep dismay among the Flemish Nationalists and played a huge part in their decision to form their own party. Leopold had achieved a majority of almost 58 percent in the referendum, but in the industrial centres of Wallonia and in Brussels only a minority supported the King. When despite this Leopold returned to the throne violent protests and strikes broke out, resulting in three deaths in the Liège area. Partly because of overt threats of separatism in Wallonia, Leopold and the CVP ultimately caved in and the King handed over power to his son Baudouin. According to the Christian trade union leader in Flanders, this outcome had 'created more anti-Belgians than the two world wars'.

The driving force behind the move to found a new Flemish nationalist party was the Brussels lawyer Frans Van der Elst, who had gained a good deal of prestige as the defender of VNV leader Elias. On 21 November 1954, he and a small group of like-minded nationalists formed The People's Union (*De Volksunie* – VU), which described itself unequivocally as a Flemish Nationalist party with federalism and amnesty as the main elements in its programme. Without repudiating tradition, the VU adopted democratic principles, seeing the parliamentary route rather than a pointless anti-Belgian stance as the only way to create a federal Belgian state. The VU had learned from its loaded past, but it failed to make an electoral breakthrough in the early years, gaining just one seat – in Antwerp, not coincidentally the city where many former collaborators had been forced to start a new life. As the party had made amnesty for political offences one of its main themes, it was for a long time distrusted as a 'VNV in a new guise'. This changed only slowly when Wallonia, in difficulties economically after the General Strike of 1960/61, began to demand federalism explicitly

Bart De Wever (left) with
Johan Vande Lanotte, (Minister of
Economy in the new
Belgian government) in the
Belgian Senate, 2011.
Photo by Filip Claus.

for socioeconomic reasons. At the same time the Flemish Movement, with its
two Marches on Brussels (*Marsen op Brussel*), was demanding the definitive
fixing of the language frontier between Flanders and Wallonia. That demand
was met in the early 1960s, but in the eyes of the VU the Flemings had paid
too high a price for it, among other things with the introduction of 'language
facilities' (for example, according Francophones living in Dutch-speaking
municipalities the right to use French in official dealings). The 1965 elections
brought a breakthrough: at a stroke the VU moved from five parliamentary
seats to twelve. Flanders was on the crest of a wave economically, too, and
the younger generation were impatient and eager to move forward. Research
showed that at least a third of those who voted for the VU were not driven by
Flemish nationalist motives, but were attracted to the party's modern, non-
conformist image. It was Catholic students who in 1968 pressured the Flemish
CVP to split Leuven's university into a Dutch-speaking and a French-speaking
institution. This immediately led to the break-up of the unitary Catholic party,
followed shortly afterwards by the Liberals and Socialists. The VU triumphed
and opened its ranks to independent members (verruimers), mostly of a
centre-left persuasion. It proved to be an auspicious move; in 1968 the party
achieved 20 seats and became larger than the Liberals. But a small hard core
of right-wing Flemish nationalists, for whom federalism was merely a means
to an end, began to show their dissatisfaction with the way the VU projected

itself as a 'policy party': which was willing to make compromises with the Fran-cophones. In 1971, led by Karel Dillen, they resigned from the VU. The seeds of a deep split had been sown.

New Flemish Alliance becomes the largest Flemish party

Like the VU, the federalists in Wallonia and Brussels also recorded major suc-cesses. In 1970 the unitary Belgian state went to its grave. In order to halt the march of the VU, the dedicated federalist Wilfried Martens was elected chair-man of the CVP. Martens was the chief architect of the 1977 'Egmont Pact' which, with support from the VU and the Socialist Party, transformed Belgium into a federal state. Many people in Flanders felt that the VU in particular had made too many concessions in the Brussels peripheral municipalities during the federalisation process; ultimately it would take until 1993 for Belgium to become a truly federal state.

The VU was punished at the ballot box for its willingness to compromise, and in 1979 Karel Dillen founded a new Flemish nationalist party, known initially as *Vlaams Blok* and later relabelled *Vlaams Belang* (VB). Dillen was resolutely in favour of Flemish independence and achieved a spectacular breakthrough in 1991 when his party played the immigration and security cards to the full.

The VB became substantially bigger than the VU. After Belgium was transformed into a federal state in 1993, many VU members faced an existential problem. Their most important aim had been achieved; now the internal right-left conflicts began to rear their heads, eventually leading to the party's demise in 2001. Many office-holders had already left the party by then. Those who remained fell into two small groups: the left-wing *Spirit* faction, which was absorbed by the socialists after running in a cartel at the elections, and the hard-core Nationalists, who founded the New Flemish Alliance (*Nieuw-Vlaamse Alliantie* (N-VA)), which gained just one seat. Like Vlaams Belang, N-VA called for separatism, an independent Flemish state. But the new party set its face against Vlaams Belang because of the latter's extreme right-wing ideas. As the Christian Democrat opposition fell into disarray, a cartel was negotiated with N-VA. The Flemish CVP changed its name to CD&V (Christian Democratic & Flemish), and called for a confederal Belgium. The cartel formula proved fortuitous: the Christian Democrats once more resumed their leadership at regional and federal level. Things went badly wrong in 2007, however, following the failure to push through a reform of the state, and after lengthy negotiations the N-VA broke up the cartel. In the end the CD&V was forced to go to the electorate empty-handed. Bart De Wever had become the charismatic chairman of N-VA. At the early elections called on 13 June 2010, he profited to the full from the ineptitude of the other Flemish parties and the stubbornness of the Francophone parties, who opposed any further state reform or the mandatory splitting of the bilingual electoral district of Brussels-Halle-Vilvoorde. To their own amazement, the N-VA became the biggest party in Flanders, with 27 seats. It was a historic moment, the first time ever that separatist nationalists had achieved such a result.

By doing so the radicals have placed their old dream firmly on the political agenda. Separatism is no longer a taboo subject in Belgium, even though many of those who voted for the N-VA have no desire to see the end of their country; while the French-speakers, for their part, are taking the idea of Flemish independence increasingly seriously.

The outcome was that after the elections of 13 June 2010 Belgium experienced the longest government crisis in its history. The differences between the French-speakers and the Flemish nationalists were irreconcilable. Though French-speakers did realise that the Brussels-Halle-Vilvoorde electoral district had to be split and that a sixth round of state reform was unavoidable. But they did not want to lose out financially either. King Albert was extremely creative in sending out new conciliators time and time again. After more than a year of negotiations the Flemish Christian Democrats took the decision to stop running after the N-VA. Then slowly but surely things started moving. On 11 October 2011 Elio Di Rupo, a French-speaking Socialist charged with forming a new government, presented a communitarian agreement. On 6 December 2011 the government, under the same Di Rupo, was sworn in. Belgium will undergo new and profound changes, with more power and money for its constituent states. The federal level will be further dismantled. The Flemish nationalists are on the sidelines for the time being, but from the Flemish Government, to which they do belong, they can make things pretty difficult for the Belgian federal government. Already there is talk of a seventh round of state reform within ten years. ∎

Translated by Julian Ross

Jan Vanriet and the Beauty of Evil

Painting is War

[ERIC RINCKHOUT]

The recent work of the Antwerp painter Jan Vanriet (b.1948) is embedded in the violent history of the twentieth century. His focus is especially on the development of powerful ideologies and their effect on the common man and the artist. The Second World War, the concentration camps, the pogroms, Stalinism and Nazism – in a word evil, the horror and its persistent memories: these are subjects that keep recurring.

In a conversation at the end of 2009 Vanriet said that in the past ideologies were communal projects that gave a line to be followed, though unfortunately it was usually a line of march. In the same interview he listed his themes as 'social problems, history, memory, reflection ... the human condition, in short, to use a loaded term'. Jan Vanriet calls these his storylines. Is he a literary painter? That is a title he is proud to bear. For Vanriet the story he wants to tell is just as important as the style of the painting.

That is not the only reason he is a literary painter. Vanriet prefers working in series, around a large subject, and he does research for it the way a writer does for a book. And in fact he loves books and regularly produces handsome publications with and about his work.

His work also contains quotations – both conscious and unconscious – from Art's mighty reservoir of images, the trash can of memory as he once called it.

On top of which Vanriet's work has a message, a concept that according to him has for too long been derided in art.

Still, it's not always immediately clear what a Vanriet painting is about. The images are unsettling, the signs ambiguous. Vanriet invites us to take a long, slow look. The painter mixes, transforms and assembles images until new meanings appear. Vanriet doesn't showcase his message, he does not yell out his displeasure or that he's right. There is a lot going on beneath the surface of the paint. In these paintings there is often a deafening silence, regardless of how many people are milling about. His work has a strange, poetic beauty. But it is the beauty of horror, the poetry of disaster.

Madonna, Closed Doors.
© Jan Vanriet.

A many-voiced choir

Take the beautiful, seemingly simple painting, *Madonna, Closed Doors* (Madonna, gesloten deuren) from 2004. With soft, light brush-strokes Vanriet has given form to a woman carrying a baby in her arms. We see the two figures from behind, they are warmly bundled up, it must be winter. The drabness of their clothes and the simple carrying bag of the woman make us suspect they are refugees, migrants from the East, people without papers. Contemporary, probably.

The woman is caught in a purely graphic representation of a corridor with many closed doors, which are only sketchily drawn. A simple repetitive motif, that rings in our ears like a succession of hammer blows. The doors are thinly painted, yet on the canvas they look to be carved in stone.

The doors are closed and will stay closed. The woman is looking at the child, perhaps trying to soothe it. Is the child crying? Is it throwing its head back? We can only guess. Woman and child stand motionless in a hateful poisonous green, in an oppressive space, the suffocating perspective of a narrowing corridor. There is no way out, no escape route, no future.

This story of refugees echoes the mythical story of a woman and her child, Mary and Jesus, a story about unwanted strangers that has happened thousands of times since then and is still happening every day.

Past and present are inextricably linked in Vanriet's work. History, large and small, is always on the move. An image or a newspaper photo will touch on other images from art, myths or Vanriet's personal history. Anecdotes transcend themselves, gain broader relevance and validity. Memories, more and more memories push their way in through the cracks of time. Unstoppably.

Portrait of an Uncle. © Jan Vanriet.

La Doctrine. © Jan Vanriet.

Madonna, Closed Doors is one of the paintings Vanriet made in the context of a commission for a new edition of the Bible. Jan Vanriet is an atheist. He has brought the Bible, which to him is no more than a literary text, into the twentieth century and has put his Mary in a cell block of Buchenwald concentration camp. 'That narrowing, threatening corridor in that cell block forced itself on me', Vanriet has said of it. 'But you don't have to know the background, the image has to be strong enough in itself.'

Consciously or unconsciously Vanriet has also used the dramatic perspective which the 16th century Venetian painter Tintoretto employed so brilliantly in *The Removal of St Mark's Body* (1562).

However contemporary Vanriet's work may be, it is always interwoven with tradition. The artist himself pointed this out in the ambitious exhibition Closing Time. In 2010 Vanriet was given the opportunity to take control of an entire museum. The Royal Museum of Fine Arts in Antwerp, which has closed its doors until 2017 for an expansion and major renovations, offered him the chance to work with its entire collection of old and modern masters, from Jan van Eyck and Rogier van der Weyden to Rik Wouters and James Ensor. Vanriet became both painter and curator, transformed the museum, turned the chronology on its head, drew paintings out of the stock rooms and told his own story as well.

By starting a dialogue, harmonizing but also confronting and contrasting his work with that of old and not-so-old masters, he showed their work in a different light. And the old masters in turn brought out different meanings in Vanriet's paintings. Both dialogue and dialectic, then, in a kaleidoscopic exhibition, resulting in a many-voiced choir. And the proof that the meaning of a work is never set in stone. The viewer experiences the eternal now of the art of painting.

However aesthetic Vanriet's work may be, the one constant factor is his ethical position. Call it humanism - Vanriet stands up for human dignity. He is sensitive to the vulnerability of the individual in the face of the big constructs that surround him. All too often he has seen the common man, and the artist too, being crushed between the jaws of merciless ideologies.

Apart from the contrast between ethics and aesthetics, there are other areas of tension. Jan Vanriet is a loner, he lives and paints in solitude and yet the world is very present in his paintings. He is often described as an enlightened misanthrope, a relativist melancholic, but at the same time he has a passionate love of humankind.

And there are other paradoxes. His work is emotional and cerebral, he is an involved and a detached observer. His paintings are sombre and often depict horrors and catastrophes, the power of the crowd over the individual. But at the same time his work has an unmistakable lightness.

Vanriet weaves all these seeming or real contradictions into works that are highly charged and, in the words of art critic Marc Ruyters, display a cool synthesis. That applies at least to his work from the mid 1980s on. The year 1986 brought a significant change. Vanriet himself refers to it as a rupture.

Samizdat

But let's start at the beginning.

Vanriet has always been politically and artistically committed. But for a long time he kept this commitment out of his work. He preferred to express it in writing. As he himself says: `My roots are in literature.'

Jan Vanriet grew up in a left-wing environment in Antwerp. His father, a former Communist, joined the then Belgian Socialist Party (BSP) and was one of the founders of the magazine *Links* (Left), of which Jan was an editor.

Later he would write for various other magazines, but eventually it dawned on him that his journalistic work was a joke that had got out of hand.

In his youth Vanriet hung out with writers and he has continued to cherish such friendships. Hugo Claus was an extremely close friend, Cees Nooteboom still is. Vanriet has spent the biggest part of his life in literary rather than artistic circles.

Vanriet has collaborated on projects with both Claus and Nooteboom, and also with Benno Barnard and Stefan Hermans, In 1979 he illustrated *The Sign of the Hamster* (Het Teken van de Hamster), a book of poems by Claus, and in 2007 *Red Rain* (Rode Regen), a collection of short stories by Nooteboom. An example of Vanriet's youthful commitment is the Anti-Censorship Evening that he helped organize in Antwerp in 1968, at which Hugo Claus, Ivo Michiels, Jef Geeraerts, Paul de Wispelaere and Remco Campert all spoke out against the then rampant government censorship.

Although Vanriet still occasionally expresses himself in poetry – in 2008, for the first time in 20 years, a book of his poetry, *Storm Light* (Stormlicht), appeared – he is a painter through and through. As he has been since the age of ten.

His first painting was a copy after Van Gogh, a landscape in Provence. *Parcours,* an overview of his work by Marc Ruyters, features an oil painting from 1966, when Jan Vanriet was only 18. It is a view of hills in Bohemia, painted with a deft virtuosity. And in fact Vanriet was never to lose his love of landscape.

After completing his studies at the Antwerp art academy in 1972, his work is especially influenced by English Pop Art. There is quite a lot of David Hockney and Peter Blake in Vanriet's figurative paintings and water colours from that period. A little later he starts introducing strange elements into his work. He makes assemblages and collages, embellishes an image or a story line with odd forms and objects, like a sphinx or a billiard table, that give the whole a surrealist look. But his work always remains transparent and extremely aes-

thetic. It is also just a bit naïve, revealing the optimism of the 1960s. Vanriet himself has said of this: `Flower power was still in the air. European Pop Art was more playful than the American kind and David Hockney really spoke to me. You can sense that in my work. In Hockney I found the same pure line as in Picasso and Ingres: simple and direct.'

Soon history enters his work. From childhood Vanriet had been acquainted with left-wing culture: the songs of Bertold Brecht and Kurt Weill, interpreted by the singer-actor Ernst Busch, the songs of the poet Vladimir Mayakovsky and the work of the artist Vladimir Tatlin.

Vanriet himself refers to his romantic-leftist sympathies, but adds that he was fascinated by the dynamic in the Soviet Union shortly after the revolution of 1917: the enormous creativity, the boundless exploration of the possibilities in art, the avant-garde in theatre, typography and photography with someone like Alexander Rodchenko.

The Tatlin he paints in 1979 still fits perfectly with the colourful and lyrical pop art-like portraits. In 1986 this approach changes radically. Vanriet changes the paper on which he paints for canvas, which already makes the work less delicate, but he also starts to paint his portraits, like the one of Mayakovsky, in a heavier, harder, less aesthetic style.

The painting *Portrait of an Uncle* (Portret van een oom, 1986) is a key work. The twin brother of Vanriet's mother had barely survived Dachau concentration camp and died of exhaustion soon after. He used to play the accordion. Jan Vanriet lays the instrument down flat and depicts it as a factory.

The painting *La Doctrine* (1986) represents an even more fundamental break. Vladimir Tatlin is portrayed in black and white, looking anguished, but it is a domestic iron that, like some foreign body, takes the lead role. Moreover, the painting is dominated by drab, blue-and-white vertical stripes that refer to the garb of concentration camp inmates and are at the same time a favourite pattern of the French artist Daniel Buren. The iron is a symbol of doctrinairism: everything is ironed flat. The painting combines figurative with emblematic and symbolic elements. It is a powerful rebus.

Decision-Making. © Jan Vanriet.

There are a number of explanations for the change in Vanriet's work. Up till then the artist had mostly kept his personal history out of his work. In 1986 he realized he could exorcise the World War II events in which his parents had been involved not only through his writing but also through his painting. Ultimately, what happened in the concentration camps had a marked effect on him. His father was a Communist and a member of the Antwerp Resistance. He was betrayed and ended up in the German camps. His mother's parents were couriers in the Resistance. His mother was also betrayed and transported to the east. It is no coincidence that *Transport* is the title of a later series of thematic paintings by Vanriet. His mother and father met in Mauthausen concentration camp; before that his mother had already been a slave labourer in Silesia.

But why did this change only come about in 1986? Jan Vanriet had at that time a studio in New York. But that city had nothing to do with the change. Vanriet gives the following explanation: 'Perhaps it was only then that I had acquired enough history.' He was 38 in 1986. What certainly also played a role was the dismal state of painting at the time. In that period, when conceptual art was on the rise, painting was no longer seen as a natural artistic occupation. On the contrary. A painter was stupid and paint stank. Painting was regarded as a bourgeois activity. In the 1970s and 80s painters were sneered at.

'You had to go underground,' according to Vanriet. 'It was just like samizdat. The people who were always going on about freedom called what we did old-fashioned nonsense. They banned us from the profession.'

It was precisely through his resistance to this that Vanriet found the strength and the fervour to continue and to create, from that time on, his most powerful works.

Who is using whom?

After that Vanriet's work goes in different directions: sometimes more symbolic, at other times pure storytelling. He makes collages, uses icons, patterns and stencils, experiments with Korean Hanji-paper, watercolour and

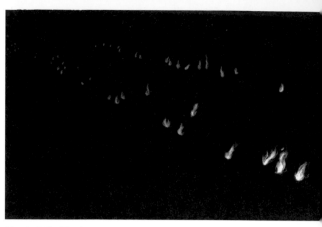

Contre Jour. © Jan Vanriet.

March. © Jan Vanriet.

lino-cut, puts in references to old masters like Jean Fouquet, to contemporary artists like Daniel Buren, René Daniels, Sol Lewitt and Luc Tuymans, and to history. He explores the boundaries between the figurative and the abstract in a series like *Last Snow* (Laatste Sneeuw, 1999).

Symptomatic of the early 1990s are two large series. On the one hand Vanriet works on monumental projects like the ceiling paintings for Antwerp's Bourla Theatre, the decoration of the De Brouckère Metro station in Brussels and a 110-metre-long mural at the KBC headquarters, also in Brussels. On the other hand he produces 35 paintings based on the Gospel of St. John. That series grows into a book project for which Benno Barnard writes the epic poem *The Castaway* (De schipbreukeling, 1995).

One question continues to fascinate Vanriet: the relationship between the artist and the powers-that-be. Who is using whom?

This fascination too has its roots in his personal history. Jan Vanriet's father had been in the same camp as Antonin Novotny, the later president of Czecho-slovakia. They knew each other well. Later, during the 1960s, the Vanriet family regularly visited Czechoslovakia.

`We moved in circles that were normally closed to people from the West', Vanriet relates. `In Marienbad there was a separate Kurhaus for the Communist nomenklatura, that's where top officials were received in luxurious sur-roundings, officials from Italy as well. While the common man in Marienbad lived in humble circumstances. Celebrated state artists enjoyed a posh life-style and kept their money in dollars, while younger critical artists had trouble making ends meet. I found this strange for what was, after all, a Communist system.'

The complex situation of artists under regimes like the Soviet Union and Nazi Germany has been the subject of several major series and exhibitions by Vanriet.

The elaborate suite of paintings, *Poet's Death* (Dichterdood, 2006), is about the Soviet Union. `I am no longer able to make paintings as independent art-works', says Vanriet. `I need something to guide me, a theme, however cryptic it may be.'

For a series of paintings about the Russian poet Vladimir Mayakovsky, Vanriet was inspired by a silent film in which the poet is murdered as the result of a love affair. In real life Mayakovsky committed suicide. Did an impossible love have something to do with it? Or was the poet slowly crushed by a stifling ideology he had initially endorsed?

The series was rounded out with older work from 1988 in which he had painted Lily Brik, Mayakovsky's infernal beloved, as a ballet dancer between two floodlights (from a concentration camp?), and with archetypal images of workers going to the factory and Party members climbing the steps en masse on their way to a congress. Not one of them has individual characteristics.

The paintings are reminiscent of Eisenstein's films, although the painter says that he was primarily inspired by television documentaries and old photographs from Soviet propaganda from the 1930s.

Colour is defining

In the exhibition *Cockchafer, Fly* (Meikever, Vlieg) of 2008 Vanriet investigated the position of the artist in Nazi Germany. One of his starting points was a little film the painter had found on YouTube. In it the children of Nazi bigwig Goebbels sing innocent children's songs. Eighteen months later their mother killed them because, supposedly, after the Third Reich no better life was possible.

Still, the exhibition in Vanriet's regular gallery *De Zwarte Panter* (The Black Panther) was dominated by several monumental works. An unsettling torchlight procession in pitch darkness, in which not one person can be seen. Across from it hung a black work and a red one, both with the same motif: a white-hot fire consuming a building. One motif executed in various colours is a recurrent element in Vanriet's oeuvre: it shows the defining role of colour in the perception of a work and a situation.

The world is on fire, the hordes are on the march, innocence will be murdered. And: *Life is a Cabaret.* For Vanriet also paints the singers, actors and dancers of the German revues of the 1930s. He portrays the infamous Mefisto, Gustav Gründgens, who collaborated with the Nazis, and he also paints a portrait of the Communist singer and actor Ernst Busch, who was saved from execution by that same Gründgens – however unlikely it may seem.

In 2009 Vanriet held a small exhibition in which he explored the mental landscape of his youth: football gods, cinema and social housing in the Antwerp neighbourhood of Het Kiel.

Yet the war continues to dominate his oeuvre: in the same year he had an exhibition in Düsseldorf with works centred on the Villa Hügel, the property of German steel magnate and Nazi sympathizer Alfried Krupp, and in *Closing Time* (2010) he showed his most recent paintings: a series of portraits based on photographs of people who were deported. Painting is, and remains, war. ■

Translated by Pleuke Boyce

FURTHER READING

Closing Time. Jan Vanriet, bilingual (Dutch/English) catalogue
of the exhibition of that name in the
Royal Museum of Fine Arts, Antwerp,
24 April-3 October 2010 (Antwerp. Ludion, 2010)

Revealing the Clear Secret

Harry Mulisch (1927-2010)

[ARNOLD HEUMAKERS]

Only when a writer dies does 'irrevocability set in and the reading become serious', writes Harry Mulisch in *Food for Psychologists* (Voer voor psychologen, 1961). Well, that happened on 30 October 2010 and now the Netherlands has to manage without him. For the last few decades Mulisch, more than anyone else, has been *the* symbol of literature, the perfect embodiment of the writer. All over the media whenever literature was involved. This was due not only to his well-groomed appearance, but also to the fact that he was read by an unusually large public. Some of his novels, like *The Assault* (De aanslag, 1982) and *The Discovery of Heaven* (De ontdekking van de hemel, 1992), reached hundreds of thousands of readers – which is exceptional in a small country like the Netherlands.

In both cases they are exciting, accessible novels. That is true, too, of *Two Women* (Twee vrouwen, 1975), which was distributed massively - free – a couple of years ago. Not coincidentally, all three novels have been successfully filmed. They contain everything to appeal to a large public. Two Women offers a dramatic love story, in fact, as the title suggests, between two women, typical of the feminist seventies of the last century. In *The Assault* Mulisch summarizes more or less the entire post-war history of the Netherlands in a series of exemplary moments, intertwined with a meditation on fate, coincidence and guilt. In *The Discovery of Heaven,* his biggest and most ambitious novel, the whole of Western modernity is portrayed against the background of the increasing hegemony of technology, the disappearance of religion and the decline of politics.

What do these novels have in common? At first glance that is not so obvious. We find Mulisch's signature, as well as in the supple, almost 'classic' style beneath the surface of the narrative, in the surreptitious references to what he himself once called his 'hermetic underworld'. His whole oeuvre stems from that and bears witness to it. In *Two Women* we find that underworld in the analogy of the story with the Orpheus myth, which is extremely important in Mulisch's 'mythological' view of authorship; in *The Assault,* perhaps his least 'hermetic' novel, the prehistoric lizards, who fatally influence the course of history with their 'eternity', signify it; and in *The Discovery of Heaven* the underworld resides, paradoxically enough, mainly in the gnostic or Neoplatonic guise of the heaven that apparently governs all earthly activity.

Harry Mulisch with
his son Menzo.
Amsterdam, 12/1/1998.
Photo by Klaas Koppe.

Averting death

Mulisch has always claimed that his 'scribbling' (as with characteristic non-chalance he liked to call it) did not come 'from literature'. He never wanted to become a writer, it just turned out at a certain moment that he was one – because he wrote his first story. In that story (*The Room*/De kamer, published in 1947) a man tells of his youthful fascination with a particular room, in which a window was always open; you could see a bookcase and 'hear a piano playing through the open window'. Forty years later the narrator returns to the city of his birth and it turns out that he has rented the very house in which this mysterious room is located. Only later, when he is struck down by a fatal illness, does he understand the reason for his fascination: 'It's my death chamber'.

Mulisch wrote this story when he was only nineteen, but it already contained one important theme that reappears in his later work: the beginning that is only to find its completion in the ending. Later on that becomes the eternal, endless moment of death. Because no one can say of himself 'I *am* dead', Mulisch concludes that dying has no end and is therefore outside time. Within our rules-and-regulations-bound lives it offers access to another reality, where anything is possible. That other reality is, of course, the world of the imagination, but it is typical of Mulisch's 'mythologizing' way of thinking hat he associates freedom of the imagination with dying. Right where man as mortal seems to hit rock bottom, he finds his greatest triumph.

Harry Mulisch and King Albert II at the Royal Palace in Brussels for the award of the *Prijs der Nederlandse Letteren*, 23/11/1995. Photo by Klaas Koppe.

In this way, one might also say, Mulisch tries to avert death – the ambition of poets and writers since time immemorial. In a programmatic text *Foundations of the Mythology of Authorship* (Grondslagen van de mythologie van het schrijverschap, 1987) he argues that literature, as a manifestation of the written word, stops time and therefore conquers death. Because the text that the author writes is there forever. If a sentence is good, 'it's suddenly 1000 years ago that it was written down', Mulisch says in *Food for Psychologists.* The writer is an Orpheus who does succeed in saving his Eurydice. The only thing is that afterwards he no longer knows how he did it - Mulisch's way of incorporating into his own thinking the typically romantic notion of the genius that creates his masterpieces subconsciously.

Magnifying the enigma

Literature is a game for Mulisch, albeit a serious game. There is always something at stake; his writing has nothing to do with *l'art pour l'art,* art for its own sake. That is immediately clear from his debut novel *Archibald Strohalm* (1952), in which the main character is destroyed by the madness the writer has transferred to him. 'You've taken up my cross, my little saviour. I shall succeed where you must fail', writes the author, intervening in his own story. The saviour is sacrificed so that the writer can save himself. From what? From the madness, or the 'broken dikes' that had overcome him, Mulisch claims, in 1949. In *Food for Psychologists* he writes: 'I had ended up in a shower of meteors. Fireworks were going off in my head, brick red, Prussian blue, white as the sun, some as black as birds; there were sparks from my hands if I touched anything; where I trod the earth was scorched. [...] I knew everything. I understood everything. From early morning till late at night my time was filled with a feverish jotting down of insights, visions, enlightenment, euphorization, all with the intensity and certainty that I tried to portray later in *Archibald Strohalm*'.

Here we see the method that Mulisch often used against the dark, the occult, the evil threatening him: he tried to overpower it, to 'colonise' it, to tame it in a literary fashion, without it losing its mysterious lustre. 'Art reveals the clear secret', says Mulisch. How? By 'magnifying the enigma'. Mulisch's most systematic attempt at this would result, in 1979, in *The Composition of the World* (De compositie van de wereld): an explanation of almost everything based on the enigma of the musical octave, which functions in this philosophical colossus as a 'tough fundamental paradox'; the octave, in which the second note is 'not identical to the first, but not not-identical either'.

Using this method of colonisation Mulisch even dared confront the phenomenon of war crimes in 1959. Already in *Archibald Strohalm* we read: 'If I didn't write, perhaps I would be a mass murderer, a citizen gone wild, a fascist, who makes lampshades with leather from women's breasts, the nipple exactly on the top, with a push-button switch in it'. The war criminal in *The Stone Bridal Bed* (Het stenen Bruidsbed) is an American pilot who took part in the senseless bombing of Dresden. Mulisch puts himself in his shoes, the 'ruins man', without any noticeable distance between them. But that is only possible thanks to literature and its 'timeless' presence beyond history. The bombing of Dresden, like Hitler, Attila the Hun, Tamerlane and other mass murderers, is located there also, in an 'anti-history' that is at odds with what Mulisch, with a nod to Hegel, calls the 'history of the mind', history that brings progress.

Between literature and progress, then, there is a fundamental difference. It is from that difference that literature gets its freedom: in principle it can tackle anything. Only in literature can man indulge his most murky fascinations. In Mulisch's case that includes his fascination with Hitler, who continued to prey on his mind right up till his last novel, *Siegfried*, from 2002. Only in *Siegfried* does he manage to conquer that fascination, by catching Hitler in a 'net of fiction' and eliminating him as the incarnation of 'Nothingness'. But, as in *Archibald Strohalm*, this is at the expense of the main character, who does the dirty work in the story. Mulisch's alter ego, Rudolf Herter, is destroyed by the spiritual struggle with Hitler, whereas the writer, Mulisch, continued to live, victorious, nine more years after the completion of his novel.

The reader completes the book

Mulisch did not always succeed in averting terror with the aid of literature. A crucial year in his life and oeuvre was 1961, when he reported from Jerusalem for a Dutch weekly on the trial of Adolf Eichmann, the organiser of the Final Solution. To his surprise he had to acknowledge, like Hannah Arendt, that there was nothing devilish or demonic about the accused; instead Eichmann seemed more like an unimaginative, over-conscientious civil servant. With this insight his surprise turned to horror. Because this Eichmann could no longer be parked in 'anti-history', on the contrary, he became 'the symbol of progress' as it is called in *Criminal Case 40/61* (De zaak 40/61, 1962), the embodiment of technology in its most disturbing form. This must have unleashed a sort of moral panic in Mulisch: would man's future be like Eichmann perhaps? Man turned machine, pure functionality without a will. This spectre had already appeared in the story *The Embellished Man* (De versierde mens, 1955): man at risk of losing his humanity because he becomes completely merged with his technical resources. In *The Composition of the World* that is the sombre prediction for the future: humanity will make way for what Mulisch calls the '*corpus corporum*'. The total union of man and technology, the great futuristic dream now turned into a nightmare.

Funeral of Harry Mulisch. Amsterdam,
6/11/2010. Photo by Klaas Koppe.

In the seventies and eighties technology as a threat assumed a more direct and specific form: the nuclear weapons against which Mulisch actively protested outside the context of his novels. And sometimes, too, in his novels, as at the end of *The Assault*. Usually he was able to keep commitment and literature carefully separate. In the turbulent sixties, when Mulisch thought he had found a salutary alternative to a future full of little Eichmanns in the 'playful' resistance of the Amsterdam Provos (*Message to the Rat King*/Bericht aan de rattenkoning, 1966) and the 'new man' in Castro's Cuba (*The Word and the Deed*/ Het woord bij de daad, 1968), he hardly wrote any novels, except for his most experimental novel, *The Narrator* (De verteller), published in 1970.

However, that does not mean that there is a complete absence of resistance in the literature. On the contrary. But the resistance lies in the literature as such rather than a protest or a subversive message being delivered in the novels and stories (or in the poetry he suddenly started writing in the seventies). Moral or political messages do not belong in literature. Mulisch says it already in *Food for psychologists*, the autobiographical and poetic book that could be considered the secret machine room of Mulisch's oeuvre. It contains a look back at the path already trodden and announces what is still to come. 'Books that prod one to do good', he writes categorically, are like 'moral pornography'. They have nothing to do with literature.

Literature can be a 'counterweight to technology', even, according to Mulisch, the 'only' counterweight that still exists because literature (and art in general) is an artefact that, unlike the technological artefacts, is psychologically enriching rather than impoverishing. Literature appeals to readers' power of imagination, and their power of imagination is at least as important as that of the writer. Only the reader completes the book, by bringing the story and the characters to life in his own head. The writer provides the material for this exercise, in which people must call on all the capacities latent in them. In the past this role was fulfilled in a slightly different way by religion, but since secularisation only art and literature are left to resist man's impending end.

Own inalienable universe

In his novels Mulisch manages to stimulate the reader's imagination in a masterly way, partly because, as mentioned above, his prose has various layers. Beneath the narrative surface there is always a glimmer of the depths of the hermetic underworld, where it teems with references, suggestions and conjectures. There modern man can connect with disciplines that have disappeared such as alchemy, Neo-Platonism and esotericism, not forgetting mythology which, like literature, knows only an eternal present. There the neglected gods and heroes still live and are sometimes willing to grant man a glimpse of their wonderful existence. Therein lies the romantic game Mulisch plays with his readers.

Sometimes it is done with great show, as in *The Discovery of Heaven*, where science, religion, mythology and politics are combined into one fantastic whole. But Mulisch also does it in a more restrained, more intimate way, as in his sublime story Old Air (*Oude lucht*) from the collection of the same title, from 1977, or in *The Elements* (De elementen), from 1988, a short novel thematically related to it.

In both Mulisch describes a couple in a dead-end marriage, and in both it is the man who does actually die, finding the ultimate fulfilment of his life in death, following Mulisch's now well-known recipe. In *Old Air* the man, called Arnold, recounts how in his youth he thought he was on his way 'to one event, one very particular, awesome event that would occur on a particular day'. Surprised, his wife Merel asks what he is thinking of and Arnold answers: 'Something like a total orgasm of the whole world rolling over me'. According to Merel, Arnold is talking about his death, and of course she is proved right when Arnold dies in an accident in the final scene and feels, posthumously, on his way to the mysterious 'inferred garden' (a symbol of Mulisch's underworld and perhaps also of Freud's subconscious), that he is being 'lifted into a secret'.

In *The Elements* (in which the reader and main character are addressed in the second person singular) the impressionable advertising man Dick Bender recalls the 'small ecstasy' that came over him as a boy, when he pulled the blankets over his head at night to look at the fluorescent face of his new wristwatch: 'You couldn't stop, even though you had to get up early for school the next morning – it was as if, in that light, which had nothing to do with anyone else, you first realised that you existed, in a big world full of secrets...'. In the novel he visits Crete with his family, the mythical island where a feather from Icarus's wings still floats down to earth when Dick and his children are visiting the Palace of Knossos. The apotheosis is just such an 'eternal' moment as is Arnold's lot in *Old Air*. Plucked from the sea by a fire-fighting plane, Dick is dropped above the burning forest, as the four elements (water, fire, earth and air) are united and Dick, in dying rapture, ascends a 'light' that cannot be expressed in words and which is therefore printed with a cross struck through it by Mulisch.

These works repeat the theme of Mulisch's first story, *The Room*, in an infinitely richer way. This underlines, once again, the cohesion of his oeuvre, despite the considerable – mainly stylistic – differences to be found in it: wild and experimental to start with, balanced and classical later on. That oeuvre offers a view of an inalienable individual universe which, wherever you look, is immediately recognisable as Harry Mulisch's universe. I cannot imagine a better proof of literary greatness. Since 30 October 2010 Mulisch's universe has been irrevocably complete, apart from a couple of additional posthumous publications that will appear in the next few years.

The serious reading can begin. ∎

Translated by Lindsay Edwards

From Utopia to Vinex Estate

The Transformation of the Bijlmermeer District in Amsterdam

[MARIEKE VAN ROOY]

Bijlmermeer. Renovated flats with metro.
Photo by Domenico Mangano.

'*What our forefathers built in the seventeenth and eighteenth centuries was splendid, and we hope that our descendants will also be able to experience what we are building here as splendid. Different in many ways, perhaps even impossible to compare, but after a century the citizens of Amsterdam should at least be able to refer with respect to the way the Bijlmermeer was built in the nineteen-sixties and seventies.*'

Mayor Van Hall, on laying the foundation stone for the housing development in the Bijlmermeer district in Amsterdam on Tuesday 13th December 1966.

This quote represents the expectations its initiators had for the new Bijlmermeer housing district in its early stages. A city for the future, with spacious homes, free of traffic and full of greenery. Since then time has caught up with this utopian vision. If the people of Amsterdam are able to speak about

Bijlmermeer with any respect around 2066 it will be mainly due to the radical renovation work launched about twenty years ago. Anyone who had seen the Bijlmermeer in the seventies and revisited it today would look round in amazement. The modernist design of that time, characterised by the strict separation of types of traffic, extensive green public spaces and imposing high-rise blocks has all gone. Instead, the cyclist and the motorist travel alongside one another again, the honeycomb flats have been demolished or amputated and the more intimate scale of the new terraced houses looks like a way of uniting the inhabitant with his immediate surroundings. The Taibah mosque, near the Kraaiennest underground station, is designed like a Dutch fantasy of the one in the Orient, and leaves no doubt as to the faith practised here. It contrasts enormously with the very first places of worship under the parking viaducts, which had voluntarily conformed to the architectural restrictions of the all-embracing functionalist design.

The regeneration of the district is almost completed, and the proposals for the approach to the last original block of flats, the Kleiburg, and the Kraaiennest combined car park and shopping centre are currently under discussion. But when that is resolved, the last surviving link with the original informal Bijlmermeer will have vanished forever. This article will outline the construction and demolition of this radical housing project, which is an important chapter in the general and architectural history of the Netherlands.

The original design

The Bijlmermeer is a former polder which was used for agriculture before it was taken over. The area is about fifteen kilometres south-east of the centre of Amsterdam and was part of the boroughs of Weesperkarspel, Ouder Amstel and Diemen. The expansion of the city in a south-easterly direction was not part of the original 1930s expansion plan for Amsterdam. It was thought that the city would grow to about 960,000 inhabitants by 2000 and that they could be housed within the boundaries of the city. However, this view was revised after the Second World War. As a result of a reduction in the average number of people in each household, an increase in sites for industry and recreation and the renovation of run-down houses in the inner city and the nineteenth-century belt, more homes were needed than had been expected. In the revised version of the expansion plan, the idea of the concentric city was abandoned and replaced by the concept of an urban core with projecting lobes. One of these 'fingers' was the Bijlmermeer.

The state did not wish to agree to expanding the city's boundaries without some serious consideration, so the city council launched a campaign to gain support for the project. For example, a letter was sent to the 320,000 inhabitants of Amsterdam explaining why the development of the Bijlmermeer was so important to the city. Here is an extract from the letter, making clear the wretched state of Amsterdam housing at the time: 'Have you ever reflected on the problem of 25,000 Amsterdam families whom an in-depth study has shown have to live in unacceptable housing conditions, because their 'homes' are in fact slums? Did you know that 38,000 Amsterdam families still live in 'homes' with only two rooms? You can imagine that we – who run your city from day to day – are now extremely concerned that we may perhaps no

Bijlmermeer. Mosque.
Photo by
Domenico Mangano.

longer be able to carry out our plans to clear the slums and get rid of the almost inhuman housing conditions if the government continues to refuse to build new homes in the Bijlmermeer? Your fine city of Amsterdam – and who among us is not proud of this city? – has to be able to build new houses as soon as possible for at least 100,000 fellow citizens. (...) Amsterdam needs the Bijlmermeer! NOW!' According to the Information Department it was the first time that the council of a major city in the Netherlands had addressed its citizens directly on such an important issue by means of a letter.

In 1964 the conflict between Amsterdam and Minister Toxopeus was settled with a compromise. Behind the scenes work was going on to put together a corporation for the conurbation of Greater Amsterdam, and Bijlmermeer might later become an independent borough within this framework. As a temporary solution, the Bijlmer could be annexed to Amsterdam for a period of 12 years. In 1966 the transfer was complete. (The administrative change never actually took place, and 12 years later the Bijlmer was definitively merged with Amsterdam.)

In terms of programme, architecture and urban planning, the Bijlmermeer is the most radical housing project to have been implemented in the Netherlands. 90% of the project consisted of high-rise structures and 70% was designed for the social sector. The project was based on the division of functions as designated in the Athens Charter (1933) formulated by members of CIAM (*Congrès Internationaux d'Architecture Moderne*). It was very much influenced by the urban planner Van Eesteren, who was secretary of CIAM from 1930 to 1947 and worked in Amsterdam's Urban Development Department. Despite its huge scale, one of the sources of inspiration was the concept of the garden city. To quote from a brochure issued by the *Federatie van Woningbouwverenigingen* (Federation of Housing Associations): 'It may sound strange, but you will soon be able to live outdoors in Amsterdam. The Bijlmer will make this possible. The urban plan for the Bijlmer is not what we are used to. It will not be a city with some greenery in it, but greenery with some city in it.'

The design for the Bijlmermeer originated from the Urban Development Department, which developed it very largely independently. This department laid down the basis for the greenery, public space, infrastructure and the division of land for housing. *The Woningdienst* (Housing Department) was permitted to work out the details of the housing, but they did not have much room for manouevre. On the one hand there were the Urban Development Department's guidelines and on the other the strict conditions laid down by the builders of modular housing, of whom the Housing Department had so far had little experience.

The heart of the project consisted of high-rise blocks of 11 storeys in a honeycomb pattern laid out in a park landscape. In line with the wishes of the Urban Development Department, the young Housing Department architect Kees Rijnboutt designed an arcade (also known as a 'dry walkway') that would link the high-rise with the car parks, which would also house spaces for communal activities. Eight storeys of homes were scheduled above this indoor street. Due to financial restrictions, Rijnboutt's plan was later watered down. An extra storey was added, taking the total to nine, and the number of waste shafts

Bijlmermeer.
Photo by
Domenico Mangano.

and lifts was reduced. This design formed the basis for the plan's remaining blocks. The solutions Rijnboutt had come up with to achieve the requested savings were repeated in each case, and sometimes implemented even more drastically.

The design for the infrastructure was decidedly progressive for the Netherlands; the different types of traffic were separated and the immediate surroundings of the blocks of flats were car-free. Elevated roads provided direct access to the car parks, which were located on the periphery of the housing areas. These were also the points where public transport, shopping centres and other amenities were grouped. Cycle and pedestrian routes were laid out in meandering patterns throughout the district, and the viaducts were essential in this respect. No traditional streets were laid, and addresses were to be located by means of the names given to the buildings. The following passage from the Collective Block Amenities Document gives a good idea of what was expected of the Bijlmermeer: 'With regard to the home and the

Bijlmermeer. Kleiburg.
Still to be renovated.
Photo by Domenico Mangano.

housing environment, the Bijlmermeer plan is intended to satisfy such general human needs as individuality and recognisability. In the plan, the endeavour is to achieve this by arranging the high-rise blocks so that the open spaces are differentiated by shape and by their location in relation to infrastructure elements, and furthermore by significant differences in the design of the open spaces. The plan provides clear contrasts whereby quiet living in green surroundings without motor traffic contrasts with the liveliness of the indoor street and neighbourhood centre. The plan is also intended to satisfy the need for both public openness and privacy. As a place exclusively for pedestrians, the indoor street is experienced much more as a communal amenity than is a traditional street. The same applies to the wide variety of possibilities for active and passive use of the large outdoor spaces, compared to the communal gardens in garden cities. In the layout of the blocks with an indoor street, several of the disadvantages of highly regulated working-class housing can be overcome by adding elements to the indoor street that increase the flexibility in the use of the home (e.g. guest rooms) and moving activities that are a nuisance to the neighbours outside the home. Such facilities as refreshment bars with patios will benefit the communal time spent in the indoor street and outdoors.'

Even though the Bijlmermeer was later often characterised as an anonymous concrete city, the designers had definitely devoted attention to the social aspects of the plan. For instance, a separate document was put forward on the uses to which the pavilions for communal activities would be put. A whole list of purposes was mentioned, of which these are just a few: refreshment bar with seating, hobby area, crèche, homework room, consultation room, rehearsal room, youth club, play area for children, and guest rooms. The neighbourhood centres combined with car parks were considered suitable for club activities, service centres for the elderly, spaces for doctors' group practices, crèches and places of worship. For the main centre they planned such amenities as an indoor swimming pool and a theatre in addition to a shopping centre. The intention behind these amenities was clearly defined in the document, as was the cost of it all. But what was not made clear was how it was all to be financed. As far as the amenities in the pavilions were concerned, it was assumed that the inhabitants themselves would develop activities. It was suggested that rents be raised so that the residents would help pay for both the implementation and the development of the activities in the pavilions. But there was resistance to this among the residents. For the construction of the first pavilion, called *Hofgeest,* the Ministry of Culture, Recreation and Social Work gave a subsidy as part of welfare experiments in four cities: Rotterdam, Enschede, Apeldoorn and Amsterdam. But the grant given for this pavilion was the only one. The consequence was that through lack of funding the building of the remaining pavilions – the core of the collective element of the Bijlmer – was abandoned.

Exotic residents

Despite the fine promises in the brochures, criticism of the district soon snowballed. Its problems were raised at two public hearings, held in November 1970 and March 1971, at which time the work had not yet been completed, even though people had been living there since 1969. The residents, who had formed an action group, criticised the rent rises, the parking problem, the poor provision of public transport and the unfinished shopping centres. In the media the Bijlmermeer was soon portrayed as a disastrous project.

To make matters worse, the target group showed hardly any interest in moving into this suburb of the future. The Bijlmermeer was originally intended for working-class families, but because of the high rents and the alternative housing available in garden cities around Amsterdam, they failed to appear. The district became attractive to others who had trouble finding a spacious home in Amsterdam. In 1970, while the number of single-person households in Amsterdam was 18%, in the Bijlmermeer it was almost 40%. One of the very first doctors to practise there described the pioneers as follows: 'It is quite possible that a higher percentage of psychological conflicts occurs here. But this is not so surprising, because what the people here have in common is a certain non-conformism. Lots of people here are not married, lots of lesbians, lots of homosexuals, because here they can live anonymously, though they pay a lot for it. And lots of young intellectuals, who are also to some extent non-conformist. At the last elections (in 1970) we had one of Amsterdam's highest percentages of votes for the *'kabouters'* (an anarchistic countercultural movement).' The Bijlmer was a free state for non-conformist behaviour.

Another side to this story soon appeared. Apart from the eccentric Amsterdammers, the Bijlmermeer became a refuge for immigrants from Surinam who came to the Netherlands after the former colony gained its independence in 1975. It then became an attractive place for other immigrants to settle, both legal and illegal, since they found compatriots there and were able to live in relative anonymity. There are currently people of about 140 nationalities living there. An informal economy developed in the district. Some homes were used as soup kitchens or brothels. At the same time it became home to about eighty different faith communities, a place where exotic products from all over the world could be found, and where young rappers honed their skills in their own Bijlmer style. This informality remained the custom until the buildings were literally demolished. The new plan provides hardly any space for such things as small improvised businesses run by immigrants.

In the eighties the district had a negative media image because of its criminality and the drug trade. The police appeared to have lost their hold on the area. There were a series of practical problems too: public transport did not operate properly, amenities were completed too late and the housing itself lacked the planned quality. The Bijlmer thus had a bad name and was the last place in the Netherlands where anyone who had any choice in the matter of housing would want to live. In the eighties all sorts of strategies were tried to bring an end to the criminality. Managers were appointed and flats restyled by, among other things, giving them new names. The future of the Bijlmermeer appeared to be in serious doubt.

Restyling the Bijlmermeer

But there were 'Bijlmermeer believers' too. In 1985, for instance, the architect Rem Koolhaas argued that the district should be upgraded. In his view, one of the biggest problems was the archaic nature of the public space, which did not comply with the wishes of the contemporary city-dweller. The problem would largely be remedied by intensifying the urban activities in the space between the blocks.

Koolhaas' ideas were not taken up. The privatisation of the housing companies in the early nineties gave the owners more freedom to radically update the site. The housing associations opted for demolition, and this came about sooner than expected as a result of a tragic accident involving an Israeli aircraft that crashed into one of the blocks, killing 43 people. Over the course of this radical redevelopment, which is gradually nearing completion, little of the functionalist urban planning and architecture has survived. Elevated roads were brought down to ground level, high-rise blocks replaced by terraced houses with front and back gardens, and the multi-storey car parks were demolished. The all-inclusive approach was abandoned. The district was divided into segments and, under the watchful eye of the municipal project group, this has resulted in a patchwork of urban planning and architectural visions reminiscent of the Vinex expansion districts that are appearing all over the country. (Vinex (*Vierde Nota Ruimtelijke Ordening Extra*) is the title of a policy document issued by the Dutch Ministry of Housing, Spatial Planning and the Environment in which large outer city areas were designated for massive new housing development to accommodate the increasing population near existing town centres.)

The only part to be preserved in its original state, apart from a few changes intended to breathe new life into the buildings, is what is ironically enough called the Bijlmer Museum.

It is not only the architecture that no longer has anything to do with the original design, but the programme too. Homes for sale and to let have replaced social housing. The percentage of social housing complies with the present requirements for expansion districts in the Netherlands, but now forms only a small part of the whole. The multicultural nature of the district has been

Bijlmermeer.
New Shopping Mall
Ganzenhoef. Photo by
Domenico Mangano.

retained, however. The origins of the residents of the new terraced houses correspond to the mixed population that previously occupied the high-rise buildings.

To the romantic fan of this remarkable housing district, which was founded on the international principles of the postwar functional city, this redevelopment – which he probably regards as a mutilation, is indisputably a thorn in the flesh. To the developer, the local authority and the administrators this radical renewal is undoubtedly a breath of fresh air. The residents have been given a safer environment on a more intimate scale, though the downside is that there is less room for their own unregulated initiatives. The rise and fall of the Bijlmermeer shows up the discrepancy between the drawing board and reality, between a visionary image of the city and the way a city and its inhabitants actually function. Large-scale anonymity has been swapped for small-scale cosiness. The regeneration of the Bijlmermeer signals the final end of the 'city of the future'. ■

Translated by Gregory Ball

Searching the Poems as a Suspect Element

The Poetry of Charles Ducal

Once I sat naked at the table, sucked dry
by the will to make something out of nothing,
made wife and sweetheart but with a cold eye,
two stones on my native soil

On which I could sharpen myself ceaselessly,
a father and mother, raised up
on my own language, four eyes to keep me small
if proof was needed the strongest one was I.

Now I sit empty at the table, pumped full
with the I that you brought with you.
And everything I am is put in words.
And everything I'm not is neatly scrapped.

The poem 'You' (Jij) from *Tucked up with a song* (Toegedekt met een liedje, 2009), the most recent collection by Charles Ducal (1952), is a neat summary of a writer's life. It gives the reader an excellent picture of the evolution – it is no exaggeration to call it a total volte-face - that the author has gone through.

Wife and Sweetheart

The man sitting naked at the table in the opening stanza of 'You' is the protagonist in *Marriage* (Het huwelijk, 1987), Ducal's first collection, which was a *succès de scandale.* In it one can hear echoes of the sacrilegious tone of the famous poem, also entitled 'Marriage', by another Flemish poet, Willem Elsschot (1882-1960). The not exactly romantic titles of series such as 'Out of Respect for the Law' (Uit eerbied voor de wet) and 'No Further Obligations' (Verder geen plichten) leave one in no doubt that marriage is a burdensome duty for the protagonist while the title of a series such as 'Community of Property'

Charles Ducal.
Photo by Merlijn Doomernik.

(In gemeenschap van goederen) forces the reader to ask whether any community of minds is involved.

The simple answer is that there isn't. Much more than a husband, the protagonist is a poet. From the top of his ivory tower in the middle of his home he looks down on his lawfully wedded wife who is the personification of banal reality. Rather than his wife, it is his sweetheart, the muse, who represents the imagination and embodies a world of unknown possibilities. To escape the gilded cage of hearth and home and indulge in his artistic passions is a vital necessity for the slave of this divinity. Freedom is a relative notion here. As an image for the fact that as a man of the imagination the poet is sufficient to himself, Ducal uses masturbation. In doing so elements from the Christian tradition are perverted. From the poem 'Whitsun' (Pinksteren): 'Then there arose in me great faith. / I felt how God suffered in me, / a sinful pain that stirred my hands. / For him I gladly spilled my blood'.

In *The Duke and I* (De hertog en ik, 1989), Ducal's second collection, the protagonist's sweetheart takes a more concrete form. The second part is devoted to the mistress of his dreams. The gulf between imagination and reality is also prominent *within* the 'I' figure. The duke of the title (a reference to his pen name, Ducal) is an *alter ego*, a figure from the subconscious who is much more powerful than the everyday I. The latter is a total coward – in this collection he is primarily afraid of *la belle dame sans merci* and of the father. He is the prisoner of them both – he cannot escape his fascination for the enchanting witch and he needs the terrifying father to protect him.

A father and a mother, bred out of one's native language

The father of the child that is the subject in the first part of *The Duke and I* seems to be the only one who can protect his son against the uncanny outside world. But the result is that the *pater familias,* the lord and master of the farm that is the setting of these poems, himself becomes terrifying. It would seem a paradoxical bargain: the almighty one offers protection to the frightened little fellow in exchange for which he must be feared himself. It is not a coincidence that the first cycle of *The Duke and I* is entitled 'The God on the Mountain' (De God op de berg) – there are plenty of similarities between him and the almighty Father of the Old Testament.

As an adult the protagonist continues to look at the world with fear and trembling. He is now a father himself, and yet he is the inferior of his own son, as is apparent in the series 'God's Parents', (De ouders van God). Power sometimes skips a generation. The lyrical I is only the almost invisible hyphen between two potentates.

In *Mother Tongue* (Moedertaal, 1994), Ducal's third collection, it is the mother who plays the part of the antagonist. Although less powerful than the father, the narrator can never entirely break free of her. The umbilical cord is tied round his neck for ever.

The woman is a 'wet nurse' in various ways. Of course she feeds her children in the most literal sense. In 'Victuals' (Provisie), by means of a metonymic shift, it is a matter of 'a good mother, lovingly / with food for bellies and teeth, / a cupboard we may strip bare'. In 'Bread' (Brood) we are told: 'She is silent, closed off / like an egg, hard shell /turning inward, / towards us, her brood / that may eat from her body / until it's all gone, play with her heart / until it's done for / and the shell breaks'. Despite or maybe precisely because of the woman's enormous self-sacrifice, the prevailing atmosphere of the poem is one of suffocation. In other verses physical decline makes her less threatening. But only death can rescue a son from the loving clutches of his mother.

The second way in which the mother feeds her children comes down to passing on a hereditary disease. It is not that this woman doesn't love her children; it's just that she isn't used to translating her love into words. Her domestic devotion has to suffice as a declaration of love. The first-person narrator has this inability to communicate in his genes, but he does his best: "I teach my mouth to say 'sweetheart' and 'darling'. / Next to me a woman lies, cross and tender, / just as distant from me". From the two last lines one can deduce that the relation of the I with his mother has set the tone for his relations with other women, something that makes an *alma* of the *mater* for the third time.

Finally, the mother figure is associated with the writer's work. She is a source of inspiration as one can see in 'Muse' (Muze). She is also the seat of the mother tongue, but this is not unproblematic. The real mother tongue is the Flemish dialect in which the narrator was raised and in which he is kept small. The Standard Dutch language is the knife that he has acquired to cut himself free from it. Language and writing means growing up and emancipation, as one reads in 'Standard Dutch 2' (ABN2): 'Fed on Flanders, a giantess, / a glutton body of milk for love. / I bottle her up. I live in secret, / my hands guilty, my mouth pursed thin. // I want to get out of here. I write poems / to reach as far as Amsterdam, / to bud there, far from the trunk, / in a language that doesn't tell me who I am, // no mother tongue, no breast in the mouth, / but instruments, a grammar and / a dictionary to graft an I on, / loveless, but lording it over the earth'.

And everything I am is put in words.
And everything I'm not is quite scrubbed out.

There are three poems in *Mother Tongue* that seem not to belong there. In 'Judged by God' (Door God gericht) the poet denounces the consumer society. This series is just one of the provocations in Ducal's early work that show that he is keen to find a way out of the ivory tower. In *Towards the Earth* (Naar de aarde, 1998) this movement is made explicit.

Marriage (Het huwelijk) ends with a play on the Dutch poet Remco Campert's celebrated line, 'Poetry is a way of saying no'. For Ducal – or rather for Frans Dumortier, the man behind the pseudonym – there was the world on the one hand and poetry on the other. The latter was the refuge where the poet could exact revenge on 'real' life with its requirements and duties, the searching gaze of wife, father, mother and so many others. In the course of time however cracks developed in his poetic bunker. Poetry, or rather the literary world as represented by critics and awards, developed into a monster that with its questions and expectations kept the poet, who was by now addicted to applause, under scrutiny and so left him paralyzed. Through the cracks came the call of the outside world. For a long time Ducal has kept poetry and his left-leaning political ideas strictly separate. Even though he wrote radical columns under his pseudonym, he continued to keep his poems "pure". In *The Relevance of Poetry* (De belangrijkheid van de poëzie), an essay of 1991, Ducal wrote that someone who denounced racism and the corruption of the government in a book of poetry with a print run of a thousand copies soon made himself ridiculous. But as the years passed this situation proved schizophrenic and impossible to maintain. More fresh air entered Ducal's poetry, more engagement, even if it remained primarily metapoetic, and in this sense his work became a poetry of inner poetic conflict.

In Ducal's fourth collection the descent to earth represented, among other things, reconciliation with his wife. In 'Towards my wife' (Naar de vrouw) the first-person narrator begs her: 'Take me away out of this head, / this image of myself I cannot sustain, / stop the applause, enter the room / and make your husband readable again, [...] because I can no longer live my me, / I've shut my body down, it's a disgrace / no one can read what it means // to spit in one's own face'. It is his sweetheart who saves him with her love when his own self-love deserts him and he finds himself in an impasse through his own assertiveness, a fever that the narrator was already familiar with as a child. The series 'Lean Years' (Magere jaren) describes the time spent in a strict boarding school; in the poem 'Primus Perpetuus' the promising lad dreams of 'the little village that looks up and greets / the halls, the papers and public squares, / the thousand, thousand clapping hands, / the undying muse, the fruit in the ear'. All of this proved to mean nothing. Pride leads to a fall, or to a leap in the void.

Inherent in Ducal's next collection, *Dipped in Ink* (In inkt gewassen, 2006), which was not published till eight years later, is the idea of purification. But ink by its nature remains dark, something that reminds the reader of the mysterious layers of the soul that were so important in *The Duke and I*. In the metapoetic poems, which again make up the bulk of the volume, the world of the imagination and the real world are played off against each other. The narrator now stands with both feet on the ground and can think himself lucky, but it remains a close call – the poet sometimes has to tie weights to his feet in order not to fly off in search of higher realms. The artist who is with difficulty cured of his elitism and the politically engaged pen-wielding citizen struggle here for dominance: "Is it possible for one to become another // by hiding oneself away like a passport / that is no longer valid? To avoid / a mirror as though one was ashamed / of oneself? To search the poem // as a suspect element?"

The school of pornography

The confrontation between imagination and reality is embodied in the tragic dream woman Lolo Ferrari, the protagonist of the series 'Lolo'. The porn star who lets her body be moulded to gratify the fantasy of thousands of men, making them crazy, and yet who – when reality claimed its rights – swallowed an overdose of antidepressants.

'Lolo' is a preamble to the series 'The School of Pornography' in *Tucked up with a Song* (Toegedekt met een liedje, 2009). In it Ducal makes certain connections. Pornography is poetry. It is a form of art, or seems to inspire the making of art. In 'www.openwide.com' one reads, 'She's widened herself to a hole / as though something in her must shine. / The eyes that prise her open are mine. / I know the depths, so scheming that // she responds to the excitement on this page'. 'www.brutalviolence.com', a poem that, amongst other things, with its enjambment after the word 'good' looks like a review of an SM film, is also about the artistic side of things: 'There are the boots and there is blood / and the liquid whistling of the whips. / A woman's crying, she's crying well and good // rid of all imperatives / provided by an invisible voice, / soon to be tucked up with a song: / *Warum betrübst du dich, mein Herz?*' A repressed concern prevails here about how such scenes may alter our perceptions: 'We could call this a horror story. [...] // But it's only a trial or study, / an innocent exercise with the lens: / high-heeled, made up and manicured / that makes us artistic for violence'.

Pornography is poetry, but because both of them reveal at once too little and too much, the reverse is also true: poetry is pornography. As in certain websites, poetry allows the interested party to see what he wants to see. Anything he doesn't like is left out. The poem 'www.doglove.com' makes clear the perverse proportions that the re-creation of reality can assume, and how bestial a human being can be: 'Like syllables finally capsized / to make up this unnatural word, / tail on tailbone till the knot subsides. / It's difficult to believe // but then one sees the woman's paws / and the dog with human eyes, the same breed. / I, that hypocrite I, stand and gawk / because there's nothing it would like more // than to have the guts to cut loose from speech / like a god in the depths of his own flesh'. In the title poem of the series we read that 'Pornography is the mother of politics' and the poet is found to be at least complicit: 'All we are is this boy's voice / biting in the milk. Music of power. // Child's play.' Whether one bites in the milk, in the breast out of protest or gluttony, remains an unanswered question. The idea of poetry being a cover-up operation is in any case tainted with guilt feelings. The last stanza of 'Unprepared' (Onvoorbereid) reads: 'We too were silent, only caring / about the plumb line in the ink / to gauge the unfathomable depths in us / and not to notice that it stinks'.

Schlechte Zeit für Lyrik

In those poems by Ducal that deal with the outside world, the approach is not one of hard-line Stalinism but of ethical concern. Once more he draws on religious motifs, for instance in 'Subhuman' (Ondermens): 'There is also a god of rubbish, / a god of failure, of scum, / that on the day without number / who created a Man that skulks, // the self-polluted angel who remained / in the garden and who knows full well/ created out of disdain / he is nothing but dust and a bad smell. // He never ate the apple / which lies rotting under the tree, / he has never wanted to measure himself, / he has no knowledge of the dream. // He is the creature of day nought, / still able to love and to write, / but like a sweaty stench or skin complaint, // and the rod is always right'.

As in *Marriage* in the series 'Too close for poetry', (Te dicht voor poëzie) which includes the poem 'You', reality takes on the guise of a woman. Unlike Ducal's first collection, here there is a feeling that life in a minor key might be sufficient. The fact that the loved one cannot be captured in art, as is already clear from the title of the series, would appear to be a victory of fleeting reality over the creations of the imagination. The balance of power and all other relationships have shifted. If there must be poetry, there must also be more authenticity

Charles Ducal's poetry offers a constant questioning of the medium itself, an unrelenting criticism of the figure of the poet who feels he has ducked his responsibilities in what Brecht called a 'Schlechte Zeit für Lyrik'. The conflict between verse and responsibility ensured a crisis *in poeticis* right through a couple of collections. It should be clear by now that over the years Ducal has renewed himself, while always remaining true to himself. One strong feature of his work is that his struggle with poetry often occurs in lines that are extremely poetic – if at least 'poetic' may be defined as a passionate, if primarily formal engagement with language and tradition. Ducal is at his best when his forms fit him perfectly and he demonstrates what he can do with the quatrain and half-rhyme. In short, Ducal's doubting of poetry is, willy-nilly, the ultimate affirmation of it. ∎

Translated by Donald Gardner

Five Poems
By Charles Ducal

Misunderstanding I

Recently there's been a woman in my house.
She calls me 'sweetheart' or else 'darling
                                             man',]
fusses over my uncut fingernails and under-
                                          wear]
and puts down unfinished that book of mine.

She smiles indulgently when I write my
                                       poems]
and doesn't notice I'm two-timing her.
She refers to you as a ghost or an old grief:
I think she simply doesn't grasp our code.

On sunny days she sits out on the lawn
and turns for an even tan from side to side.
Deep in the dark indoors I invent your body.
The two of us grow pale self-gratified.

And yet

Does your wife like this? his friend asked
on being shown his poems to read.
He looked for an excuse. There wasn't one.
What was said there was said. And with some
                                          need.]

Still he stayed on without quite knowing why.
He no longer missed the dusty roads
and far-off women only for form's sake.
I love you. He uttered it in the void,

for when she looked it sounded heavy on the
                                       tongue,]
an excuse for years of letting go.
Yet she was the only one who was wanting.
Poetry is a way of saying no.

Misverstand I

Sinds kort dwaalt hier een vrouw in huis.
Zij noemt mij 'schat' en 'lieve zoet',
bekreunt zich om mijn nagels en mijn ondergoed
en leest het boek dat ik haar geef niet uit.

Zij duldt dat ik gedichten schrijf
en merkt niet hoe ik haar bedrieg.
Zij noemt u een fantoom, een oud verdriet:
ik denk dat zij de code niet begrijpt.

Op warme dagen ligt zij buiten in de tuin
en wentelt zich een kleur om te behagen.
Diep in huis vind ik uw lichaam uit.
Wij worden bleek van zelfbehagen.

From *Marriage*
(Het huwelijk. Amsterdam: Atlas, 1987)

Toch

Vindt je vrouw dit leuk? vroeg de vriend
aan wie hij zijn verzen liet lezen.
Hij zocht een excuus. Het was er niet.
Er stond wat er stond. Met reden.

Toch bleef hij en wist niet waarom.
Hij miste niet langer het stof op de wegen
en verre vrouwen alleen voor de vorm.
Ik heb je lief. Hij sprak het uit in de leegte,

want als zij keek klonk het dik op de tong,
als een excuus voor jaren gewenning.
Toch was zij de enige die niet volstond.
Poëzie is een daad van ontkenning.

From *Marriage*
(Het huwelijk. Amsterdam: Atlas, 1987)

Vespers

Wind and rain blew shut the shutters.
We sat there kneeling at the hearth
in the form of worship we were heirs to.
The woman to whom we owed our birth

spoke incantations to make us small.
Her voice nagged nonstop in our necks.
We sat there dumbstruck, just baptized.
As for the man who'd begotten us

he raised his hand. We bowed our heads.
He pressed his thumbprints on our brains.
Wind and rain fuelled the dream.
Wolves and witches beneath our beds.

Avondgebed

Wind en regen sloten de vensters.
Wij zaten geknield bij de haard
in de godsdienst die wij zouden erven.
De vrouw die ons had gebaard

zei formules om ons te verkleinen.
Haar stem zeurde taai in de nek.
Wij zaten stom, pas ingewijden.
De man die ons had verwekt

hief de hand. Wij boden het hoofd.
Hij prentte zijn duim in de hersens.
Wind en regen bestookten de droom.
Onder bed sliepen wolven en heksen.

From *The Duke and I*
(De hertog en ik. Amsterdam: Atlas, 1989)

Wife 2

Let this poem be imperfect, read
a hole in the language, summon me alive.
I've been refining these hands such a long
time that your body has become mislaid

(something naked seen in the morning
lying in the bath, with moistened cheeks,
that one avoids resting one's eyes on
 so as not to be drawn into making love).

Scratch the gloss off my soul. Scrap
the woman of paper I write down
to take possession of me. Wipe the ink
from my lips. Stir up enmity

between me and my poetry.

From *Towards the Earth*
(Naar de aarde. Amsterdam: Atlas, 1998)

Tot de vrouw 2

Maak dit gedicht onvolmaakt, lees
een gat in de taal, roep mij levend.
Ik heb deze handen zo lang veredeld
dat je lichaam zoek is geraakt

(iets naakts dat men 's ochtends ziet
liggen in bad, met vochtige wangen,
waaraan men vermijdt de ogen te hangen
om niet tot de liefde te worden verplicht).

Krab de glans van mijn ziel. Schrap
de vrouw van papier die ik opschrijf
om mij te bezitten. Veeg de inkt
van mijn lippen. Wek vijandschap

tussen mij en mijn poëzie.

Revolution

is not the same as insurrection
with barricades, drunken masses
and the blood ablaze.

The city is calm and surfeited,
a little lethargic from the sun,
shining in all its streets.

People are out there shopping,
at ease with the day and the times,
deaf and blind.

A young lad shouts out something against
all that brandishing a newspaper aloft.
There's something despairing about it, but
                                        still,]

it's a start.

From *Dipped in ink*
(In inkt gewassen. Amsterdam: Atlas, 2006)

Revolutie

is iets anders dan opstand maken
met barricaden, dronken massa's
en opgezweept bloed.

De stad ligt kalm, weldoorvoed,
een beetje lam van de zon,
in haar straten te blinken.

Mensen lopen te winkelen,
in vrede met uur en dag,
doof en blind.

Een knaap roept daar iets tegenin
en steekt een krant in de hoogte.
Het heeft iets wanhopigs, maar toch,

het is een begin.

All poems translated by Donald Gardner

Lievens and Rembrandt

Parallels and Divergences

[AMY GOLAHNY]

Rembrandt van Rijn (1606-1669) and Jan Lievens (1607-1674) share a home town, various acquaintances and patrons, and the cultural milieu of Amsterdam. The trajectories of their lives and careers converge at various points. Both were born in Leiden and trained by two foremost artists there, before studying with Pieter Lastman in Amsterdam. As young artists they associated closely, and critiqued each other's production in painting and etching. Dutch writers often considered them together, although eventually Rembrandt's reputation eclipsed that of Lievens. This article examines how their very different artistic personalities are evident in their early work, and what authors wrote about Lievens.

After 1631, their paths diverged. Lievens went first to London (1632-1634), and then to Antwerp (1635-1644), where he associated with artists in the circle of Antony van Dyck and Adriaen Brouwer. He returned to Amsterdam in 1644-1654, lived in the The Hague for five years, and finally moved back to Amsterdam. Rembrandt had settled in Amsterdam by 1633, moving house on several occasions, and both lived on the Rosengracht at various times. Their works often show up in the same collections, a circumstance that can be traced to similar tastes among collectors and shared acquaintances. Lievens was not an art collector, perhaps because he did not have the income to support the habit and perhaps because he moved frequently, but Rembrandt collected compulsively, even though he did not always have the means. In 1656, Rembrandt had nine paintings and one folio of prints by Lievens among his extensive art collection.

Both were immensely successful, yet in different ways. Lievens, not Rembrandt, received commissions for Leiden Town Hall (1641), the Huis ten Bosch (1650), the meeting rooms in Amsterdam Town Hall (1656) and the Statenzaal, The Hague (1664). Rembrandt, not Lievens, received commissions for grand group portraits, the foremost of these being the Night Watch (Rijksmuseum, Amsterdam), and for numerous private portraits, both painted and etched. Lievens portrayed the elite of Amsterdam in his finished portrait drawings, some paintings, and a few etchings. On a few occasions, Rembrandt and Lievens portrayed the same patrons or their relatives, including the Trip family, Johannes Wytenbogaert, Lieven Coppenol, Ephraim Bonus, and Rene Descartes. The poets Jan Vos and Joost van den Vondel wrote about their works, but both selected Lievens, not Rembrandt, to portray them. Lievens and Rembrandt were each allotted one painting in the Batavian

Lievens, *The Feast of Esther,*
ca. 1625. Oil on canvas,
130.8 x 163.8 cm.
North Carolina Museum of Art,
Raleigh.

series of Amsterdam Town Hall, yet only after Govert Flinck's untimely death in 1660. Their reputations may be charted in the literature, to reveal the vagaries and selective attention of critics.

Llevens in the literature of his time: from glowing praise to scathing criticism

Two contemporary writers offer assessments of Lievens and Rembrandt as a pair that frame their careers. Constantijn Huygens (ca. 1630) and Gerard de Lairesse (1707) provide high praise and sharp criticism respectively. Other authors apparently considered the two independently of one another: J. J. Orlers (1641), Philips Angel (1642), Joachim von Sandrart (1675), Samuel van Hoogstraten (1678), and Arnold Houbraken (1718). Huygens, Orlers and Angel praised Lievens as effusively as they praised Rembrandt. Yet Von Sandrart, Van Hoogstraten and Houbraken gave Lievens short shrift; this may be due to their closer contact with Rembrandt, or because that artist's brilliance eclipsed that of his associates. After Houbraken's biography of Lievens, the literary reception of Lievens fell into obscurity.

Constantijn Huygens' private diary of ca. 1630 reveals that Lievens matured earlier than Rembrandt, pushed himself to experiment with artistic forms and styles, and had great self-assurance. Even as they may have learned from each other, the two young artists assimilated external impressions, including monochrome tones, Rubens' inventions, and dramatic lighting and themes.

Rembrandt,
*Judas Returning
The Thirty Silver Pieces*,
1629. Oil on oak panel,
79 x 102,3 cm.
Private Collection.

Huygens contrasted the qualities and abilities of the two still-beardless young men:

'One would be rendering [Lievens] good service by endeavouring to curb this vigorous, untameable spirit whose bold ambition is to embrace all nature, and by persuading the brilliant painter to concentrate on that physical part which miraculously combines the essence of the human spirit and body. In ... history pieces, the artist, his astonishing talent notwithstanding, is unlikely to match Rembrandt's vivid invention....I venture to suggest offhand that Rembrandt is superior to Lievens in the sure touch and liveliness of emotions. Conversely, Lievens is the greater in inventiveness and audacious themes and forms. Everything his young spirit endeavours to capture must be magnificent and lofty....Rembrandt, by contrast, devotes all his loving concentration to a small painting, achieving on that modest scale a result which one would seek in vain in the largest pieces of others.'

Huygens regarded Lievens' art as forceful on a large scale, and his character as ambitious and impatient; Rembrandt's art was expressively vivid on a small scale, and his character patiently inventive. These assessments are corroborated by Lievens' Feast of Esther and Rembrandt's Judas Returning the Silver [Figs. 1 and 2, 2008-09 cat. No. 6; ca. 1625; The North Carolina Museum of Art, Raleigh; 1629, Private Collection]. In Lievens' Feast of Esther, four figures crowd around a table. They are dressed in richly textured and brilliantly coloured robes. Behind them is a luminous curtain, crafted in loosely brushed strokes. Lievens has given extraordinary attention to each component of this scene, the moment just after Esther's revelation of Haman's treachery. Haman reacts in horror, and Ahasuerus will immediately condemn him to the gallows. Esther is illuminated, while Haman is shaded, to indicate their respective virtuous and malicious natures. But it is the king, Ahasuerus, who dominates. As Ahasuerus realizes the treachery of his favored courtier, he clenches his hands and stares at Haman. Ahasuerus' hands indicate Lievens' approach to painting: he studied how the fingernails dig into the palm and how the knuckles bulge, and he arranged the hands within the painting so that they frame the corner of the table. Although Lievens lavished attention on the particulars of the hands, he did not consider the placement of the king's right hand upon the table, between the pie, bread, and plate. As the king clenches his fist, as if to hang it on the table, it has no place to fit between the pie and bread. Consistently, Lievens focused upon details at the expense of integrating the whole within a coherent spatial arrangement. Rembrandt, on the other hand, considered the overall unity of a group of figures in a spatial arrangement, as in the Judas. There, each figure is placed with respect to the others, and each reacts differently to the main action of the remorseful Judas. Huygens considered the two young men stubborn to a fault. Although he stated as much in the matter of their not travelling to Italy, he may well have generally thought that the two rejected others' advice. Rhetorically, he remarked that if only they would spend a few months travelling through Italy, they would quickly surpass the Italian artists, and give the Italians reason to come to Holland. Huygens lamented: 'If only these men, born to raise art to the highest pinnacle, knew themselves better!'

As intermediary for Stadhouder Frederick Hendrik, Huygens arranged for six of their paintings to be in the Noordeinde palace by 1632, and may also have made possible other commissions. When in Antwerp, Lievens was in contact with Huygens' sister-in-law, and informed Huygens of Rubens' death (May 1640).

Speaking in Leiden in 1641, Philips Angel was interested in elevating the art of painting, and in demonstrating that artists were learned. Angel named Lievens, along with Rembrandt, and several others, as capable of rendering histories with knowledge and appropriate reflection. Angel admired these artists for their display of learning in devising original compositions of familiar stories. As an example of Rembrandt's erudition, Angel gave Samson's Wedding Feast, and concluded that Rembrandt read the story properly and examined it with 'lofty profound reflection.' [1636; Gemäldegalerie, Dresden]. Then Angel immediately discussed two paintings by Lievens that he praised for depicting a familiar theme in a novel, thoughtful, and learned manner.

Angel discussed a grisaille of Lievens' Abraham sacrificing Isaac, in which the patriarch embraced his son, in line with Josephus, Jewish Histories, Book I, Chapter 13. The grisaille is lost, but a grand painting reflects its composition. [Fig.3; Herzog Anton Ulrich-Museum, Braunschweig] In the biblical account, Abraham bound the hands of the boy, and the angel of the lord called to Abraham and stopped him from laying the knife upon the boy; after Abraham had sacrificed the substituted ram, he and Isaac went home.

Josephus amplified this account, with lengthy conversations between father and son. Abraham told his son how much he loved him and how he was obligated to obey God, and Isaac understood that he was to obey his father and be the sacrifice himself:

'And with that he went straight to the altar and would have allowed himself to be slaughtered for the offering, and immediately would have been dead, if God had not opposed it.'

God bestowed his blessing upon father and son, and produced a ram for the sacrifice:

'So Abraham and Isaac ... kissed one another; and after they had sacrificed, they went home to Sarah and lived happily together, and thanked God for all they had received.'

The slaughtered ram, with its organs already burnt on the altar, lies in the lower left corner. Lievens implies that Abraham sacrificed the ram before he and Isaac embraced. Although this contradicts Josephus, it is in keeping with the

Lievens, *Abraham Embracing Isaac*, ca. 1636.
Oil on canvas,
180 x 136 cm. Herzog Anton
Ulrich-Museum, Braunschweig.

focus on dramatic moment of halting the slaughter of Isaac and of revealing the sacrificial ram.

Angel proclaimed: 'One may read more than one book in order to gain a deeper understanding of the subject.' Although the Bible was the prime authority, it was amplified by another account, that of Josephus.

Lievens' Bathsheba exemplified an artist's embellishment of a text. Angel explained how Lievens deviated from the biblical text in three ways: Bathsheba holds a letter sent by David, an old woman as a procuress stands in the background, and a cupid in the sky shoots love's arrow. The known version of this painting lacks the Cupid [Fig. 4; 2008 cat. No. 27; Cooney Collection, Studio City, California]. Angel reasoned that it was appropriate for Bathsheba to receive a letter, even though this contradicts the Bible, which explicitly mentioned that a messenger summoned her to David. The letter motif allowed Bathsheba to become flushed with a 'sweet blush of honourable shame' and thereby the painting gained in expressive power. Indeed, Lievens' buxom, blond Bathsheba has flushed cheeks.

Angel further analysed the situation:

'First, he [Lievens] reflected that no matter how powerful a prince might be, no one need be prepared to be at his service in sin. Accordingly there must have been a hot fire of passion in Bathsheba when she was entreated by the king.'

The deviations from the Bible in the letter, old woman, and cupid were legitimate, for they added to the overall effect. Angel regarded the letter as Lievens' innovation in representing Bathsheba, but he was mistaken. Earlier artists included the letter, among them the Amsterdam painter Francois Badens (1571-1618), little known today but much appreciated in his own time. Badens' lost Bathsheba Bathing and Receiving a Letter was praised by Karel van Mander. Although Lievens read Josephus for his Abraham embracing Isaac, he most likely followed a pictorial model for his Bathsheba.

Angel chose two unusual cases in which Lievens actually did demonstrate thoughtfulness in reading, sufficiently so that Angel was justified in considering the artist as learned. This was the exception rather than the rule in Lievens' practice. Lievens read the Bible, Josephus (but only for the rendering of Abraham), and some popular literature, but not much else. Angel's judgement of Lievens' learnedness, based upon a highly selective view of the artist, endured, although it was undeserved.

Jan Jansz. Orlers' biographies of Lievens and Rembrandt reveal much about their youth, but nothing about their association with one another. Orlers noted that Lievens demonstrated a remarkable ability at an early age, and also a single-minded and driven motivation and concentration. In 1621, Lievens, then aged 14, made a portrait of his mother at which everyone marveled, and in 1631 he went to England where he portrayed the royal family (in paintings now lost). For Orlers, Lievens was an accomplished artist, from whom one could expect great works yet to come.

Joachim von Sandrart's compendium of artists' lives includes a brief passage on Lievens which indicates some familiarity with his works, but a general ignorance about his life, which included sojourns in England and Antwerp. Von Sandrart emphasized Lievens' remarkable achievement as an artist who had not travelled abroad:

'Of those who have been nowhere but in their Fatherland, without even travelling through the territories of the Netherlands, was also Johannes Lievens of Leiden, who is among those following the highest paths. In large histories he made many heads after life, which were well painted, and had good knowledge of colours. There is not much after the antique to see in his studies, rather, in his works he maintains his own and not frightful manner. From his hand there is much to see in Antwerp and Amsterdam, where, according to my knowledge, he is still living.'

Von Sandrart accurately noted that Lievens studied heads from life, that he did not incorporate ancient models in his work, and that he had good ability with paint with colour. His style was uniquely his own, and as Von Sandrart stated, 'not frightful'. His assessment of Lievens is a short, positive spin of several aspects of his own much lengthier passage on Rembrandt, whom he judged deficient in knowledge of ancient history and literature, antiquity, Italian art, and academic practices.

Van Hoogstraten praised Lievens as one of the best artists of his time. Demonstrating his grasp of the differences in the distinct painterly styles of Lievens and Rembrandt, Van Hoogstraten noted that Lievens was expert in gaining effects of smeared pigments and varnishes, and in the depiction of moonlight landscapes.

In his Groot Schilderboeck of 1707, Gerard de Lairesse paired Lievens and Rembrandt in two pithy statements, one sharply critical, the other highly praising. Taken together, these remarks indicate how difficult it must have been to grasp the variety of Lievens' art and the complexity of Rembrandt's. De Lairesse criticized the two artists together:

'[one should not paint] in the manner of Rembrandt and Lievens, whose colours run down the piece like dung.'

De Lairesse was familiar with Rembrandt's late paintings, which include the portrait of himself by Rembrandt of 1665 (New York, Metropolitan Museum of Art), and Lievens' two paintings for Amsterdam Town Hall (Brinio and Fabius Maximus). Rembrandt applied paint thickly, in layers, and with palette knife as well as brush. Lievens used brushes of various sizes, loaded with impasto, to get an uneven surface, pronounced highlights, and heavy shading. De Lairesse's remark that paint 'runs down' the canvas surface is accurate for the late works by Lievens, according to Melanie Gifford, the conservator who examined Lievens' works for the 2008

Lievens, *Bathsheba Receiving a Letter From King David*, ca. 1631. Oil on canvas, 135 x 107 cm. The Cooney Collection, Studio City, California.

exhibition. Although Rembrandt applied pigment thickly, he never allowed the paint to 'run down' the canvas. De Lairesse may have linked the artists in recognition of the long-enduring reputation of their early activity in Leiden, but he may also have known that the two associated later in Amsterdam as well.

On a more positive note, De Lairesse connected Rembrandt and Lievens by contrasting their genius of invention with mediocre artists of his own time:

'...but we do not find, now-a-days, Wits who endeavor to distinguish themselves among the knowing, by new Inventions. We had several of them some time since, of whom I shall name but two, Rembrandt and John Lievens, whose manner is not entirely to be rejected.'

De Lairesse here separated artistic invention from paint application. If he attributed the paint running down the canvas, a quality of Lievens' style, to Rembrandt, he then recognized Lievens as an artist equally inventive with Rembrandt. Here, too, his judgment reflects Angel's praise of their genius.

Houbraken provided an informative account of Lievens' life and work, adding details of Lievens' London and Antwerp years, including his marriage to the daughter of the sculptor Michiel Colyn. Houbraken noted that he made many renowned, large altarpieces for Catholic churches and prominent people, and included poetic tributes by Joost van den Vondel and Jan Vos. Houbraken concluded by citing Franciscus Junius on the shared purposes of painters and poets: 'Painters and Poets are driven by one spirit, often to undertake something new.' This surely reflects Angel's discussion of Lievens' Abraham and Bathsheba, which that author presented as novel renditions of familiar themes. Aware from Angel that Lievens was important, Houbraken neglected him in comparison to Rembrandt.

Lievens' personality must have been ingratiating and forceful, and his network of acquaintances broad. His range of subjects is fairly limited by comparison to that of Rembrandt; while both rendered subjects from genre, the Bible, character heads, and exotic figures, Rembrandt depicted more subjects from history and myth. Lievens, indeed, benefited from his association with Rembrandt in the accounts of Angel and De Lairesse: as a lesser artistic force that catches some of the reflected glory of Rembrandt. ■

FURTHER READING

Braunschweig 1979: R. Klessman et al., *Jan Lievens: ein Maler im Schatten Rembrandts,* Braunschweig, Herzog Anton Ulrich-Museum, 1979

Washington-Milwaukee-Amsterdam 2008-09: A. K. Wheelock, Jr. et al., *Jan Lievens: A Dutch Master Rediscovered,* Washington, National Gallery of Art/ Milwaukee, Milwaukee Art Museum/ Amsterdam, Museum Het Rembrandthuis, 2008

Kassel/Amsterdam 2002: E. van de Wetering *et al. The Mystery of the Young Rembrandt,* Kassel, Staatliche Museen/Amsterdam, Museum Het Rembrandthuis, 2002

Coutré 2009: J. Coutré, "Vanquishing the Shadow: Jan Lievens Comes to Light after 250 Years," Dutch Crossing, Vol. 33 No. 2, October 2009, 135–151

Golahny 2006: A. Golahny, "Lievens' Reading: Some Observations on his *Mucius Scaevola before Porsenna,*" in: R. van Straten and M. Roscam Abbing, eds., *Around Rembrandt/Rond Rembrandt, Leiden* 2006, 191 204

Schneider-Ekkart 1973: H. Schneider, *Jan Lievens, sein Leben und sein Werke*, with supplement by R. E. O. Ekkart, Amsterdam 1973

NOTES

1 Kassel/Amsterdam 2001, pp. 51-53.

2 Schneider-Ekkart 1973, 292: letter from D. de Wilhelm to Constantijn Huygens, 6 June 1640.

3 Philips Angel, *Lof der Schilderkonst,* Leiden 1642, 44; For the English translation, see Philips Angel, *Praise of Painting,* tr. M. Hoyle, *Simiolus,* vol. 24, 1996, no. 2/3, 245.

4 Angel 1642, 48-49; Angel/Hoyle 1996, 246. For the original text of Josephus, quoted *above,* see *Flavij Iosephi Historien und Buecher...,* Strassbourg, 1574, 13, and A. Golahny, *Rembrandt's Reading,* Amsterdam, 2003, 172. For Lievens' intellectual gifts and limitations, see Golahny 2006.

5 Washington/Milwaukee/Amsterdam 2008-09, cat. 27, as ca. 1631.

6 Karel van Mander, *Het Schilder-boeck,* Haarlem 1604, 298v.

7 For this passage from Joachim von Sandrart, *Academia Todesca,* 1675, I, 313, chapter 19 (vol. 1, part 2, book 3) see Schneider/Ekkart 1973, 300.

8 Samuel van Hoogstraten, *Inleyding tot de Hooge Schoole der Schilderkonst...,* Rotterdam 1678, p. 238; see further Schneider-Ekkart 1973, 300.

9 Gerard de Lairesse, *Groote Schilderboek,* Amsterdam 1712, Book V, p. 324, translation from Kassel/Amsterdam 2002, p. 53 and p. 57, n. 109.

10 Gerard de Lairesse, Groote Schilderbook, quoted in English from Fritsch translation, 1758 ed., p 253.

11 Arnold Houbraken, *De Groot Schouburgh der Nederlantsche Konstschilders...,* Amsterdam 1718-21, vol. I, 396; see also Schneider/Ekkart, 301.

Piet Hein Eek

The Value of Sustainability

Piet Hein Eek is one of a number of students graduating from Dutch design academies in around 1990 who created examination projects that were an immediate hit. They rejected the aesthetics of modernist design, countering it with playfulness and honesty. The contrary approach to design taken by both Sottsass (1917–2008) and Sipek (b. 1949) made an impact in the 1980s, with unconventional ideas and a vivid visual language that new designers found very stimulating. These were forms in which you could lose yourself. They created a sensation of boundless freedom and a delightful optimism that objects could be redesigned, free from the old, accepted laws.

New Dutch design

The young designers who experienced this shift during their studies believed that objects should first and foremost be imaginative, social and communicative, and that humour and playfulness could be expressed in the design, through the reuse not only of forms (the light bulb and the simple milk bottle) and ideas (Duchamp), but also of materials. They also felt that the environment mattered. Perfect beauty, extravagance and luxury were no longer the norm. Design acquired a new meaning, a new narrative that could be regarded as much warmer, more straight and personal.

In autumn 1995 Piet Hein Eek participated in the Dutch Design Café at the Museum of Modern Art (MoMA) in New York, along with other designers who included Tejo Remy (Milkbottlelamp), Rody Graumans (Chandelier 85 Bulbs), Henk Stallinga (Bubble Lamp) and Joep van Lieshout (Bussing Stations). During MoMA's Piet Mondrian retrospective the design studio OPERA reworked the museum's Garden Café to create a space featuring Dutch-designed tables, chairs and lamps, other fixtures and furnishings, and a display of typography and posters by Dutch graphic designers on the walls. Eek supplied aluminium tables, chairs and stools for the space, with an industrial form and a pop rivet joint as a distinctive design feature. This showcase event marked the beginning of a growing interest in Dutch design in the US. It was the era of Clinton and Dutch prime minister Kok: the economy was flourishing and all was well.

Scrap wood cupboard,
scrap wood, final exam, 1990.

After the fall of the Twin Towers, Dutch Design really came into its own. Its philosophy and approach were appealing, offering comfort and an interesting design experience. Increasing numbers of museums and individuals bought pieces. From Milan to New York, this new Dutch design was appreciated for its simplicity and dry humour. It conquered the world. Credit is due to the Droog creative agency, founded in 1993 as a platform for independent Dutch designers, for bringing this new Dutch design to countries where design was not an everyday concept.

The visual impact of scrap wood

Piet Hein Eek (b. Purmerend, 1967) graduated in 1990 from the Eindhoven Academy for Industrial Design (since 1997 known as the Design Academy), where, after following an inspiring foundation course, he was taught by Ed Annink and Gijs Bakker. At that time the content of the lessons was strongly influenced by the tutor's own artistic preferences, as was the case in all Dutch design academies. The educational system did not offer a broad curriculum and everything was decided on an individual basis. Bakker in particular wanted to hear stories from his students, a narrative that would explain their designs. But for Eek stories were not a priority. His concerns were more pragmatic. He wanted to find out more about craftsmanship, about form and function and

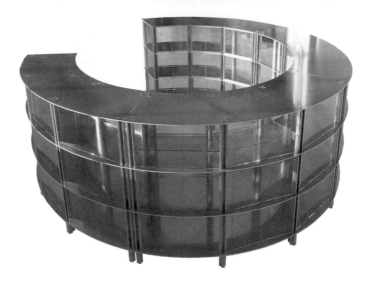

Cabinet curved,
aluminium and glass, 2011.

design systems. His notions of design were shaped by his recollections of his father using scrap wood to repair his garden shed. The art of finding, sawing and shaping old planks was etched into his memory. His imagination was full of sheds, with their plank walls, windows, doors and hinges. While his fellow-students discussed their clever gimmicks and concepts, he attempted to find a balance between thinking and doing, a form of design that would be of value in any era, like the design of a rabbit hutch or a piece by Eames. He started working with wood himself. For his final exam in 1990, he used reclaimed wood to build his now famous scrap-wood cupboard, a tall and narrow cabinet of weathered planks, doors and drawers, in which the layers of old paint and the arrangement of the strips of wood gave the piece a painterly look.

Eek's cupboard was the product of a process in which design, technique and material all interacted. This picturesque scrap wood became a characteristic feature of his work. In the years that followed he used this sturdy material to make tables, chairs, benches, beds and sideboards, both as commissioned one-off pieces and collections for the open market.

Since then, Eek's clients have come from all over the world. His furniture is available not only in its own natural colour with a thick layer of clear varnish, but also with a white or black finish.

The robust wood gives his furniture a monumental impact, as can be seen in the 'enormous scrap-wood armchair', which Eek made in 2000 using the wood from an old shed. With a basic block shape, wide planks and gently curving back and seat, this chair has the aura of a throne. Its dimensions have been selected with the skill of a sculptor, countersunk screws make the joints visible, and the signs of use, the paint and nail-holes all contribute strongly to the appearance of the piece. Thick varnish provides a smooth and practical surface.

Aluminium and glass

Eek's metalwork is also uniquely robust and simple. In 1993 he discovered the possibilities of the CNC (computer numerical control) machine, a computer-controlled lathe that allows shapes to be copied in metal with seamless precision. Eek worked with the factory that owned the machine to produce a light-grey, almost graphic aluminium chair, an industrial gem composed of flat, folded sections held together with pop rivets. He used the same approach for the matching table that he went on to design, and exhibited both table and chair in New York. These pieces were revolutionary because, although their appearance suggests otherwise, they are in fact extremely lightweight and stackable. The cold-construction method of assembly, using bent edges and rivets, is an allusion to the beauty of the functional construction of factories, bridges and machinery in the late nineteenth century.

Two years later Eek made a metal storage unit based on the rectangular glass doors of a lab cupboard that he found on a Philips dump. This became one of his most successful designs. Just as the rhythmic arrangement of the planks of his wooden cupboard are reminiscent of structures in Cubist painting, the modular cadence of the Philips cabinet reflects the identical series in the work of the American minimalist artists Andre, Judd and LeWitt in the 1960s, who based their sculptures on the rhythms of the grid and the automation of the production process.

Just as elementary in form, but of a dazzling elegance, is Eek's 'aluminium curved cabinet', a long undulating glass form that he designed in 2011 and exhibited at the Salone Internazionale del Mobile in Milan. The piece is based

Ticket office of the Museum Kröller Möller,
Otterlo, 2000.

Restaurant (2010) with various furniture, tubes buffet, lamp of Léon Stynen and the 'Old lamp shade lamp 'Ball'(2008).

on a curved aluminium unit that Eek had recently made for a shop. Restricted by the rounded shape of the setting within which the unit had to function, he devised a construction that allowed straight glass sections to be placed within a curved aluminium frame. The result was this glittering piece of furniture, which appears completely transparent, with its reflections of aluminium and glass. It is an arrangement of metal sections with glass sheets mounted within a series of crystal-clear segments which can be extended endlessly in any direction. The interplay of old and new is a key feature of this piece: the glass and sculpted lines give this unit a character that owes much to functionalist architecture, but its aluminium construction and resultant elegant form lend the design an entirely contemporary look.

Discovery, design and production

Piet Hein Eek's furniture appeals to the imagination. His pieces appear on television shows, at trade fairs, in reading areas at exhibitions and by 1995 they had already found their way to MoMA in New York. He researched his ideas in what he refers to as his 'free work', in which he has experimented with different materials, imitating wooden furniture in steel, attaching veneer to steel objects and making a cupboard out of sticks and a treehouse from scrap steel. He nearly always bases his work on something that he has happened to find – old wood, a piece of metal, a heap of glazed windows or an unusual object. He recently took a stack of heavy beams, which he'd come across years ago and kept in storage because he liked the way they looked, and piled them up to create a unique group of benches and chairs. His company showroom is full of seats and tables made from leftovers of the production process, as though in a protest against wastefulness.

In 1996, prompted by his love of old doors and his father's sheds, he designed his own first garden houses, buildings whose appearance is determined by their intended function. One outstanding example of this work is the ticket-sales kiosk in the woods at the rear entrance of the Kröller-Müller Museum in Otterlo, which he made from left-over materials in 2002.

Not only are his designs based on found forms and materials, his approach to construction solutions also relies on serendipity. Every technical discovery that leads to a remarkable result is painstakingly recorded for the long-term benefit of the company's design processes and profits.

Eek finds room for reflection and taps into new ideas within the free association allowed by his experimental work, where no external demands influence the process. He believes that research, design and manufacture form a single whole, just as the pop rivet in his metal products represents both the form and the construction. For Eek, design is all about finding the right balance in the calculating and creative process. Because a design has no value if it is not economically feasible.

Company finances

Since 2010 Eek en Ruijgrok BV, the official name of the company that Eek set up in Geldrop in 1996 with his fellow-student Nob Ruijgrok, has been based in one of the palaces of industrial construction on Strijp R, a former Philips factory site in Eindhoven. The factory, renovated by Eek himself, covers an area of 10,000 square metres and consists of five large halls, divided between two blocks that are connected by a transport corridor. The building, originally a ceramics workshop for the lighting industry, has high ceilings and a lightweight construction of concrete and brick, metal and glass. Sunlight streams in through the glass roof. These transparent spaces present all of the different facets of the company: design studio, production floor, shop, showroom, administration department and exhibition space, where Eek also displays work by fellow artists and designers.

Eek en Ruijgrok BV is a completely independent operation with an annual turnover of 4 to 5 million euros. It is a successful creative industry employing fifty people. The organisation has a holistic structure that allows an easy overview of the entire design process of Eek's products, from the initial pencil sketches to the computer development and the manufacture of the result.

Eek views the creation of his own company in Geldrop as the most successful moment in his design career so far. It enabled him to combine everything under one roof, which proved hugely successful in terms of quality and sales, because it gave Eek control over both the price and production standards. And this has led him to believe that designers are exceptionally well qualified to take the lead in a new approach to business. Their work gives them the ability to take a broad economic view. Right from the initial sketches, they are able to visualise the final product and the stages required to get there. Eek feels that the business world could benefit from applying the creative concepts and qualitative aspects of design. And indeed, increasing numbers of artists and designers are now working successfully in think-tanks for innovative projects and in this way they could also contribute a great deal to the renewal of the economy.

Tubes buffet, old pipes, 2010

For Eek, sustainability is a non-negotiable aspect of his business. The quality of his work depends on it. He is currently considering purchasing an area of woodland in the Dordogne, where he has already bought and renovated a dilapidated watermill, so that he knows where his wood comes from and that it was sourced responsibly.

The restaurant

The premises also house the company restaurant, where Eek's own designs mingle with antique furniture. The look of this space, with its high ceiling, is determined by lots of natural light, a colourful bar unit and an unusual group of hanging lights made from old lampshades. The bar unit was made by Eek and consists of a horizontal stack of gas, water, air conditioning and heating pipes in their original colours, which had been reclaimed from the Philips factory. A monumental light in a simple, vertical form hangs dramatically in the middle of the restaurant. It is a design by the Flemish architect Léon Stynen (1899–1990). This hanging lamp, with its long lines of glass and metal, is a monument in light, surrounded by smaller, more playful lighting designs. Eek's decision to install this colossal piece, with its architectural allusions to the middle of last century, at the centre of his restaurant, may be a reference to the balance that he is seeking, a notion that is constantly apparent in his work: the balance between architecture and furniture, between then and now, in search of the eternal form. His lampshade-lights hang daintily around this piece, circling in a dance of elegant glass shades found by Eek in second-hand shops.

As we have already seen, Piet Hein Eek's independence and his open cultural attitude, his conceptual vision and his craft, and his ability to make rapid associations with what he sees are all important factors in the development of the

Tubes chair, old pipes, 2011.

designer's work. The objet trouvé always plays a vital role. Found elements inspire Eek in his creation of associations, connections and new designs that, all being well, will result in the production of objects. This is how all his designs came about, from the scrap-wood cupboard in 1990 to the Philips cabinet in 1994 and last year's 'aluminium curved cabinet', which was developed on the basis of the same design, via the 2003 oak display cabinet. He used the pipes he found in the old factory not only to make the restaurant bar unit, but also a number of tube chairs and benches, thus linking him, in his own unique way, to Marcel Breuer (1902–1981), who made his first bent tubular steel chair in 1925.

Above the factory shop and design floor is an immense exhibition area for art and design. In this loft-like space, Eek shows the work of artists and designers with whom he feels an affinity. The Van Abbe Museum has used the display case in the middle of this space, which was designed by Eek, to present pieces by El Lissitzky, René Daniels, Henk Visch and JCJ Vanderheyden. These are small, important works in which the conceptual and visual values of the artistic concept unite in a way that everyone can see.

Eek's designs reveal his warm relationship with elements of modern visual art. His connection with Judd and Andre has already been mentioned, but the bright spirit of Mondrian is also prominent in his work, and is expressed in the dimensions and scale of his designs. The metal table he designed in 2004 as a development of his scrap-wood tables reveals his affinity with the artist. Its staggered pattern reflects not only the structure of the scrap-wood table surface but also the interlocking patterns painted by Mondrian in 1918 and 1919, when he was tentatively feeling his way towards his own universe. In his paintings Mondrian sought to find absolute harmony of body and spirit. In the rich sustainability of his designs and in his company's approach to business, Piet Hein Eek is doing the same. ∎

www.pietheineek.nl

Translated by Laura Watkinson

Charley Toorop

A Deeper Longing

Anyone looking at a list of contributors to Dutch art exhibitions during the early decades of the last century might be surprised at how many female artists were active at the time. However, it was only the rare exception whose name would enter the annals of art history. Art, after all, was a male activity, as the art critic Jan Engelman observed, and very few women were ever allowed to enter that particular citadel.

Charley Toorop (b. 1891 Katwijk; d. 1955 Bergen, N. Holland) succeeded in doing so with flying colours, in spite of regular splutterings of protest from the critics who simply could not get their heads around her work. On the occasion of her first solo exhibition at the Amsterdam Stedelijk Museum in 1927, the same Jan Engelman wrote: 'Charley Toorop does many things badly and sloppily, but she has a core of such masculine fearlessness that revelations emerge that do more than merely charm, they move'[1] One of the first to be won over by her work was the influential older critic Albert Plasschaert. He had been hugely irritated by an exhibition put on by a group of painters in 1926 and wrote indignantly: 'What kind of creatures are they? What is Charley Toorop doing among people who only want to stay out of the wind in a quiet corner [... Compared with them] Charley Toorop speaks another language, expresses a deeper longing, and I ask myself: 'Charley, how could you leave *your* Rotterdam and get together with this elderly, prim and proper lot?'[2]

Charley Toorop was neither elderly nor prim and proper. She dared to create paintings that many people thought ugly and even distasteful – and still do today. She did not try to charm; she sought soul, and that involved more than the careful imitation of reality. Eight years after her debut in a group exhibition of 1909, she had decided where she was going and described her ambition in rather cryptic and high-flown words: 'Being a part of the cosmos involves recognising the natural element that leads to inspired vision'[3]. By this she meant that, unlike Mondriaan and the De Stijl group, she would continue to depict reality, but for her the challenge was to penetrate more deeply into it so as to express its *soul*, which was, in the end, to find a way of expressing how she herself saw and experienced reality.

There was no ready-made recipe for this. She had to discover it herself through trial and error, by falling over and picking herself up again. Conse-

quently Charley Toorop's work is not uniform; hers was a compulsive quest for a form of expression, a style, that she could make her own. Looking back on her body of work, one can distinguish three periods: a period of orientation from 1909 to 1926; a crystallisation phase from 1927 to 1945; and a final period of maturity from 1946 to 1955.

Charley Toorop,
Farming Family in Zeeland,
1927. Oil on canvas,
120 x 150 cm.
Stedelijk Museum, Amsterdam.

Orientation, 1909-1926

Charley Toorop was eager to try out the new styles which avant-garde artists introduced in the early 20th century. First of all, luminism, the Dutch variant of post-impressionism of which her father Jan Toorop was a leading light; then cubism, in which Jacoba van Heemskerck and Piet Mondriaan were her exemplars; and finally expressionism, which as it turned out appealed to her most of all. It was not so much the French Fauves who inspired her as the symbolically-laden semi-abstract expressionism developed by Van Heemskerck and the Utrecht artist Janus de Winter on the basis of Kandinsky's art and ideas. For four years, from 1914 to 1918, Toorop painted works in which she tried to depict the 'aura' of objects, landscapes and people, as for instance in the painting to which she gave the abstract title of *Composition* (1917). In that

Charley Toorop,
Three Generations, 1950.
Oil on canvas, 200 x 121 cm.
Museum Boijmans
Van Beuningen, Rotterdam.

work, which shows flowers, a man's head, a bent figure and a bottle, she was probably expressing her feelings about her alcoholic husband.

Her marriage to Henk Fernhout did not last long. She was already pregnant with her first child when she married him in 1912. Her parents were dead set against the union and had forbidden any contact between them. But in vain. Charley was extremely strong-willed and stubborn. She went her own way and would continue to do so throughout her life, self-willed and certainly not afraid of making mistakes. The marriage with Fernhout undoubtedly had its happy moments. Three children were born: two sons, Edgar who took up painting at a young age, and John who thanks to Joris Ivens became a cinematographer, together with a daughter, Annetje, who was emotionally neglected by her alcoholic and largely absent father and her egocentric mother. The marriage held together for five years. Fernhout proved unable to accept that his wife's primary concern was for her art and not for him. In his outbursts of rage he cut her paintings to shreds – which only had the effect of driving Toorop even more into herself and her work. In 1917 it was over; Toorop walked out. Until the 1940s she had a number of affaires but none developed into a firm commitment; her painting always came first. For a man like Arthur Lehning with whom Toorop had a passionate affaire between 1928 and 1932, it was not enough: he demanded a level of obedient devotion that Toorop was quite unable to give him.[4]

In 1919 Toorop went to live in North Holland, where she knew a number of artists. Her contact with them influenced her style, and she began to use dark glowing colours and heavy contours. In 1920-21 she took six months off to go to Paris to paint and catch up with the latest developments in the art world. The Belgian art critic André de Ridder, an acquaintance of her father, and the writer and poet Paul-Gustave van Hecke visited her there and promptly invited her to exhibit in Brussels. They also organised an exhibition for her in a Paris gallery. During the next few years Toorop would visit Brussels regularly; she was an enthusiastic networker.

In Brussels she met old acquaintances and made new ones, one of whom was Edouard Mesens, a poet, musician and organiser of exhibitions. She revived her contacts with the painter Gustave De Smet whom she had met when he was living in the Netherlands during the First World War. De Smet was an important influence on her. In the 1920s, after a dark expressionist phase, he adopted a style similar to the French constructivists, combining it with 'naïve' figurative work. After Picasso's discovery of Henri Rousseau, artists were showing a great interest in so-called naïve art.

De Smet's new work provided a fresh stimulus to Toorop's stylistic development. In 1926-27 she painted a series of views of Amsterdam, the Rotterdam docks and the Middelburg fairground which in their visual language, composition, brushwork and use of colour are naïve in conception. She also employed constructivist simplification and stylisation of form in a number of still lifes.

In this way she gradually developed a style of her own and freed herself from the masters who had once served as her exemplars. Jan Toorop, Jacoba van Heemskerck, Janus de Winter and Gustave De Smet were the most important of the artists who had influenced her. But her interests had always

Charley Toorop, *Medusa puts to sea*, 1941. Oil on panel, 60 x 70 cm. Kröller-Müller Museum, Otterlo.

been wide-ranging: she had explored the world of the avant-garde with an open mind. For a long time, her knowledge of it remained limited, coloured by what was being exhibited in the Netherlands. Symbolism was a basic undercurrent in Dutch avant-garde art, and like other artists Charley Toorop was convinced that art should reveal what was hidden from the eye. Expressionism seemed appropriate for the task.

So in Paris in 1920-21 it was an eye-opener for her to discover that it was not necessary to twist oneself into all kinds of contortions to achieve expression.

The instant she saw Picasso's new neoclassicist work in the Rosenberg Gallery it became blindingly obvious to her that it was simply a question of clear insight. What you must express is *your own* view of reality, your personal understanding of what you see. In a letter written to a friend from Paris: 'one thing I know, that I am shocked by the paintings which are sent to me from Holland [...], it's very distressing! I want everything to become steadily clearer. And I want, whatever the cost, to create things that are happy and radiant. I mean inwardly radiant, yet austere and quiet.[5]

Crystallisation, 1927-1945

Charley Toorop,
Self-Portrait with pallet,
1933. Oil on canvas,
119.5 x 90 cm.
Gemeentelijk Museum,
Den Haag.

Solutions are found where they always seem to lurk, surprisingly close at hand. It is just a matter of seeing them and being aware; but developing that awareness can take time, sometimes years. So although on her return from Paris and Brussels Toorop may have had her insights, she had not yet progressed so far that she had her own language, her own painterly style. So for the time being she fell back on points of reference. When she was still in Paris, she had seen the Fayoum portraits in the Guimet Museum, realistic late-Egyptian portraits of the dead. She wanted to achieve in her own work the same magical power that radiated from them. That realism, together with the clear simplicity of Picasso's current work led to another point of reference: the painting of Vincent van Gogh.

Through her father she had long been familiar with van Gogh's work, but only now did his painting come alive for her. Was he not also searching the depths of human existence? Van Gogh, like her, had fumbled and enquired his way through life – Vincent was a soul-mate.

In 1927 Charley Toorop painted her first masterpiece, a version of Van Gogh's Potato Eaters: *Farming Family in Zeeland [Boerengezin]*. For its style and inner symbolism Toorop seems to have drawn heavily on her father's monumental chalk drawing *Faith and Earnings* [Geloof en Loon] of 1902. It is a remarkable coincidence that in both works the space is restricted and the heads intersect powerfully, while the father's head is placed precisely in front of the cross formed by the bars in the window beyond which one can see the land from which he scrapes a living. The composition sets the farmer on the far left and his wife and children in the right half of the picture. It is striking how the children appear to be almost riveted to the mother to form a single unit. The oldest daughter is on the far right, forming the antipode of the father on the left. She is combing her hair and gazing sullenly out of the picture. Behind her hangs a mirror. Thus Toorop creates a certain psychological tension between the hard-working farmer ground down by his labours and the daughter who is growing up with very different interests.

The work is not 'inwardly radiant, austere and quiet'; but it is certainly powerful and full of expression. In the years that followed Charley Toorop would produce many more such paintings. They are the works that one immediately recognises as hers and with which she established her reputation.

The years between 1927 and 1933 were extremely productive, when Toorop not only produced her best work but was also actively involved in the art world. In 1926 she went to live in Amsterdam where she took the initiative in setting up a new artists' association, a progressive society for architects, painters and

Charley Toorop,
*Self Portrait with Edgar
in Paris*, 1921.
Oil on canvas,
73.2 x 60.2 cm.
Stedelijk Museum, Alkmaar.

sculptors. She was also actively involved in the setting up of a Film Society in 1927, a club for writers and artists who disliked the commercial films coming out of America, for whom evenings were organised to view French and Russian 'cinema', which was considered to be avant-garde. In 1929 she moved to Paris. She also lived for a time in Berlin. In both cities she met various avant-garde artists such as Sophie Tauber-Arp and Hans Arp, Amedée Ozenfant, Naum Gabo and László Moholy-Nagy. In Paris she spent a lot of time with her old friend Piet Mondriaan and regularly helped him out. Before finally returning to the Netherlands in 1931 she spent time in Brussels where she visited the international exhibition *L'Art vivant en Belgique* in the Centre for Fine Arts (BOZAR). A year later she was back in Brussels taking part in a major exhibition of a century of Dutch painting. Edouard Mesens had meanwhile become the Exhibitions Officer for the Centre for Fine Arts and invited her to put on a solo exhibition which took place at the end of 1933. André de Ridder wrote in his introduction to the catalogue: 'As an artist Madame Charley Toorop is more virile than many of her male colleagues, and she will astonish many critics and visitors with her objective and realistic vision, her unflinching composition and the austerity of her palette.' [6]

In retrospect, the exhibition proved to be an end-point. Not a single painting was sold and the reception was lukewarm[7]. De Ridder had probably accurately anticipated what the reaction of the public and the critics would be: as the work of a woman, Toorop's muscular language was at the very least unsettling. But it was also becoming clear that a new age was dawning. Europe was experiencing the painful effects of the 1929 financial crash. In Germany, the consequences were catastrophic – the disastrous economic situation brought Hitler to power. In other countries too, reactionary conservatism was on the move. For the arts this meant that modernism almost disappeared; it virtually went into hiding and just barely survived in very restricted circles.

Charley Toorop also felt the effects of the financial crisis and the shift of society to the right. There was no longer a market for her paintings of muscular farmers. To earn money she turned to other genres: still lifes, bouquets, paintings of fruit trees and portraits. She pressed her friends and acquaintances to sell her work and obtain portrait commissions. Incidentally, she not only looked after herself but also helped other artists when they turned to her – her son Edgar most of all.

Toorop did not close her eyes to political developments. In 1938 she started on a small work, a head of Medusa. As soon it was completed in 1939 she started work on another version, *Medusa puts to sea* [Medusa kiest zee]. They are two remarkable paintings. Whereas Toorop in her portraits and paintings of people had always placed the emphasis on wide-open staring eyes, the eyes of her Medusas are left blank. They emanate a blind menace.

When the Second World War sucked the Netherlands into its maelstrom of destruction, she initially cherished a hope that something good might come from the 'upheavals', because 'Dutch life and its fossilised forms had run to seed'[8] That hope gradually gave way, not to a lazy acceptance of the situation, but to an unyielding resistance to the new regime that the Occupier had imposed. She refused to register with the Kultuurkamer and was ready to help others, including Jewish friends and needy artists. Life became difficult for her when she had to leave her house in Bergen in February 1943. Until the Liberation in May 1945 she drifted from one address to another : in Amsterdam, in Blaricum with Bart van der Leck, and with farmers and acquaintances in North Holland. In spite of the circumstances she continued to paint – painting again became, as it had been during her marriage, a form of escape, this time an escape from having to socialise constantly with her hosts.

Maturity, 1946-1955

For Charley Toorop the Liberation in May 1945 meant regaining her own space, her 'privacy' as she described it in a letter. Her existence as a continual 'lodger' had brought her to the end of her tether and she was overjoyed to be able to return to her own home. Artistic life gradually got going again. Amongst other things, in 1946 Toorop was invited to take part in a London exhibition of *Dutch Art During the Occupation*. Three of her paintings relating to the war, including *Medusa puts to sea*, were selected. Toorop visited the exhibition and also took the opportunity to visit her aunt, the sister of her dead mother, who lived in London. But while there she fell downstairs and suffered a brain haemorrhage. That marked the start of her physical decline. The war years had taken too much out of her.

In the years that followed she had a series of strokes; these were so serious that it was only with a great effort that she eventually made a partial recovery. Her speech was affected, she walked with difficulty and her left arm was paralysed. She must have considered herself extremely fortunate that she was right-handed, because she was still able to paint. And paint she did. In 1941 she had decided to paint a large canvas on which she would immortalise her father, herself and her son Edgar. It had been difficult enough to make a start on it during the war, but her physical condition did not make it any easier afterwards. Nevertheless, she did manage to work on it and in the autumn of 1950 she completed the massive painting. She called it *Three Generations* [Drie generaties]; it was her last major work.

The composition of *Three Generations* is again significant. Toorop painted herself, her father and her painter son as if they 'were nailed to the cross' – as she has been quoted as saying. Her father Jan, to the left of the painting, is represented by the bronze bust of him made by the sculptor John Rädecker whom she greatly admired because of his ability to capture the *soul* of reality. On the right stands Edgar, palette in hand, and below, between the two of them, sits Charley herself with a paintbrush in her hand as if applying paint to the canvas. A significant detail is that she painted Edgar as he posed for her, but she portrays herself in mirror image, so that in the painting she looks left-handed. The composition of the Father on the left and the Son on the right leads one almost naturally to complete the Trinity: the *Spirit* is in the midst.

Toorop was certainly spiritual in the sense that she was enormously motivated. Towards the end of her life she came upon the writings of the philosopher Nikolai Berdyaev, in which she must have recognised herself completely. Berdyaev believed that man could only become truly free when he had freed himself from materialism and discovered the spiritual power within himself. For Charley Toorop that was precisely the motivation that had driven her to paint. Throughout her life, painting had helped her to break free and not only develop a personal vision of reality, but also achieve self-realization. ∎

Translated by Chris Emery

NOTE

1 Jan Engelman in *De Nieuwe Eeuw*, 18 June 1927.

2 Albert Plasschaert, 'Schilderkunst. De Brug', *De Groene Amsterdammer*, 25 September 1926.

3 Charley Toorop, 'Iets over nieuwe schilderkunst' [Something about the new painting], *De Forens*, 1 December 1917.

4 Arthur Lehning was an anarchist, writer and founder of the intellectual journal for art, literature and politics, *i10*. For his affaire with Toorop see T. van Helmond-Lehning, *Zelfportret van een liefde. Charley Toorop en Arthur Lehning*, Amsterdam 2008. See also M. Bosma, Charley Toorop. Dessins – Lettres, Fondation Custodia, Paris 2010.

5 Charley Toorop, letter to A. Roland Holst, Paris 30 January 1921.

6 'Artiste plus virile que beaucoup de peintres masculin, Madame Charley Toorop surprendra bien des critiques, bien des spectateurs par le coté objectif et réaliste de sa vision, la fermeté de son dessin et l'austérité de sa palette.' André de Ridder, in *Charley Toorop*, cat. Brussels (Paleis voor Schone Kunsten) 1933.

7 Exhibitions were always selling exhibitions; artists were contractually obliged to pay the exhibition organisers a percentage of any sale. In addition they paid room hire. As for its reception, I have been unable to find any reviews in the press of the time.

8 Interview 'Charley Toorop: 'I am not a pessimist', *De Telegraaf*, 31 July 1940.

Dredging

What Two Small Countries Are Really Big In

Take a good look at the commercial contours of the Low Countries and you'll notice a striking difference between Dutch and Belgian companies. The Netherlands has more multinational businesses that catch the imagination with whole strings of products. Take Philips, for example: active around the world in consumer electronics, light bulbs, and communications and medical equipment. Or Unilever with its wide range of consumer products, including such well-known brands as Dove soap, Lipton tea, and many more. You rarely find companies like this in Belgium.

Belgian multinationals do exist, of course, but they usually focus all their energy on one type of product. Take Bekaert, which has its headquarters in Belgium and is active from Venezuela to China. This multinational produces steel wire – in hundreds of varieties, of course, but even so: steel wire for car tyres, steel wire for cutting solar panels, steel wire shaped into crucial bra components. Belgian companies may not be champions when it comes to diversity, but they do extremely well in detail. Imec, a world player in the world of nanoelectronics and nanotechnology, is a perfect example. Another is Stageco, a company that builds stages for the very biggest concert tours of groups like U2. With their products they form a small but indispensable cog in a much larger machine. While Dutch companies provide ready-made end products, Belgian enterprises tend to be subcontractors.

But there's one other interesting feature on the economic landscape of the Netherlands and Belgium: both countries are world leaders when it comes to dredging. And dredging is big business. The worldwide dredging market today has a turnover of ten billion euros a year on average. The US, China and Japan together account for half of those sales, but they are closed markets. No foreign dredging company is ever given a contract there. This may raise some eyebrows, particularly with regard to the US as the champion of the free market, but in those countries waterways and harbours are regarded there as strategically important, so foreign companies cannot be made responsible for their maintenance. This policy is even enshrined in law in the Jones Act. As a result, however, American dredging companies are lagging behind technologically because of the lack of competition.

In the other, 'free' half of the dredging market, European companies account for 85 percent, with Belgian and Dutch companies taking up three-quarters of that amount. Between them they also have the largest and most modern dredging fleet in the world. Royal Boskalis Westminster, a Dutch company with some 8,000 employees, is generally regarded as the world's largest dredging business. Another Dutch company, Van Oord (4,500 employees), and the Belgians Jan De Nul (4,300 employees) and Deme (3,500 employees) are among the world's largest dredging firms. But there are also hundreds of small companies in the Low Countries that work regionally or locally. The world players often compete with each other for contracts, leading to fierce conflicts on more than one occasion. But they're also increasingly aware of the need to cooperate in order to bring major projects to a favourable conclusion.

©Boskalis.

Queen of the Netherlands.
© Boskalis.

From mud mill to steam dredger

It's not surprising that the Low Countries are such mighty dredgers. Throughout their history the Netherlands and Belgium have constantly had to defend their land from water and flooding. And the Netherlands in particular has also reclaimed land from the sea and held back the water to maintain polders and habitable areas. About one-quarter of the Netherlands is below mean sea level, and that says everything about the importance of dredging in those regions.

Over the centuries, the Low Countries have had to struggle with an endless series of floods and breached dikes, so since the early Middle Ages the inhabitants have been forced to think about how to control the water. Dikes were erected, but in addition lakes were drained, harbours built, waterways dug and deepened, and land reclaimed. And it always came down to dredging.

For a long time dredging was done by hand. Silt and sewage were removed from rivers and watercourses by means of some kind of scoop net, often consisting of a long stick with a leather bag attached to it known in dredging jargon as a *baggerbeugel* or dredging brace. Canals were dug with shovels and spades. Wheelbarrows always played a major part. But at the same time, of course, people were constantly thinking how they could make dredging more efficient.

In the sixteenth century especially, when technological innovations were taking place in Europe in countless other areas, great progress was made in dredger development. One of the best-known designers was Joost Janszoon Bilhamer (1541 – 1590), a military engineer, surveyor, sculptor, engraver, cartographer and master builder. In 1575 Bilhamer invented a mud mill. This consisted of two flat-bottomed barges with a conveyor-belt sort of construction fixed between them which was powered by a treadmill. Mounted on the belt

Widening and deepening of the Pacific entrance
and South approach of the Panama canal.w © Deme.

were a whole series of buckets that scooped up the mud from the sea- or river-bed. Later on the brothers Tymon and Adrianus Kater produced a new version of the mud mill that could dredge to a depth of five metres.

In the earliest designs, the treadmill was operated by four strapping fellows (sometimes these would have been convicts). But the deeper the dredging went the more energy was required, so horses were substituted and were given a brief rest after every hour's work. Later versions used steam power, and later still diesel engines were used. The history of dredging and the development of dredgers through the centuries is beautifully illustrated in a permanent exhibition in the Baggermuseum, or Dredging Museum (www.baggermuseum.nl), in the Dutch town of Sliedrecht, which is generally regarded as the cradle of dredging in the Low Countries.

In the Middle Ages dredging operations were the result of local or regional initiatives, but in the sixteenth century they increasingly became the responsibility of the provincial or national government. The great leap forward was made by King Willem I of the Netherlands (1772 – 1843), also known as the 'Merchant King', a man with a reputation for commercial insight. He saw that the Netherlands was lagging behind and attempted to stimulate the Dutch economy on several fronts. To this end he developed an economic policy that relied heavily on the creation of a solid infrastructure. From 1820 on he devoted a great deal of attention on the construction of canals and on making the harbours of Ghent, Amsterdam and Rotterdam more accessible.

Willem I was also personally involved in the development of a steam-driven dredging machine. In 1824 the first steam dredging mill was completed, and the king put it straight to work deepening the harbour of Antwerp. Not long afterward, however, the boiler exploded, and even after it was repaired the mill never worked properly. Until the mid-nineteenth century dredging was still mainly a manual operation and the dredging brace was the tool most frequently used.

The Belgian Revolution of 1830, which would result in an independent Belgium, put an end to the great infrastructure projects. The Dutch coffers were empty and political entanglements caused the national debt to rise, bringing the development of the dredging industry in the Low Countries to a temporary halt. Even so, the nineteenth century saw the construction of hundreds of kilometres of canals, the creation of numerous polders and the dredging of many harbours and rivers so that ever larger ships with ever greater capacity could make their way inland.

Since the Middle Ages the Dutch have been renowned for their expertise in water management, and even then foreign monarchs were seeking their advice on the reclamation of marshy areas or the draining of wetlands. In the eighteenth century Dutch engineers travelled to Germany, France, Italy, Spain,

Offshore wind farm, Ostend, Belgium. © Deme.

England and Russia to help build dikes and reclaim land. They then expanded into other continents such as South America and especially Asia, where the Dutch were particularly interested in their overseas territory, the Dutch East Indies.

In spite of dredging's early internationalisation, Dutch dredging companies didn't really begin to make headway internationally until the end of the nineteenth century. According to specialist historians, it was only then that the policy established by King Willem I took effect, partly because at that time the Dutch economy was picking up. Bigger and heavier ships were being built, with a consequent demand for deeper harbours. In addition, the Dutch now knew how to construct steam engines that didn't explode. So in the nineteenth century small-scale manual labour in the dredging sector was slowly but surely pushed aside and replaced by wealthy firms that were able to deploy large dredgers. Internationalisation was rapid during that period: between 1890 and 1900, Dutch

Dubai Plam Island.
© De Nul.

dredging firms received commissions to work in India, China, Japan and South Africa. A great deal of money could be made on such international projects, making it possible to invest in better and better dredgers. As a result, Dutch dredging companies gained a headstart on their foreign competitors, from which they still profit today.

International growth in the dredging sector stalled with the outbreak of the First World War in 1914, revived somewhat during the period between the wars, but came to a standstill again in the recession of the thirties and the Second World War that followed. So for the dredging industry the first half of the twentieth century was a turbulent and often depressing period. Things didn't really pick up until after the Second World War. Until then, dredging was largely confined to large infrastructure projects such as the construction of canals, the deepening of rivers and the building of sluice complexes. But after 1945 methods were developed for transporting sand over long distances through pipelines. The result was the development of a new kind of dredging activity: the raising of land levels by means of sprayed sand.

Creating land at sea

During the same period, dredging companies were also being asked by the oil and gas industry to construct pipelines overland or under rivers. And when oil production in the North Sea began in the 1960s, dredging companies with their dredging experience and maritime expertise had all the work they could wish for. They were hired for such tasks as securing pipelines to the seabed and then safely running them to the shore.

In the seventies there was another successful episode. The environmental problem was gaining public attention, and dredging companies were asked to clean up the pollution. Every now and then, however, the companies

Alexander von Humboldt
rainbowing. © De Nul.

themselves got into hot water for allegedly harming the environment, for instance by disturbing underwater life during the dredging process or disposing of the polluted silt improperly.

Another activity for which dredging companies have been consulted more and more since the seventies is the creating of land in the sea. At first this mainly involved creating islands for oil production or building new industrial zones. Starting in the nineties, however, larger land creation projects were launched, mostly for the construction of airports and other infrastructural elements. The creation of the partly artificial Chek Lap Kok island, on which Hong Kong International Airport would be built, is probably among the best-known of these projects. Certainly it was described at the time as 'the dredging contract of the century', and Dutch and Belgian companies worked on it together. Then in the Middle East interest began growing in large-scale land reclamation and in the creation of artificial islands for the purpose of tourism. The most well-known of these are perhaps the megalomaniacal projects in Dubai, where islands known as The Palm and The World were created.

This new development went hand-in-hand with significant technological progress in dredger design. Until the 1960s, the bucket dredger was the workhorse of choice for dredging companies. This vessel had a long, continuous chain of metal buckets that – with a great deal of noise – scraped up sand, clay, solid ground and even large stones from the seabed and transported them to the surface. But as demand grew for ways of moving large amounts of sand easily and quickly, a new type of dredger – the trailing suction hopper dredger, or TSHD – became the focus of interest and investment. The first TSHDs had been built after the invention of the centrifugal pump in 1851, but they didn't really take off until a century later. The TSHD works by pumping up the sand from the seabed and depositing it in a hopper. A variant of the TSHD is the cutter-suction dredger, which appeared in the seventies. The cutter-suction dredger has a cutter that breaks up hard clay or rocky parts of the seabed into fine fragments, which can then be removed.

As already noted, the big dredging companies of the Low Countries undoubtedly owed their great international success to the fact that their home market offered them so much interesting work, enabling them to build up a vast amount of experience over the centuries. Another significant aspect of this development was that in the late nineteenth century the Dutch government encouraged dredging companies in a variety of ways to invest in dredging equipment. Until the beginning of the twentieth century, dredgers were often second-hand ships with cobbled-together equipment, but from 1900 on the dredgers were increasingly better designed, and today they're technological masterpieces full of computers.

United we stand, divided we fall

All this naturally requires enormous investment, which makes the dredging world highly capital intensive. As a result, internationalisation and economies of scale are absolutely essential to keeping the whole thing running: today a dredging company with aspirations has to have a large, versatile fleet at its disposal, and has to be able to deploy those dredgers at a number of places in the world simultaneously to justify the capital outlay. But the risk involved is immediately evident: if the world economy comes under a bit of pressure and the demand for dredging drops, then the dredgers – with their astronomical price tags – are used less frequently and dredging quickly becomes less profitable.

That's why all the dredging companies, including those in the Low Countries, are anxiously watching developments in China, as are all companies currently active in the international market. The skyrocketing Chinese economy is in need of more and more land, quays and waterways, and that, of course, means more work for dredgers. The Chinese dredging market has traditionally been closed to outsiders, but there is so much work to be done there that the Chinese companies cannot manage it on their own. Some Dutch and Belgian companies have already been active in China, but almost always in a supporting role. They're hoping that China really will open up its dredging market, and that they too will be able to benefit handsomely from the Chinese economic miracle.

The four top dredging companies in the Low Countries – Boskalis Westminster, Van Oord, Jan De Nul and Deme – are all world leaders in the field, and they are all in competition with each other. Sometimes things have got pretty rough. But today the jobs are often so big and challenging that a temporary partnership is set up, in which companies work together in various combinations. For the dredging companies are well aware that small countries can only be big in something if the companies concerned don't destroy each other but engage in healthy competition, which actually makes each of them stronger – and, when necessary, to shake hands on a collaborative deal that is to their mutual benefit. ∎

Translated by Nancy Forest-Flier

Disruptive Images, Historical Friction

On the Work of David Van Reybrouck

Will things work out well for David Van Reybrouck? The awards that have rained down on this young writer (°1971) in a scant ten years feel like a tropical storm. And that, please note, in the Low Countries! Has the literary climate lost its way? Or has our literature made a U-turn in the last decade, from focusing primarily on itself to looking more to the wider world? If success is a barometer, then Van Reybrouck is at the focus of that shift. But even if that would prove to be a vain illusion, for him what matters is not to give way under the pressure. By which we mean: not the pressure of being famous, but that of what initially and *à la limite* is an all-dominating commitment, perhaps even a 'mission': to protect the public arena as the heart of democracy, not least by reviving our collective memory, through literature. This is the portrait of an archaeologist who gave up his academic career to become a writer, and since then has given shape in word and deed to the hopes of many a Flemish intellectual. If only that can actually work out, in an age of anti-intellectualism.

Midas and his asses' ears

The signs are favourable, though. The literary non-fiction of *The Plague. The silent gnawing of writers, termites and South Africa* (De plaag. Het stille knagen van schrijvers, termieten en Zuid-Afrika, 2001) immediately earned Van Reybrouck three prizes, including that for the best first book. For the inspired dramas *The Soul of the Ant* (Die Siel van die Mier, 2004) and *Mission* (Missie, 2007) he received no fewer than four awards. His controversial *Plea for Populism* (Pleidooi voor populisme, 2008) added two essay prizes to his haul. And *Congo, a history* (Congo, een geschiedenis, 2010) – in both literary and historical terms an unparallelled tour de force - was yet to come. In 2010 it won him the Libris History Prize and the prestigious AKO Prize for Literature – the first person to win both for the same book – as well as a shoal of lesser prizes and nominations which may seem hardly worth mentioning, but which would have had many authors jumping for joy.

Rather less than that might make you feel that the sky had fallen on you, even if to the public it might seem more like the seventh heaven. Whatever Van

Near Kükes, Albania, 1999.
Photo by Stephan Vanfleteren.

Reybrouck touches turns to gold – or so it seems. But of course that comes at a price. Combined with the totally distracting media interest that is the inevitable result of all those prizes it doesn't just create pressure, as we said: how do you start afresh after you've written a history of Congo, how do you surpass yourself yet again when 'everyone' is already praising you to the skies? On top of which, staying with the image of King Midas, some people would rather set asses' ears on his head than a crown. By regularly making his views known in public debate the writer brands himself as an 'opinionist' who is spoiling the literary craft for more reserved, less mediagenic colleagues, since by comparison they are sidelined as autistic. And the content has also attracted criticism. The reproach that in *Congo* 'Western interventions are smoothed over' led to a vicious attack on his historical and literary methods. 'Nicely put together, but not an accurate reflection of the facts' was the pithy comment. As though for (literary-)aesthetic reasons Van Reybrouck was playing tricks with the truth.

This is a frequent criticism, and it goes to the heart of his position as an intellectual. In an attempt to make a good book Van Reybrouck has allegedly separated truth from beauty. His only novel, *Cast Shadow* (Slagschaduw, 2007), and his assorted poetry are supposed to illustrate this, little though they have in common with the commitment he demonstrates elsewhere, for instance both as chairman of PEN Flanders and in his more opinionist work. But this is not just the result of faulty reading by his critics, it is also based on a dogmatic refusal to appreciate the true power of his commitment. Rather than being disconnected from each other, Van Reybrouck's writings and actions are linked by the constant focus on preserving, and where necessary restoring, the public arena as a precondition for democratic debate. Of course, that does not mean that everything he writes is a success: his play *N* (2006) and his novel are certainly no world-beaters. But it does help if one considers his words and actions on their own 21st-century merits, from his experiment with collective poetry up to and including his dedication to 'consultative or deliberative democracy'.

Disruption, steadily increasing

Perhaps there is no better way of understanding the (actual) relationship between aesthetics and ethics in David Van Reybrouck's work than through the essay he wrote for *TLC 13* in 2005 about a war photo by Stephan Vanfleteren. The photo shows three Albanian Kosovar women who are fleeing the violence in their province after NATO started bombing Serbian targets in Spring 1999. Van Reybrouck describes how for five years he lived with that photo before his eyes, shaken as he was at the first sight of it, being confronted above all with the moral dilemma that NATO's use of force, with its 'humanitarian' motivation, posed for him at the time. 'What I do remember is disillusion, so immense, so furious that it had to be masking a deeper sorrow.' And also: 'Stephan Vanfleteren's photos left us in no doubt. In the context of the discourse about the horror of ethnic violence, they confirmed precisely the motivation for going to war [...]. We regarded those women with cool compassion. It was dreadful, but it would turn out all right.'

Five years later those feelings have disappeared. Only the piercing stare of the old woman in the foreground is left, along with the seemingly banal clouds in the background, to reflect Van Reybrouck's changed perception. Today he cannot describe his earlier reaction to the photo ('affected by its beauty, moved, touched') without 'a feeling of perversion'. Pictorial aesthetics and photographic analysis are replaced by international politics and retrospection: searching for the true facts as a historical antivenin for the appearance of beauty. The result of that retrospection is anger. 'But,' Van Reybrouck at once concedes, 'belated anger is also embarrassment.' And in his eyes it is precisely that 'Structure of Shame', as the essay's title puts it, that the photo exposes: a feeling that goes far deeper than merely being moved: 'That assumes some measure of resolve, steadfastness, even superiority', as he says it. 'Being moved is the melancholic counterpart of a smile, it is being briefly but superficially affected by an incident in the outside world. Being moved is also the empathetic side of pity.'

Averse both to being moved and to indignation ('which is yet another of those good-hearted sentiments'), with regard to his shame Van Reybrouck speaks at the end of the article of a steadily increasing sensation of disruption. And disruption seems to me to be the right word to describe the ethical relationship which results from the friction between an (aesthetic) image and its history in Van Reybrouck's work. That very clearly covers more than just an insight into the futility of what happened and the relativity of every point of view: roughly speaking, the realisation that what seemed good at first turns out on closer inspection to be bad, and vice versa. Van Reybrouck was reproached for something like this by his fellow-writer Joris Note with regard to *Congo*. The images he uses in reconstructing the story of Lumumba, in particular – on the motorbike with Mobutu *in tempore non suspecto*, or the hand which is said to have stuck up for a while out of his grave – precisely because of their inclination to aesthetic effect they betray an ideological fiction which comes down to this: that any hope of change is pointless. 'A refined form of blinkered conservatism', so Note states flatly. In the end all that remains is *belles lettres*, a deftly told historical tale full of kitsch images, designed to promote... yes... melancholy.

The disruption is more fundamental than this, however. It is not a matter of an established, *a priori* insight into the relativity of things – as postmodernism asserted regarding Truth. On the contrary, it implies the experience of being wrenched out of one's superior point of view, including the idea that truth does not exist, so that room for discussion and consideration is again emerging; in short, so that once more such a thing as truth is in the debate. Disruption relates, then, to the emergence of a radical openness because truth is at work in someone: not as an established fact, but as a summons that enforces an ethical relationship, even if that means that to your genuine shame you have to acknowledge that you had it wrong. The basic condition for that is a sense of involvement. And that being so, it is no mere chance that when he looks back at the NATO bombing of Serbia Van Reybrouck refers to the tragic accident with the ski-lift at Cavalese in Northern Italy, close to the air force base from which the bombers took off and the place where a year earlier he lost five childhood friends - though he does not mention that. After all, for Van Reybrouck history is precisely that confluence of circumstances where sooner or later the small story impacts on the large one, an impact that on occasion can suddenly become visible in an image. History is complexity which implicates 'us'. And wherever this is revealed, however improbably, we find ourselves already 'involved'.

Van Reybrouck's involvement, though, goes further than that. Since it is a precondition of disruption, it also finds its goal in the openness that disruption creates. In other words, his involvement is not only the starting point of Van Reybrouck's work, the ultimate goal of his 'commitment' also relates to the room for discussion which that involvement creates, i.e. insofar as it is so profound as to cause a sense of disruption and is fundamentally receptive to other people's thinking. Van Reybrouck, then, is anything but the 'neutral middleman' that some people take him to be: someone whose work is, because of his uncritical treatment of both sources and words, neither historiography nor literature. Rather, he is a man who by exploring the friction between history and literature opens up a 'space' for negotiation between them, so that the topic in question again becomes a subject for discussion, the gage in a political battle. So this has nothing to do with ideological dithering. Now that our Western democracy is in crisis, partly due to the inability of our 'representatives' to abandon their fixed positions and engage in discussion, it seems to me to be quite the reverse: an emphatic gesture of contemporary commitment.

The most obvious example of that contemporary commitment is Van Reybrouck's involvement in the organisation of the G1000 Burgertop in November 2011. This was a voluntary civil initiative by a group of independent thinkers and doers who wanted and worked for a supplementary model of consultative democracy, as a response to the political crisis in Belgium and the crisis in representative democracy as a whole. The aim was 'to feed fresh oxygen into the political impasse and to show that democracy can be restored' by means of 'a frank and wide-ranging discussion between free citizens.' For according to the people behind the G1000, the root of the crisis lies in a short-circuit in the lines of communication between citizens and their politicians, not because of any gulf between them but because of overheating caused by the effect of the new media society. 'Citizens,' Van Reybrouck says somewhere, 'are more vocal but at the same time more powerless than ever, while the politicians are more high-profile but at the same time more desperate than ever.' By organising a genuinely meaningful discussion between free citizens, even if that lack of alignment was also their Achilles heel, they hoped to change matters for the better.

The G1000 was tailor-made for Van Reybrouck, as was apparent from the enthusiasm with which he used his literary fame and his energy in its support. And it follows seamlessly on from earlier work that had already demonstrated his concern for the functioning of press and Parliament. The volume of essays *What Belgium Stands For. A vision of the future* (Waar België voor staat. Een toekomstvisie, 2007), which he compiled with some of his 'brothers-in-arms', is a prime example of this. But in fact there is a continuity between his opinion-forming and his more literary work, and has been from the very beginning. A very early column he did for radio about a fatal explosion in the Nigerian capital Lagos, which killed far more people than a firework disaster in the Dutch town of Enschede, begins, seething with outrage: 'The Flemish quality papers each gave it a couple of lines.' The business logic behind this is something the first-person narrator of *Cast Shadow* (2007) will later experience for himself. As a freelance he notices how his suggestions for reports more and more often lose out to sponsored travel and leisure notes that fit in with the seasonal feelings of the reader, or rather the consumer. 'Private vices do not lead to public virtues', the Lagos column says. Fortunately, there exists a form of resistance called 'writing'.

That in his literary and essayistic utterances Van Reybrouck is looking for an alternative to the talk of privatisation that through the media has increasingly hijacked political speech – so much is evident. The monthly 'threatening letters' which he has written with Jeroen Theunissen in the journal MO* since being elected chairman of PEN Flanders are proof of that, directed as they are at those of questionable commitment, such as the rocker Bono and Wikileaks guru Julian Assange. Sadly, with their direct, colloquial style the letters are not really convincing. Precisely because they thus seem to be addressing only the local reader, they have something of the playground bully about them. Better, then, *The European Constitution in Verse* (De Europese Grondwet in Verzen, 2009) which he and Peter Vermeersch put together with the Brussels Poets' Collective. Just as in his little experiment with Facebook poetry, compiled from reactions to a posted sentence from a newspaper about the formation of a government, here too the goal was through a harmonious multiplicity of voices to promote the speaking of a different language, as an alternative to the uniform

David van Reybrouck (1971).
G1000: citizens discussing
politics, Brussels,
11 November 2011.
Photo by Stephan Vanfleteren.

language used by the political and media hegemony. This did not always produce high-quality poetry, but perhaps that was not the intention; it is 'poetry from below', analogous with his historical writing in *Congo*.

The most recalcitrant example of Van Reybrouck's activism on behalf of voices 'from below', though, is his intellectually 'outrageous', politically incorrect *Plea for Populism* (Pleidooi voor populisme, 2008). He had already touched on the problem the previous year in *Cast Shadow* when the journalist-narrator, wondering about the interest in Flemish folklore-figures in his own reports, asks himself: 'Weren't we keeping ourselves busy providing the paper's well-educated, prosperous readership with a weekly helping of unadulterated authenticity from *La Flandre profonde*? Are we not guilty of the romantic glamorizing of all poor, uneducated or provincial people?' *Plea for Populism* opens with a scene which goes more deeply into the question: Van Reybrouck and his highly educated friends laughing with the common folk at the seaside. On the one hand the image is meant to be didactic, as elsewhere in Van Reybrouck, serving to illustrate the neglected problem of the gulf in education which in his pamphlet he identifies as the root cause of 'dark' contemporary populism. On the other hand, that same image also acts as an example of disruption, holding up to the intellectual, which Van Reybrouck himself first and foremost is, a mirror which forces him to fundamentally revise his original patronizing attitude.

Faced with a populism that threatens our very democracy, we are compelled to realise that the supposed cultural gap between right-thinking Left and narrow-minded Right actually follows the contours of a harder fault line: that between the highly- and the less well-educated. The success of the populist Right turns out to be mainly a case of powerless poorly-educated masses who are consistently cold-shouldered by the highly-educated establishment for which they are supposed to vote. That certainly does not justify their electoral behaviour, but it does add to the familiar explanation – that populism takes root most easily among those who are 'afraid, angry or discontented' – a further and more profound diagnosis. A cultural impoverishment is taking place among the less educated sections of the population who, regardless of their material prosperity, are poorly integrated into the community. The result: where educated people see advantages, in globalisation for example, the uneducated react mainly with fear or resentment at equality that never materialises. The point Van Reybrouck eventually makes here is not just that this fear must be acknowledged, or that this resentment has a legitimate place in our democracy, but above all that the well-educated too have to come up with an answer to that cultural impoverishment and its current political expression. In this sense his plea for an 'enlightened populism' is an attempt to explore the gap between the well- and the relatively un-educated and make it a topic of public debate.

Entangled in history

When you come down to it, that system of research into intellectual attitudes, with the varying intermediate forms that it yields, probably provides the basic pattern of David Van Reybrouck's writing. It is no coincidence that he began to write at the precise moment that he gave up his academic career as a researcher (in cultural history and archaeology). His monumental first work, *The Plague* (2001) makes the point in a literary form that is intermediate between research, travel story, autobiography and reportage. The research began when towards the end of his doctorate Van Reybrouck stumbled upon a bizarre accusation of plagiarism: in his *La vie des termites* (1926) the Belgian Nobel laureate Maurice Maeterlinck had supposedly plundered an article by the South African Eugène Marais. The non-fictitious quest that followed, though, should certainly not be called 'literary' simply because it is 'beautifully' described, or because it deals with this *petite-histoire littéraire*. It is 'literary' because it is an account of a metamorphosis: the genesis of a figure who changes the course of his own history and exchanges it for a future as a writer, not to prove himself, but because he has become entangled in a history the topicality of which he finds more and more disruptive.

'Being gripped by a new research topic is a particular form of falling in love', according to Van Reybrouck in the prologue to *The Plague*. In the first place he is intrigued by the figure of Eugéne Marais and the story behind him. And that's not surprising: 'Anyone who tries to reconcile the impossible worlds of poetry, journalism and science can't help making my heart beat faster. He is playing simultaneous chess with the three Aristotelian virtues – the beautiful, the good and the true.' Beyond the initial recognition on which that fascination clearly rests, though, it also brings about an intellectual *volte-face*.His research into Marais sets him on the road to an experience which will radically change him:

the confrontation with present-day South Africa. The reason for this will later be tellingly summarised by the narrator of *Cast Shadow*: 'In Africa, history is not something from the past.' It is the beginning of a symbiosis between the expertise of the archaeologist and the politics of the writer which would eventually, ten years later, result in *Congo, a history*.

In fact, in the years between *The Plague* and *Congo* the same basic pattern systematically recurs, often with Africa playing the lead role. Like a 21st-century Pygmalion Van Reybrouck falls in love with a historical image which he 'brings back to life' by recollecting it, not out of nostalgia but in an attempt to have that history take a central place in public discussion. The image of the missionary in *Mission* (2007), a figure who is a composite of facts from numerous interviews, reactivates the colonial memory in order to discuss the theme of commitment and what underlies it in an age of permissiveness and fundamentalism. In his 2007 short novel *Cast Shadow,* which deals with press privatization, the narrator-journalist tries to rescue from total oblivion the historical truth behind the statue of Gabrielle Petit (a First World War Resistance heroine) on Sint Jans Square in Brussels. And the stage play *N* (2006) recounts the life of the French musician Raymond Borremans, a figure (à la Marais) whose *Grand Dictionnaire encyclopédique de la Côte d'Ivoire* is a forerunner of *Congo*, which itself appeared – not coincidentally – at the commemoration of fifty years (1960-2010) of the former Belgian colony's independence.

It is significant that time and again Van Reybrouck will dig up an image or, better, prise it out of the petrified layers of meaning under which passing time has buried it. This is not just a reminder of the archaeologist and cultural historian that he is by training. It also indicates the primordial importance of beauty, or of a pictorial experience of beauty, as a precondition of his personal involvement. There is no question here of a conflict between what is beautiful and what is true. Van Reybrouck too is someone who 'plays simultaneous chess with the three Aristotelian virtues'. His perception of beauty often relates to someone's 'life's work' or the ethical stance that it reveals: the Resistance heroine, the (socially committed) missionary. At the same time that perception serves as a starting point for research and more in-depth social analysis, because it tends to prevent jumping to conclusions and enforces further consideration.

Hopeful polyphony

Van Reybrouck's committed appreciation of pictorial beauty appears at its best in the essays he has written on the work of some plastic artists who are friends of his. In *Belgicum* (2007), the first monograph on Vanfleteren's photographic work, he is concerned less with aestheticizing melancholy for the unique progressive project that unitary Belgium once was than with critical consideration of what is being lost, insofar as it is still visible today. In *Scheiseimmer* (2009) he wrote a text to accompany what can literally be called the life's work of the artist Koenraad Tinel: a series of 240 paintings in ink that describe, 65 years after the event, the fantastic happiness that Tinel experienced as the child of a 'blackshirt' during the Occupation, and the horror that that happiness turned into when he was grown up: stigmatised for what had happened, burdened with guilt and scarred for life.

The possibility of thinking differently which an image invariably opens up for Van Reybrouck has continued into his provisional magnum opus *Congo*. Around the middle of the book Van Reybrouck recalls the moment when he and his father, who had worked in Congo for a while, saw a really upsetting photo on the table in the dentist's waiting room; he was then aged ten or eleven. 'That photographer must have been standing very close to me,' his father told him. 'It happened right outside my door.' Later Van Reybrouck discovered that it is very far from being just a photo, as he had already recognised from 'the deadly fear in the man's eyes'; it was actually 'the most famous photo of the Katangese secession'. His father had been an eyewitness of the event. When he visited the spot in 2007, though, Van Reybrouck was not tempted to assume and breathe new life into the perspective of 'the colonial'. Rather, it provided a starting point for observing and portraying the changes in Congo over the past fifty years, with the maximum of personal involvement and with no timid focusing on the 'decline'.

'The windowless garage where for five years my father had parked his Ford Consul had now become an improvised prayer-house. I attended a service there. Some thirty of the faithful sat packed together on rickety wooden benches. In the half-darkness I saw glowing colours from the praying people. I thought of black-and-white photos. 1963 and 2007 merged into each other. My father had died the year before. The people sang splendidly.' (*Congo*, pp.335-336)

Looking more closely, one cannot imagine an image that would better express the hopeful harmony of voices that as a historian the writer envisaged in *Congo*. 'Every African who dies is an encyclopedia lost', as he put it in *N*. In *Congo* Van Reybrouck puts that principle into practice by bolstering his 'history from below' with numerous testimonies by Congolese, particularly the improbably distant but surprisingly accurate recollections of the – by his own reckoning – 128-year-old Etienne Nkasi (whose picture adorns the book's cover). That choice brought him not only praise but also criticism. Especially when one of his historically spectacular conversationalists proved unreliable (the man who claimed to be the figure seen stealing King Baudouin's sabre in the famous photo taken during Congo's Independence celebrations), some critics were extremely quick to cast doubt on the authenticity of the other Congolese contacts with whose aid Van Reybrouck added colour to his reconstruction. Under the mantle of scholarship they not only came out with exaggerated generalisations about the Congolese ('When they have no more stories to tell they will think some up, just for something to do. If they see that visitors are interested in their stories, and certainly if they think that those visitors have money in their pockets, they will try to keep them hooked'). The main object was to dispute Van Reybrouck's integrity and independence ('He was once allowed to share a stage with a Congolese musical star, who was consequently given an excessively large role in his history'), especially since he also got accused of having lapsed into 'pedantry', 'as is not uncommon with intellectuals who find themselves in a tight corner'.

I don't think Van Reybrouck should feel himself driven into a tight corner by such envy. In my opinion, the fact that for some journalists the concept 'intellectual' has now become a term of abuse is a greater cause for concern. In that context the slightly ironic question whether things will work out well for him depends mainly on the extent to which as a writer, in an anti-intellectual age, he can consistently give expression to the intellectual that he essentially is. That is no easy task, especially now that after a ten-year odyssey (from *The*

Plague to Congo) the African subject-matter of his writing is more or less exhausted. For a new play In the Maize (In de maïs), which unlike the monologue style of earlier work (*Mission, The Soul of the Ant*) will continue the use of multiple voices of *Congo*, Van Reybrouck has announced a return to the Westhoek, with its Dranouter Music Festival and its scars from the First World War. One should not, though, expect this to be a self-sufficient retreat into his own locality. More than most other Flemish writers, Van Reybrouck is able to weave a global perspective into his local histories, often through the way in which globalisation plays havoc with local lives. Take the words of Albert Camus that he quoted in his speech on receiving the Arle Prize: 'The artist forges himself in that eternal shuttling between himself and the others, somewhere halfway between the beauty he cannot do without and the community from which he cannot withdraw.' One might say that by his writing Van Reybrouck has expanded the Flemish community to which he belongs into an international community affected by beauty, intrigued by history, focused on a future which rediscovers democracy. ∎

Translated by Tanis Guest

An Ode to 'What If' Thinking

The World of Mark Manders

[DAVID STROBAND]

It's not easy to explain the characteristic style of artist Mark Manders, who was born in 1968 in the Dutch town of Volkel (Netherlands) and now lives and works in Arnhem (Netherlands) and Ronse (Flanders). Opinions on his work are available, it is true, but any single descriptive and interpretative text very soon falls short of the mark.

Mark Manders' world unfolds in all manner of configurations in which every object becomes a building block in an ever broader visual poem. Coffee mugs, dangling ballpoints, teabags, tables, chairs, big, indefinable objects, imitation animals, human figures, bits of rope and drawings: these are just a handful of the many objects that bolster Manders' visual language.

Every time I come in contact with his idiom I am seized with admiration and confusion. His language makes me introspective, and leads me to question whether I am sufficiently curious and uninhibited in the way I look at the world around me. Manders once wrote of this world: 'In the past, when I went for a walk I would go through streets where there might be a clothes peg lying on the ground, or when I went inside somewhere there would be a table with, for example, a phone and an empty vase on it, in short, I found myself in a world that I had not myself arranged. I decided to construct a building alongside or, rather, inside this world. A building in which a changing stillness reigns, in which and through which I am constantly confronted with my own choices, with Mark Manders' choices'. Early in 2009 I visited an exhibition of a great deal of Manders' work at the SMAK in Ghent. I was a little afraid that the combination of so many diverse elements from this artist's world might generate a lot of disquiet and fuss. But the opposite was the case. Walking through the rooms containing the various works you seemed to have entered a domain of tranquillity where every object seemed to be whispering to you, seducing you into inner contemplation. The title of this exhibition was *The Absence of Mark Manders*: at first glance a paradoxical statement. But in fact the more you are drawn into Manders' world, the greater his absence becomes. He has left too much behind in his spaces for there to be any room for himself. At first I wanted to scream for his presence and ask him to guide me through his enigmatic world. I wanted to understand this world, and I needed the artist to help me do so. Later I realised that it was precisely his absence that I liked. It ensured that I had all the space I needed to decipher his language in my own way and to make it my own. And then, what a fantastic space it becomes.

Manders is a linguistic artist. In addition to the fact that he speaks in images, he also knows how to give verbal relief to his visual work. His comments in interviews, for example, add an interesting dimension to his work. Whereas that time in Ghent his absence gave me so much pleasure, now I am recruiting him to help tell you about his world. And so I shall be quoting him regularly in this article. Not out of laziness, but for the sake of precision. To get as close as possible to the specific language of this artist.

Finally, I have to say from my heart that I am amazed that in the last fifteen years there has not been one major solo exhibition of Manders' work in the Netherlands, the country where his roots lie, when there have been such exhibitions in the rest of the world, including in Belgium. Not surprising, given that country's strong surrealist tradition. Though this last sentence won't please Manders much. He hates any interpretation of his work that smacks of Surrealism.

Inhabited for a Survey (First Floor Plan Self-Portrait as a building. Mixed media (sculpture). Writing materials, erasers, painting tools, scissors. Variable dimensions. 1986-1996-2002. © Zeno X Gallery, Antwerp.

Self-portrait as a Building

In 1986, at the age of 18, Manders created his first work. *Inhabited for a Survey (First Floor Plan from Self-Portrait as a Building)* shows a floor plan, laid out on the floor and made up of felt-tip pens, pencils, ballpoint pens, rubbers, scissors, sponges, tubes of paint and rulers. Together the various objects form seven oblongs of varying dimensions with circular spaces at the short ends. You can interpret this floor plan as two schematised human figures; heads and trunks are there, arms and legs are missing. This plan, which as you observe it so easily turns into two rough sketches of human figures that are incapable of movement, constitutes the beginning of an increasingly sprawling world which Manders henceforth has consistently called 'Self-portrait as a Building'. Manders has this to say about this seminal work: 'This floor plan from 1986 is made up of all the writing materials I had at the time, and served as the basis for a future written self-portrait. It related to a building in which seven people together formed a self-portrait. It was to be a book without beginning or end, on which I would have constantly to keep working. I thought it was interesting that it was a dry, formal floor plan with no observable movement whatsoever. I wanted to project a mental self-portrait onto it, in which everything would play out exclusively in language. To create a self-portrait seemed like the most fundamental thing to do. However, I realised when I was writing that I didn't like the fact that I could dictate to the public, by means of written sentences, exactly what they should be thinking. I didn't want the self-portrait to become genuinely personal, it was supposed to remain abstract.'

Here Mark Manders provides a little insight into the character of *Self-portrait as a Building*. A character that is difficult to define because it contains such an infinite number of mutations. Manders has been working on it for 25 years now, and when you think you have at last discovered the path within Selfportrait as a Building, you soon find you have been deceived. Seemingly familiar objects keep coming back in varying arrangements, and within the various modules in which they operate they take on a different character each time. The substance of Selfportrait as a Building is remarkably hybrid. It has a multiplicity of inhabitants, and every new edition of this progressive work throws up new encounters: for example, with a schematic rat or fox, a sugar lump, a pan, a shoe or a collection of teabags. All these inhabitants travel the world with Manders and as a result of the continual transformations they have surprising encounters with each other.

In the catalogue for *The Absence of Mark Manders*, by way of justification the artist writes an article entitled: 'A message to the owner of this catalogue'.

'I would like to offer my apologies – this is a book about an unfinished project. Although most of the works in here are finished, they have not been photographed in the right locations. The photos were taken in museums with the wrong floors or bad light, in grubby studios and even in supermarkets. But the main problem is that never at any point is there a connection – a connection such as you get when you look at architecture and its location or style, and especially a connection in time. You can't just walk from one space to the other. I have also shown my work in group exhibitions, in strange locations, in beautiful old buildings, in old factories or schools, and it was fantastic – they fitted the space and that made me very happy. Yet these pictures have in some way been misplaced.

I have also sold a lot of work. Out of necessity. How else could I have carried on working? Now my work is spread throughout the world, which should make me happy. A lot of it is now in major collections or has been acquired by good museums, but it is impossible to buy everything back.'

Here Manders touches on the impossibility of gaining an understanding of his work in its entirety. The essence of *Self-portrait as a Building* is that it is continually suspending itself. Again and again the viewer sees fragments which, despite their seemingly orderly modular appearance of systematic exposition, still do not deliver any evolving, ordered, essentially encyclopaedic insight into the 'story' of this ever-progressing project.

If you put the words *Self-portrait and Building together*, the idea emerges of a vital investigation into the artist's own 'self'. An investigation that must ulti-

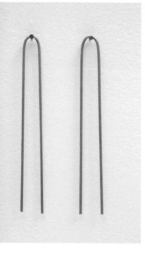

Short Sad Thoughts. Brass, nails. 2 x (22 x 3) cm. 1990. Photo by Brian Forrest.

mately be set out schematically in a ground-plan. In various statements Manders acknowledges that his artistic activity does not necessarily fit seamlessly into his personal life. Mark Manders the man is completely at the beck and call of his 'Self-portrait' and for him Manders the artist is a fictitious person.

The great, pure choir of 'Five'

Whenever you come face to face with Manders' world, you find yourself wondering just how, as an artist, he actually relates to his objects. They are the actors in his world; created by himself, or found by him and thus already in existence.

The work *Short Sad Thoughts* (1990) consists of two bent copper wires hanging on a nail. Even before you've read the title, these two wires look melancholy and somewhat mournful. It looks as if by bending the copper wire and then curling it around the nail, Manders has animated the material. Whenever he makes or appropriates objects and then positions them in his *Self-portrait*

Silent Factory. Wood, iron and other materials.
ca. 250 x 387 x 276 cm.
2000.© Zeno X Gallery,
Antwerp.

A New Entrance for the Night.
Sand, glass, bricks, shoe, fabric,
iron. 200 x 250 x 140 cm.
2002 © Zeno X Gallery, Antwerp.

as a Building, they are transformed into vessels of thoughts and feelings that are essentially foreign to them.

In 1997 *Stichting De Appel* in Amsterdam played host to a presentation by Mark Manders in which the number five played a key role. With the aid of newspaper pages made by himself and filled with a series of reproduced fives, dice with the five at the front, arrangements of five identical objects, pages containing five words and the numeral five appearing in all kinds of sculptural, reproduced or graphic forms, the visitor was conditioned to such an extent that upon leaving the exhibition the city also seemed full of all kinds of fives and multiples of five. As a viewer, moving from Manders' seemingly infinite universe you end up with a renewed, fresh acquaintance with your own fingers and toes. The work *Broom with Fives* (2001) is a perfect example of the artist's inexhaustible, possibly obsessive approach to certain phenomena that he finds fascinating. In the partially sawn-through handle of this old broom is a newspaper replete with, among other things, depictions of fives, a photo of a girl holding up five fingers and an emblem of a 'five-leaved clover'. Attached to the right-hand side of the broom-head are five red-painted nails and on the left-hand side five green ones. Stuck to the biggest red-painted nail are yet more assorted little images of the number five (some of them in red).

In its many guises, the five is a constantly recurring inhabitant of Manders' world. Of his fascination with this number, he writes: 'I found it fascinating that something outside your body has the power to make you think something specific. For example, if there are five sugar lumps outside your body, and you see them, then the number five forms in your head. It is incredibly beautiful that our brains should function like this.'

Feeling fine without arms

What's clear is that each of the inhabitants of the *Self-portrait as a Building* tells its own story. A story that is far from unambiguous. The materials from which the various objects (inhabitants) are made contribute to their wayward lives. Manders uses material not in a symbolic but in a direct, factual way. He is averse to attributing meaning to any material for fear that the use of material could acquire an illustrative and, in his eyes, masking effect. Every element of his *Self-portrait as a Building* is a quest for the bare essence of the world(s) around us.

In *Isolated Bathroom* (2003) three human figures made of clay and wrapped in plastic are lying on the ground. Beside them is a rectangular bath, full of bits of clay that look wet and unfired. In fact they have been fired and then painted the same colour as unfired clay. Manders has this to say about the work: 'The figures give the impression that they have just now been abandoned, unfinished, without arms. I love the idea that the figures look as though they enjoy being without arms. If you imagine not having arms you feel very vulnerable, but these figures seem to be enjoying their vulnerability.' *Isolated Bathroom* is one of those works which allow the viewer to make up their own story. The scenario offered to you here is so full of gaps and open spaces that any descriptive explanation is doomed to failure. The human figure in the *Self-portrait as a Building* plays the same role as a cup, a pencil, a table or a made-up cat or mouse. And in Manders' work a human figure can also have a range of cultural backgrounds. A recumbent figure (with arms) in *Coloured Room with Black and White Scene* (1998-1999) looks as much Greek, Etruscan, Egyptian, African as it does Asian. This enormous diversity of origin renders the figure abstract by definition.

Silent Factory (2000) shows three elongated tables, suspended just above the floor and supported by a number of trestles. Beside the tables there is another group of trestles bearing two massive clay factory pipes. On the tables there is a metre-high rod which ends in a shape, made of newspaper, that strongly resembles a loudspeaker. On a projection next to the factory pipes, and supported by two identical wooden chairs, lies the simulated body of a white cat. An armchair stands with its back to the tables. Behind the wooden chairs, precisely organised, all kinds of objects are lying on the floor: these include two aluminium pans, a bag of sugar, a yellow watering can, some teabags, three different-coloured wooden blocks, a beaker, a couple of cups, a bar of soap and a pair of men's shoes.

Manders describes *Silent Factory* as 'a cross between a sitting room, an organism and a factory'. The individual objects on the floor are all from the 1970s, the artist's teenage years, which he is trying unsuccessfully to recover. *Silent Factory* is a good example of Manders' very free interpretation of what sculpture can be. The tradition of sculpture is a narrative one. Historically, sculpture has always been a compact display which had to tell its story in as convincing a manner as possible. In the second half of the 19th century, sculpture acquired an 'autonomous' eloquence, epitomised by August Rodin, and eventually in the 20th century it allowed its traditional narrative function to blend into the expressive language of the visual means employed. In this way, in the 20th century sculpture became yet more abstract and in the course of the 1980s it also became more heterogeneous in appearance. Silent Factory is a wonderful example of how far notions of sculpture have evolved since the mid-1980s. All kinds of objects are brought together and at first glance seem to lack coherence. In this Manders again combines self-made props with found objects. Here sculpture is speaking a completely different language. A language that is tied up with all sorts of changing paradigms in thought and reflection in the Western cultural and intellectual world. From the 1960s and

Isolated Bathroom.
Iron bathtub with wooden tap,
water pump,
thin plastic sheeting, painted
aluminium and ceramic, wigs.
450 x 300 x 74 cm.
2003 © Zeno X Gallery,
Antwerp.

'70s onwards post-structuralist thinking gained ground. The concept of 'decon-struction', a term first coined by the French philosopher Jacques Derrida, be-gan to play a major role in many cultural manifestations. In post-structuralist thinking we come across the term 'intertextual'. A text no longer focuses on itself alone but refers to innumerable other texts around it. In any sentence it is no longer the individual words that are significant, but rather the white spaces between them, where different meanings can come together, become interwo-ven and so generate new ones. Meanings no longer have to be grasped in such a structured or linear way, but far more from the fragmentation or, in other words, from constantly changing, hybrid configurations of knowledge.

The night creeps into your shoe

The more hybrid, and possibly also more open, language of Manders' work invites the viewer to make a much greater physical and mental effort when wandering around in it and to view it as a kind of labyrinth. It is a world in which Manders can happily turn all his fantasies loose. Take for example A Place Where My Thoughts Are Frozen Together (2001). A bone from a human thigh (of painted epoxy) lies on the floor and is connected by a lump of sugar to a cup of coffee. This expressive world is enigmatic. In a brief accompanying text the art-ist attributes a kind of function to the bone and the cup of coffee: 'I like the way both of them, powerless and armless, hold tight to the sugar lump.' It's as if Manders routinely attributes human functions to his objects. He seems to want to inject them with a soul, in the tradition of animism. At first glance this enig-matic element, which is also greatly stimulated by the continuous combination of multiple objects juxtaposed in alienating positions, evokes associations with the world of Surrealism in the 1920s. As I said at the beginning: Manders rejects this reference out of hand. He regards his works as 'conceptual constructions in which poetic representations can sometimes be hung'. He compares Sur-realism rather to the 'unsupervised knitting of a tie.'

The titles of fragments from *Self-portrait as a Building* frequently seem to form poetic literary references, or they can be concrete indications of objects that play an important role in them. The titles are invariably in English, in order to have a more 'universal' significance. However, every now and again there is one that cannot be expressed in written or spoken language. A work from 1994, in which a series of animal-like shapes, a rudimentary human figure and a number of objects are arranged neatly next to each other on the ground, is entitled -(-/-/-/-/-/-/-/-/-/-/-). Here open spaces are created in the written language, too, in which every idea or interpretation can find a home. And, moreover, there are also titles where words alternate with open spaces (dashes).

In some of the titles used by Manders we see the suffix (Reduced to 88%). Some illustrative elements that feature in *Self-portrait as a Building* are reduced to 88% of their real size (i.e. reduced by 12%). According to Manders, a reduction to 88% tends to be felt rather than seen and thus has an alienating effect. The fact that he reduces to 88% and not to, for example, 85% is a matter of subtlety. Too great a reduction would soon become over-theatrical. He wants to give the viewer a different relationship to the objects. The reduction to 88% highlights the tension between the familiar and the unfamiliar. Manders determines his own realities. He does, after all, call himself the maker of three-dimensional photos.

Typical, and very early, inhabitants of his *Self-portrait as a Building* are a rubber with a pencil sticking out of it, two batteries connected together, a plug on an extension cable plugged into its own socket and an unused match lying in a cup of water. On inspection, these small gestures reveal themselves to be wonderful, self-generating worlds which, in their essence, form the heart of Manders' domain. With no objective, no function, but extremely rich in meaning. They illustrate the subtle power of images. In the 1980s Manders switched from written poetry to illustrative poetry, as he tells us in his article about his first contribution to Selfportrait as a Building. For him, illustrative objects have more dimensions than written language. Objects are obviously more tactile, while at the same time appearing more elusive.

A New Entrance for the Night (2002) is a space constructed out of large white stones. The front has a glass wall and there is sand on the floor. In the middle of the space, with its opening facing the front, is a large elongated iron box, supported at each corner by slender spreading legs. A funnel-shape emerges from the underside of the box, its point ending in the toe of a man's shoe that is lying on the ground. In a discussion of this work Manders writes the following: 'At night, if you stand in a field and take off your shoe, the night, yearning for more space, instantly creeps into your shoe, filling the area that your foot once occupied. You may be aware that the night always enters the shoe via the same entrance as when you take it off. This has been happening in the same way ever since the existence of the very first shoe. However, if you seal the shoe completely and make a new hole at the front, and you attach a funnel-like construction to the hole, then you have created a new entrance for the night, just like that.'

That, then, is how simple and strange the world can be. ∎

www.markmanders.org

Translated by Gregory Ball

Dylan's Kin in the Lowlands

'Sad-Eyed Lady of the Lowlands' is on Bob Dylan's album Blonde on Blonde (1966). The lyrics incarnated in Dutch as 'Droeve Dame Van Het Laagland' on a CD of Dylan songs translated and sung by Ernst Jansz (1948), himself of undying Doe Maar fame. He shares a birthday with Dylan and has been fascinated by his work from the very beginning.

> Met je kwikzilveren mond
> Als het missieuur begon
> En je ogen als rook
> En je gebed als een chanson [EJ]

> With your mercury mouth
> In the missionary times
> Your eyes like smoke
> And your prayers like rhymes [BD]

The original tune, which ripples along in 6/8 time, is played on an acoustic guitar with hints of tambourine and organ and lasts for 12 minutes. Nine minutes into the song Bob's harmonica enters the sound spectrum. Any listener hearing this for the first time would be startled. The first notes are piercingly high and then fall back into a lower register of inhaling and exhaling. Youtube, which limits uploads to 10 minutes, includes the beginning of this solo - which is then suddenly cut off. The curious Youtuber is then obliged to go in search of what comes next: this is what it is like to experience Dylan in 2011. Elsewhere in cyberspace Ernst Jansz explains how he *as a singer* absorbs and experiences the secrets of Dylan's lyrics.

Bob Dylan's 70th birthday was worldwide news. In our part of the world too there was a tidal wave of tributes, nostalgia and stage performances which differed from North to South. In Berchem, for example, there was *Still Searching At 70*, announced as a 'spiritual' evening featuring Dylanologist Patrick Roefflaer, author of *Bob Dylan in de Studio* (2011), along with rising stars New Rising Sun. Radio 1 broadcast a moving tribute session live from the cultural centre "De Vooruit" in Ghent; among the contributors were Gabriel Rios, Bart Peeters, Thé

Bob Dylan
Bringing It All Back Home

Lau and Roland van Campenhout. With due apologies Bart Peeters ventured on 'Make You Feel My Love' (1997), the Dylan number that became a worldwide hit for the British singer Adele. According to Peeters, to Dylan fanatics 'Omdat Ik Van Je Hou' is blasphemy: only the master's original versions – His Master's Voice – are allowed into the canon. Paradox, the centre for contemporary music in Tilburg, hosted the *Bob Dylan 70 Jaar Tribute Festival*, featuring the doyen of Dutch pop journalism and Dylan expert Bert van de Kamp, author of *ABC Dylan* (2011). The evening was one of admiration blended with nostalgia and good stories.

The *Dylan-70-event* was held in Heerenveen, with look-alike Jacques Mees and protest singer Harry Loco. Friesland has its own Dylan tradition. In 2004/5 Ernst Langhout and Johan Keus brought out two CDs of *Dylan Yn It Frysk* (Dylan In Frisian). In 2010 another cd/dvd of Dylan songs in Frisian was released with contributions by eleven Frisian acts, including Langhout and Keus. The translations for this *Earbetoan oan Bob Dylan* (Tribute to Bob Dylan) were the work of writer Baukje Wytsma and poet Harmen Wind, the high point being 'Roffel Op 'E Himeldoar' (Knockin' On Heaven's Door). So few people turned up for *Dylan-70*, that the organisers had to abandon further Dylan celebrations.

Bob Dylan, *Bringing It All Back Home*, Columbia Broadcasting Systems, 1965. Album Cover

Things went better in Groningen. A heavily attended "intellectual" happening took place at the film and debate centre Forumimages. Dylan biographer Sjoerd de Jong, who works for the Dutch newspaper *NRC Handelsblad*, gave a talk. Erik Bindervoet was there too. Together with Robbert-Jan Henkes he had translated Dylan into Standard Dutch, published in 2006 as *Snelweg 61 herbezocht, Bob Dylan Liedteksten 1962-1973* (Highway 61 Revisited, Bob Dylan Lyrics 1962-1973) and *Voor altijd jong, Bob Dylan Liedteksten 1974-2001* (Forever Young, Bob Dylan Lyrics 1974-2001) published in 2007. 'Every syllable matches and the lyrics retain their original meaning' according to the translators. The lyrics were transposed from one vernacular into the other with technical perfectionism. 'Singers they obviously are not', remarked Ernst Jansz when asked to comment. Lucky Fonz III, the up-and-coming bard who rediscovered Guido "The Flemish Bob Dylan" Belcanto for a Dutch audience, added his musical magic to the evening. Famous artists were conspicuously absent at the other tribute programmes in the Netherlands.

Lurking in the background

Guido Belcanto.
Photo by Daria Rogulska.

Almost half a century ago Bob Dylan was the fuse that ignited the powder keg of pop music. Thanks to Dylan, Flemish and Dutch folk movements rediscovered their regional traditions. Protest singers came and went. The marriage of culture and counter-culture ended up on the rocks. Those true artists who mined the same vein as Dylan survived, among them the Antwerp singer and all-round artist Wannes van de Velde (1937-2008). His experiences as a child during the World War II instilled in him the fire to rework Dylan's 'Masters of War' and make it his own. Together with blues singer Roland van Campenhout he performed 'Oorlogsgeleerden' (on *Nomaden van de Muziek*, Nomads of Music, 1999), Wannes singing in his mother tongue, Roland in Dylan's.

Oorlogsgeleerden, genies van 't kanon
Ge bouwt de torpedo's en waterstofbom
Ge schuilt achter muren en achter papier
Maar ik ken al uw kuren, uw stalen manier [WvdV]

Come you masters of war, you that build all the guns
You that build the death planes, you that build the big bombs
You that hide behind walls, you that hide behind desks
I just want you to know I can see through your masks [BD]

Van de Velde described the folk singers' profession succinctly in his songlines: 'here is a singer, his voice and his story, on his journey along the roads of language,'('Hier Is Em Terug' 2006). He knew Flemish folk music like the back of his hand, songs from the Antwerp pubs and docks and, by a marvellous coincidence, Andalusian gypsy music. Out of this musical background he created an intensely personal oeuvre, and not from any intention of becoming rich and famous. Such a profile, which fits organically from the cradle to the road leading on from it, is characteristic of the Dylan tradition which is a lot older than Bob. In 'Ne Zanger Is Een Groep' (1976) Van de Velde put it this way:

Vertelt me nooit niet meer: ne zanger is iets enig
Want da's een leugen, dat is reklaam
Ne zanger is een groep, dat zing ik en dat meen ik
Een lieke zingt ge nooit of nooit allenig
Zonder al d' ander zou dat niet gaan

Never tell me again that a singer is on his own
For that's a lie, it's only an advertising sign
A singer is a group, that's what I sing and I mean it
Never ever do you sing a song alone
Without all the others, it wouldn't work out fine.

Most of the music made by Belgian and Dutch singer-songwriters in the American folk and blues tradition would not have existed without Dylan. Even though artists are reluctant to talk about their influences and mentors out of fear of revealing themselves as imitators, many of them have Dylan lurking in the background. He hides in the sources of their inspiration, the length of the numbers, the (in)comprehensibility of the words, the freedom of expressing one's opinion, the criticism of the madness of the moment, the credibility of the person who sings. The idiosyncratic Dylan has always remained the same self-willed man, with an intuitive aversion to rigidity and predictability. Pop artists following in Dylan's wake sought out their own paths in the light of Dylan's revelations. With such a powerful model it is extremely difficult to step out of his shadow.

Musically speaking, a Dylan epigone is easily recognised. But what matters is what lies behind the notes, that coagulation of emotion and musical language, the power of expression, the will and the skill to bend the record industry and the media to one's own ends. That is why Dylan's love songs are just as important as his folk ballads and cryptic intellectual games. His symbolic B-side of love gave pop music the fragile emotions that suited the international zeitgeist better than the heavy timber of blues and country music. Dylan encouraged his followers to create self-liberating work. Not for Dylan's kin were shiny wrapping paper and ribbons to hide the great emptiness within; the Dylan-inspired type of singer-songwriter preferred the directness of a song, a voice, a sound that could lay bare heart and soul.

Serious music, and yet pop. Dylan's humour is not tainted by feeble parody or crude jokes. Even 'Rainy Day Women' (1966), renowned for the refrain line 'Everybody must get stoned' is not trying to be hilarious. 'In De Hemel Is Geen Dylan' (There Is No Dylan In Heaven, 2003) by De Nieuwe Snaar, a tune they composed to lyrics by Frank van der Linden, matches in closely with this creative balancing on the edge:

Ik weet: de Boomsesteenweg is geen Highway 61
Maar als ik weer de baan op moet, dan voel ik toch de drang
Om luidkeels mee te zingen met de kerel die verlangt
Naar een mooie Sad Eyed Lady – die bestaan ook in dit land

I know the Boomsesteenweg is no Highway 61
But when I have to take that road, then I still feel the urge
To sing along and loudly with the guy who yearns
For a lovely Sad-Eyed Lady – we have them here as well.

'Leven Na De Dood' (Life After Death, 1997), by the eminent Dutch comedian Freek de Jonge after Dylan's 'Death Is Not The End' (1988), is a doubtful case. It did get to the top of the hit parade, though. The lyrics are full of references to current events, and that doesn't work as well now as it did then. That doesn't really matter. But. the singer wants and expects to be funny. And he is undoubtedly funny. He is a master of comedy. However, this (timeless) passage is quite un-Dylanesquely lame:

De Nieuwe Snaar.
Photo by Marc Ras.

Heb je je doodsangst overwonnen
Wordt het alle dagen feest
Dus vandaag maar vast begonnen
Voor je 't weet, ben je er geweest

Now overcome your mortal fears
Throw daily parties in your honour
Start catching up on your arrears
Before you know it, you're a goner

Compare this to a fragment from the original:

When you're standing at the crossroads
That you cannot comprehend
Just remember that death is not the end.

Dylan's 'Death Is Not the End' is full of cities on fire, burning flesh, sinister visions. It might be called typical Dutch humour, poking fun at an image so apocalyptic.

Ever since his Dylan-inspired hit 'Ben Ik Te Min' (Am I Not Good Enough, 1967) the Eindhoven-based protest singer Herman van Loenhout (1946) aka

Armand has been known as 'The Dutch Bob Dylan'. He is perhaps a little too serious to be honoured as a prophet in his own country. With his guitar, hoarse voice and harmonica, his sound was clearly Dylan-inspired. The song has nonetheless become a Dutch classic, a folksong that deservedly finds its way into the repertoires of folksingers that consider Armand to be a prime mover in the Netherlands.

> Ben ik te min?
> Ben ik te min omdat je ouders meer poen hebben dan de mijne?
> Ben ik te min?
> Ben ik te min omdat je pa in een grotere kar rijdt dan de mijne?

> Am I not good enough?
> Am I not good enough because your folks have more dough than mine?
> Am I not good enough?
> Am I not good enough because you dad has a bigger crock than mine?

The contrast with the 'The Flemish Bob Dylan' couldn't be greater. It is unclear how Guido Belcanto came by that title. His favourite stylistic devices are bizarre exaggerations and crazy contrasts, all of which make you die laughing. 'Een Vrouw Zien Huilen' (Seeing A Woman Cry, 1990) is his very own 'Sad-Eyed Lady Of The Lowlands', utterly individual, instantly recognisable. This is where Belcanto's Dylan quality lies. He never became solely dependent on his model. His other ear is tuned to the French tradition of *chanson*, in this case to Jacques Brel's 'Voir Un Ami Pleurer' (To See A Friend Cry). Belcanto boasts to the point of absurdity about his dangerous hobbies and heroic deeds and then admits:

> Maar als ik een vrouw zie huilen
> is 't alsof mijn wereld vergaat
> alsof er niets meer bestaat ... dan verdriet
> als ik een vrouw zie huilen
> dan krimp ik in elkaar, is het eind der wereld daar
> een vrouw zien huilen kan ik niet

> But when I see a woman cry
> It's as if my world founders
> It's as if there's nothing but sadness, I swear
> When I see a woman cry
> I cringe, the end is nigh
> Seeing a woman cry is something I can't bear

Many have followed in Dylan's footsteps, in a multiplicity of ways. Because the Low Countries' artists need to find some creative way of compensating for the fact that we have no Bryan Ferry (Roxy Music) who uses covers on his CD *Dylanesque* (2007) and gets away with it, since what he made wasn't really a Dylan cover CD but an authentic Bryan Ferry CD. Apart from the routine buskers on café terraces making a few cents with 'Blowin' In The Wind' and 'The Times They Are A-Changing', what concerns us here is finding out 'where Dylan is'. We won't find the answer to this in any *Dylan Encyclopaedia, Rough Guide To Dylan* or *Dylan Companion*.

On the 24th of September 2011 the North Nederlands Dylan Festival was held in the former communist heartland of Oost-Groningen in the tiny village of Mussel, on the shores of the Lindenmeer, along the Ondersteveenweg. The event was in the atmosphere of the mid-nineteen-sixties. It was organised at Café De Mussel on the Musselweg where Siep Schoenmaker, who translates Dylan into Groningen dialect, and Alex Vissering, who performs Siep's work, set about assembling an excellent international line-up. In the Groningen countryside, of all places. Why? Bob Dylan went cycling there - not exactly there, but close enough. Bill Mensema fanned the persistent flames of rumour with his novel *Fietsen met Bob Dylan* (Cycling With Bob Dylan, 2008).

But first, the facts. Dylan played at the Martinihal in Groningen on 18 March 1995. This resulted in the release of a bootleg double CD. About that time Bob Dylan was supposedly seen drinking a cup of coffee at the bar of Café 't Zielhoes [Sailhouse] in Noordpolderzijl in the district of Usquert in the very north of Groningen Province, on the shores of the Waddenzee, level with the deserted island of Rottumerplaat. So not in the middle of, but on the very edge of nowhere. It is rumoured that Dylan cycled all the way to 't Zielhoes on the recommendation of an acquaintance who thought that Dylan would feel at home in the landscape. The bike is the weakest link: an American on a bike, Bob's delicate thinness, the long distance in wind and weather. The key witness, the café owner, has provided verbal confirmation. He wasn't overawed by such an important visitor. His only concern was making sure the bill was paid.

Ronald Ohlsen (1968), a published poet who lives in Groningen City, has embraced the legend. Ohlsen belongs to the 1980s generation who rediscovered Dylan from a purely musical perspective, without the idealistic baggage of the 1960s. Following his lecture on Dylan at Groningen Uiniversity he was approached by the lads from Mussel who persuaded him to do a warm-up evening for their festival. Ohlsen is no average Dylanologist. He performed with the "De Rollende Donder Revue" (The Rolling Thunder Review, a title taken from Dylan) in Vera, Groningen's Valhalla of pop. For that occasion he wrote 'Robert Zimmerman-blues', a lyric not a poem, just as Dylan is wont to write lyrics not poems. Here's a fragment:

> *Ik heb de Robert Zimmerman-blues*
> *Ik schrijf een evangelie*
> *'k Ben Judas niet maar ken hem wel*
> *Hij vroeg om peterselie*

> *I've got the Robert Zimmerman blues*
> *I'm writing a gospel, really*
> *I'm no Judas but I do know him*
> *He asked for parsley*

Now back to Ernst Jansz, who kicked off this chapter with his much acclaimed Dylan translations. In 2010 Jansz released the CD *Dromen van Johanna* (after Dylan's 'Visions of Johanna', 1966), consisting of his own translations/adaptations of twelve Dylan songs, mostly about love. A book, a DVD and a theatre programme completed the account of his research into the language of words and sounds. In keeping with the spirit of the master, Jansz added autobiographical elements.

Ernst Jansz and
The New Fools, Flemish Dylan
Coverband, at Dylan Festival
in Mussel.
Photo by Daniël Schoenmaker.

'Voor Ramona' ('To Ramona', 1964) leads the listener soundwise to Jansz's co-
lonial-Indonesian family background, in which he developed an active interest in
later life. In 1960 'Ramona' (an American song that dates from 1927) was a huge
hit for The Blue Diamonds, two brothers born in colonial-Indonesia who were
the first superstars of Dutch pop music. Jansz is the latest who has a comparable family background, although he himself was born in Amsterdam. He embedded his beautifully frayed voice in the sound of ukuleles and Hawaiian guitars.
Via Dylan Jansz has managed to create his most nostalgic colonial-Indonesian-
sounding music to date.

Jansz's Dylan interpretations were the artistic climax of the Mussel event.
The guitarist Luigi Catuogno, well known for his *Dylan Suite* (1999), came over
from Italy. The Englishman Danny Bryant played 'Girl From The North Country'
(1963), naturally. Of course The New Fools from Achel in Belgium were there
too, six men dressed in black from head to toe: arguably the best Dylan tribute
band in Europe. And following the disappointment at Heerenveen, who should
be there but look-alike Jacques Mees, runner-up in the Dylan Cover Competition
on dylanradio.com, along with singing buccaneer Harry Loco from the village of
Vries in Groningen province.

Where wonders do belong

To conclude on a personal note from this jubilee year: 'The Ballad Of Frankie Lee
And Judas Priest' on *John Wesley Harding* (1967) is a marathon of brilliant words
and phrases in a story that was way over my head back then. Following his wake-
up-call harmonica solo Dylan returns to the song: 'Well, the moral of the story,
the moral of this song, is simply that one should never be, where one does not
belong.' Oops, and for forty-five years I've been singing 'where wonders not belong', in tune with the world-view that Dylan had handed on to his eager admir-
ers. Bobdylan.com helped this girl from the North Country back into business. ∎

NOTE

The legend of Dylan in Noordpolderzijl was checked by journalist Herman Sandman, who asked Bob Dylan himself by e-mail, and received a reply. As guest radio columnist, he reported his
findings at VPRO's 3voor12 Groningen on 7 September 2009.

Translated by Alison Mouthaan

Jeroen Brouwers' Paper Monument

"My death will be the only thing I haven't described" was the concluding sentence of Jeroen Brouwers' 'Self-Portrait with Eraser', which he wrote at the age of thirty-seven. Six years later, in the introduction to *The Final Door* (De laatste deur), his book of essays on suicide in Dutch-language literature, he noted: 'I'm a writer who chronicles his own life, adding to his biography with each new book, explaining his existence, clarifying his views, in the hope that this will lead to new insights.'

Ten years on, in 1993, after the jury of the Constantijn Huygens Prize, which he had just been awarded, had mentioned his 'pre-eminently autobiographical work', he was keen to qualify that 'misunderstanding': 'In the strictly autobiographical sense, I've written scarcely anything about my own life.' It is not the content of his oeuvre that is autobiographical, he explains, but its form: 'The autobiographical element in it is the way of thinking, expressing in words, ordering, fighting various kinds of chaos, shaping. Without any concessions and with the greatest possible integrity towards oneself.'

Brouwers does not write in order to tell his life story. The term 'autobiographical oeuvre' refers not to a factual reconstruction of his life and times, but to the making of literature. That is even more apparent in the later novels, the work of the 'mature Brouwers', written after *The Deluge* (De zondvloed), his great novel of 1988.

In April 1990 Jeroen Brouwers turned fifty. In the preceding fifteen years – since he had moved to the countryside of Gelderland near the German border to devote himself full-time to writing – he had published extensively. With *The Deluge* he had completed the magnum opus he had heralded; in his own words, this novel marked the conclusion of the work he had resolved to write. Following *The Submerged* (Het verzonkene, 1979) and *Sunken Red* (Bezonken rood, 1981) the novel was also the concluding volume of the 'Indies trilogy'. Later, from 1992 onwards, the Indies novels appeared as a single volume, the realisation of a long-standing plan. From the time when he wrote the first fragments he had envisaged a book of at least a thousand pages describing his childhood in the Indies and its influence on his character and later life.

He himself had described *The Deluge* as the definitive book, the one which, as the novel says in so many words, 'summarises all my books and in which

Jeroen Brouwers (1940).
Photo by David Samyn.

everything refers to everything I have written'.

His oeuvre appeared to be finished, concluded. Interviewers and students of literature wondered aloud what possible sequel there could be. One reviewer suggested that he would have to publish his next book under a pseudonym and another even alluded to a possible suicide. After all, Brouwers' other, much heralded large-scale writing plan had also been realised: 1983 had seen the appearance of *The Final Door*, an investigation of suicide in Dutch literature, on which he had worked for years.

'What next?' was a question often put to the author, who was not yet fifty.

'I'm not dead yet, you know,' he reacted with annoyance during an interview. 'There's a whole stream of stuff on the way, but people are so impatient. You've got to let people get on with their jobs.'

A new period will probably begin, he declares. He would like to write a novel as spontaneously as he writes letters: 'It's not easy to change style, but still it's an ambition of mine. I'm not tired of life yet.' The reference to his published letters, collected in *Chronicle of a Character* (Kroniek van een karakter, 1987), is not coincidental. Those books of letters were universally acclaimed on publication. The occasional lightness of tone and the humour in particular attracted praise.

Fugal literature

In the autumn of 1990 a new novel, *Summer Flight* (Zomervlucht), appeared. In terms of content the book was again characteristically sombre – 'The theme is disappointment at growing old' – but stylistically it marked the beginning of a new period. For example, it was once again a novel with an imaginary third-person character as protagonist, and hence contradicted Brouwers' repeated assertion that he would never again write a novel with fictional characters. Brouwers was aiming for a simpler style, more laconic, more distanced: 'In The Deluge and in other books of mine it's as if I grab the reader by the hair, push him nose-down on top of the text and keep him there. It's too much me, too heavy.'

The main character of *Summer Flight* is Reiner Saltsman, a concert pianist, composer and author of a world-famous book on the art of the fugue. Although a celebrated musicologist, he is suffering from a creative block, disillusioned by life and love, a prey to melancholy obsessions. Saltsman – and the same will apply equally to all the protagonists of Brouwers' later novels – may have a completely different biography from the writer, but as regards character and attitude to life there are striking similarities. Saltsman, for example, has spent twelve summers in an isolated "backwater" to which he had retreated "at a low ebb" to write his masterpiece on the fugue. Now he feels like an old man, "who at the age of thirty-five had cut a cord, as if consciously, of his own free will, ceasing to live – but without dying. I've lived for too long in the isolation of that house, I've been for too long too completely cut off from the world, I've become alienated from reality." (The same view of life can be found almost verbatim in diary entries that Brouwers published later, for example in It's Nothing (Het is niets, 1993), and *Everything's Something* (Alles is iets, 1998), in which he writes about the inertness of Exel, where he lives: "What happens here is that life ripples on. Apart from that nothing happens.").

Summer Flight is also a novel about the art of the fugue. Saltsman explains that the art form consists of variations on a single theme: "This creates a chain of repetitions that are not repetitions, but variations, in a host of forms, on that same theme." There is also such a thing as fugal literature, he continues, in which the same technique is used, "sometimes not only within a single work, but even extended into a whole oeuvre". As Brouwers admits in interviews, it is clear that one "as it were through the mouth of Saltsman talking about music, hears Brouwers talking about his view of writing".

Of Brouwers'novels *Summer Flight* is somewhat underrated and neglected, though it was reprinted as recently as 2010 in the omnibus edition *The Seasons* (De jaargetijden). The writer himself continues to hold it in high esteem, repeatedly stating: "My favourite is *Summer Flight*. A beautifully serene book of great integrity about a man who has run out of steam."

A vicious and witty polemist

It was to be ten years before Brouwers published another novel: his bestseller *Secret Rooms* (Geheime kamers) did not appear until 2000. Diary entries show that he began work on the novel as early as 1990.

In the intervening period, though, a flood of publications appeared. Brouwers remained productive with essays, portraits, polemics, memoirs and diaries. He regularly published, in 'Rough Notebooks' and later in 'Feuilletons', his essays and stories from the preceding period.

In 1995 he was awarded the Gouden Uil non-fiction prize for *Lions of Flanders* (Vlaamse leeuwen, 1994), his collected essays on Flemish literature and language politics. The award made him very proud: "I feel first and foremost an essayist and some of my essays have given me greater satisfaction than some of my fiction."

Brouwers has always fought against the 'hegemony of the novel'. The annoying thing is that in the literary world the novel is regarded as the ultimate achievement, as he often said wistfully: 'I have written essays that I put on the same level as my novels. But funnily enough they're never mentioned.'

However, he did cause quite a stir with his polemics. That was true in the 1970s – when he made his name as a polemicist – and it remained true. In 1996 he broke with De Arbeiderspers, his regular publisher since 1976, and published a blazing polemic about it. Targeting the new managing director, Ronald Dietz, who had been appointed some years previously, Brouwers set the conflict within a wider context of the decline and commercialisation of literary publishing.

Brouwers as polemicist is severe, grumpy and vicious, but also often irresistibly witty. Literary polemics as a firework display – it is as if his brilliant style and humour are best expressed when he gets angry. That was again apparent in *The Beacons of Sisyphus* (Sisyphus' bakens, 2009), a denunciation he wrote after being awarded the Dutch Literature Prize of the Dutch Language Union. He refused the prize and the accompanying 'piddling' sum of money. In the polemic he places the matter in a wider context, that of the wretched economic situation of the literary writer, the producer of 'merchandise', who in a small language-area can scarcely live on his production.

Although by now he has been canonised, praised, showered with prizes and recognised as one of the greatest living Dutch writers, Brouwer's repeated complaint remains the difficulty of making ends meet. In published diary entries he is strikingly frank about his financial condition: 'It's not my literary production that is a failure – I've written a few good books – but my literary career, the social side of being a writer: disappointing sales of my books, hence constant poverty, hence the humiliating necessity of going cap in hand to agencies that offer subsidies, humbly, on my knees.'

In interviews one senses a certain bitterness: 'I'm getting on for sixty and I still can't earn a living from my books.' Sometimes there is a note of weariness: 'If there were a pension scheme for writers, I'd pack it in right away. I've had enough. To a great extent you write to stay alive.'

A light-hearted dreamer

In 2000 the novel whose appearance had been proclaimed for years, *Secret Rooms* (Geheime kamers), was finally published. A bulky tome about love and its unattainability, and also about deceit and adultery: the main character, the sometimes pathetic, sometimes amusing Jelmer van Hoff, is secretly in love with the mysterious and capricious Daphne.

Of course the affair ends badly, and the storyline is vintage Brouwers, but stylistically the touch is lighter than usual. In interviews Brouwers declared: 'I wanted to write a drama for a change and this is one, but in such a light tone that you sometimes burst out laughing because it's just *too* awful.'

In the same promotional interviews he stated: 'The composition is no longer as tough as rye bread,' and said hopefully: 'I wouldn't mind a bestseller that sells a hundred thousand copies.' Apart from *Sunken Red,* which has meanwhile assumed the status of an evergreen, Brouwers' books are not immediate commercial successes: 'But there's hope, hope springs eternal: that next novel, perhaps that will finally be a bit of a blockbuster.'

The reviews were surprisingly favourable. The novel was called a masterpiece, stylistically sublime, but what attracted particular attention were the light tone and wealth of action, a new development in Brouwers: 'Usually not much happens in my novels. *Secret Rooms* on the other hand is a novel with a plot, full of intrigue and mystery.'

He confided to another interviewer: 'It turned out wonderfully well; upbeat, structurally supple. Jelmer van Hoff isn't as much of a wimp as my earlier characters. He endures his fate fairly laconically.'

The novel sold unusually well and won numerous prizes. What is the explanation of that commercial success? Besides the more accessible style and lighter tone the subject may also be a factor. "It's a good book, but not my best," stated Brouwers in interviews: 'At the end of my career I'm now suddenly receiving high praise and prizes and money. Secret Rooms is my first book with the features of a bestseller.'

In 2002 sales passed the hundred-thousand mark, and the book continues to sell: it is 'the surprise of my old age – That I should have lived to see it!' He already had literary fame and prestige, but never such a degree of commercial success. He can no longer maintain that his career has been a failure: 'But why didn't this happen to me twenty years ago?'

He had written eight novels to date, said Brouwers in 2003, and there was one more to come. But first he published some memoirs: *Dustpan and Brush* (Stoffer & blik, 2004), about his time as a publisher in Brussels (1964-1970): 'I need to get a few more memoirs down on paper before the light is turned out for good.' In other publications, such as Paper Lives (Papieren levens, 2001) or *Dusk is Falling* (De schemer daalt, 2005), he again excels as a portraitist, a genre he has made his own, often in the form of an empathetically and sympathetically written in memoriam. After the death of his contemporary Freddy de Vree, for example, Brouwers wrote: 'Around me, closer and closer and in ever greater numbers, the friends, acquaintances and contacts are falling to the ground like felled trees. (....) writers and others I have known, sometimes I can still hear their voices. Dusk is falling.'

High-flown bellyaching

Brouwers was already working on a new novel, when suddenly another book clamoured for precedence. The trigger was the premature death of his eldest son. In a few months – surprisingly quickly by his standards – he wrote *Dateless Days* (Datumloze dagen), which appeared in the autumn of 2007.

The protagonist of this extended monologue is an older man who lives in a deserted wood. The novel begins as follows: 'The hundreds of things you've done wrong in your life. Not necessarily on purpose, it may have happened out of stupidity, clumsiness, thoughtlessness, by mistake, out of spinelessness, with no intention at all.'

Remorse, regret, melancholy, shame. The novel is about a troubled father-son relationship, written with such apparently nonchalant stylistic mastery that it makes a deep and even painful impression. The first-person narrator reviews his futile relationship with his son, whom he scarcely knew. Biographically the main character does not resemble the writer at all, but he does psychologically.

Stylistically the book continues the pattern of *Secret Rooms*, and unsurprisingly the critics again highlighted the surprisingly light-hearted, deft style. A characteristic of the older Brouwers, together with the apparently nonchalant but ingenious construction, with references to Classical myths and previously explored Brouwers themes. And also with clear links to earlier novels, beginning with his début *Joris Ockeloen and the Waiting Game* (Joris Ockeloen en het wachten, 1967), which was also about the father-son relationship. In *Dateless Days too* everything relates to everything else. On the second page there is already mention of 'a sun taking its leave', 'which touches everything one last time and casts a shadow.'

In 2011 the novel he had previously been planning, *Bitter Flowers* (Bittere bloemen) appeared. Brouwers sketches a burlesque portrait of Hammer, an elderly man very unlike himself in physique or biography, who takes a reluctant cruise around the Mediterranean. With cheerful cynicism and light-hearted whinging he looks back at his life as an ex-judge, ex-politician and ex-writer, until he is once again ambushed by romantic infatuation.

However cheerful it may be, and however refreshing the language, in content it is far from being a light-hearted book. As usual it is about thwarted illusions, but here couched in a sublime, well-crafted style which gives the constant moaning and bellyaching about human decay an exalted feel.

In *Bitter Flowers* Brouwers writes about the decay of old age, the treachery of the body, but thanks to the exceptional narrative perspective and exceptionally musical style manages to suggest that literature can transcend death.

In 'The Exel Testaments' ('De Exelse testamenten'), a key text from the 1970s, the young Brouwers wrote: 'I should like to make out of all my writings, even my failures, of which I'm ashamed, a paper monument, which can, somewhere, still be visited in a landscape where it is forever autumn and everything is draped in cobwebs, long after I am dead and buried. It must be possible to say of that monument: this is the life of Jeroen Brouwers. People will comment that it was full of crinkles and tears when it was put up, but that sentence about that compote and the flies and the rotting fruit isn't bad at all.' ■

Translated by Paul Vincent

An Extract from *Dateless Days*
By Jeroen Brouwers

The hundreds of things you've done wrong in your life. Not necessarily on purpose, it may have happened through stupidity, clumsiness, thoughtlessness, by mistake, out of spinelessness, or with no intention at all.

Sometimes a poisonous memory suddenly sneaks into your brain, like an intruder throwing a piano wire over your head and pulling it taut against your throat.

When such memories appear I tend to emit a very loud, sustained scream, in order to blow the scenes out of my brain, just as in spring one uses a gas gun to drive the rodents from one's newly-sown fields or the winged rabble from the orchard full of young fruit.

Actually I don't even mean the painful memories themselves, but the shame they give rise to. The older you get, the more shame you feel.

I live alone, like a hermit, in a white house in a mixed wood made up partly of deciduous, partly of coniferous trees.

In autumn, like now, the birches, beeches and oaks shed their clothes and colours and pose like pencil-sellers among the evergreen of pines and firs, which only turns a little rusty. All this needs, what is now actually happening, the thin glow of a departing sun that touches everything one last time and provides it with a shadow.

In the city, if one steps out of one's house one is at the same moment surrounded by one's fellow city-dwellers and their noise. If I walk out of my house, I'm in woods – I rarely meet anyone on my walks and I hear exactly the same as in my study: silence, silence. Just listen. Silence that nevertheless consists of all kinds of noise, but which is integral to the wood and forms part of the silence. Blank out the birds, that twittering and flapping of wings, that dull hammering of a woodpecker on wood up ahead. Pretend for a moment that you can't hear the hysterical, helicopter-like buzzing of woodland insects hovering around your ears on their way to the decomposing body of a rabbit or a hedgehog. Then it will not be silence you hear, but the uninterrupted mute yawn of death: What you hear in a hospital when the patient dies and all the machines to which he was attached by tubes and wires fall abruptly silent at the same moment, stop croaking and snorkelling as an accompaniment to the curving patterns on the monitor screens surrounding him and recording his breathing, heartbeat, blood pressure. The silence that then manifests itself with a dull sigh splashes against the white walls with their notice boards covered in postcards wishing the deceased 'get well soon' when he was not yet dead. Silence that creates echoes of silence. Deathly silence. At the moment of death everything on the monitors goes haywire, the vital-signs curves on all the screens shrink simultaneously into long, straight, horizontal lines, which would continue into infinity if one of the hospital staff did not pull a bunch of plugs out of the power-point at the head of the bed. As a result the light disappears – phut ! – from all the machines, the screens go black and suddenly look like gaping jaws exhaling silence.

Such a silence never prevails in this wood, - something is always rustling, something is creaking, a pine cone or an acorn falls onto the sandy path with a drumming sound. Something is always whispering, growling, singing, something is screaming, moving. The leaves fall with a faint sound like rustling paper. A wind gets up, like the wind in my head, where it's never still either, but never still in a different way than in the wood.

Shame at everything that has gone wrong. The older you get, the greater the expanse of your past, the more it looks as if your life has consisted of a succession of bankruptcies. It's not only bankruptcies, not everything has gone wrong, but still.

There are howlers you have committed deliberately and with premeditation, though you could have known in advance you were doing something stupid. The kind of blunder you'll be confronted with for the rest of your life, comparable with a recurring, incurable disease. When thoughts of it come charging into your brain like armed bandits with nylon stockings over their heads, there's no way of shouting it down to drown out the shame.

As you nevertheless start wailing at the top of your voice, you slap yourself in the face with the flat of your hand as you do when a mosquito lands on your cheek and drills its sting into you, you pound your head with the knuckles of both fists until stars and lightning flashes shoot across the backs of your eyes. At night I take to my car and tear along deserted motorways, past black industrial estates, with in the black spaces behind them a vague glow above black cities. Does it make me any calmer? The slurping sound of the tyres on the asphalt makes me sleepy. I enter this wood to walk the restlessness out of my body, but I know everything here too well to be distracted, I go on walking till I'm knackered and sit or lie on the ground if it's not too damp. Try to calm down by counting all the trees in my field of vision – there are more of them in autumn and winter than in summer when there is thick foliage everywhere. One, two, three, four... Or all the toadstools. I turned off onto a side-path, where the red of the toadstool caps had caught my eye like a fever. Scores, several hundred, the path was covered with them as if with a carpet floating a few centimetres above the ground. With every step I made a hole in it, as I kept

kicking over and crushing toadstools. At the end I looked round and saw my footsteps in all that red, all those shades of red – crimson, vermilion, coral, Bordeaux, amaranth, pomegranate... and in it every half-metre the havoc I had caused with my footsteps like a museum vandal who with a knife or a corrosive liquid attacked the Rembrandt red of the Jewish Bride. My eyes became hot and to my troubled gaze the red woodland path liquefied, changed into a stream in which all the tints merged into a single red.

By squeezing your eyes shut a few times you can force back your tears. What good are tears to me?

A lapping rivulet of blood; the damaged bits my shoes had left in the red filled up with it and again became invisible. When I stopped squeezing my eyes shut, so hard that my ears buzzed, and looked again, there was no longer any question of lapping and flowing: all the red had congealed as if into candle grease, all the red consisted of clotted blood.

What good are tears to me? Why do I count tree trunks? ∎

From *Dateless Days* (Datumloze dagen. Amsterdam. Atlas, 2007)

Translated by Paul Vincent

Art and Immigration

Painters should go to the Dutch School to learn the art of Painting,
as they would to a Grammar School to learn Languages.
Sir Joshua Reynolds, 1781

When the Merchant Adventurers set up their headquarters in Bruges in 1344, it marked the beginning of a long period of commercial, intellectual and artistic interactions between the Low Countries and Britain. Bruges had become a staple for merchandise sent from every part of the world, the centre of European commerce and finance. In order to defend their interests, foreign merchants united in 'Hansen', including the powerful 'Flemish Hanse of London'. Contacts were intense and beneficial. From 1463 to 1469, for example, William Caxton (ca. 1421-1491) was living in the city as governor of the Merchant Adventurers. He learned the art of printing in Flanders and on his return installed the first printing press near Westminster Abbey in 1476. The early history of English printing is identified with Caxton and hence with Flanders.

By 1460 Antwerp was one of the largest cities in Europe with a total population of some 100,000 citizens. Of those inhabitants, just twenty were recorded as being painters. A century later, as many as three hundred master painters in the city were registered as members of the Guild of St Luke. Antwerp had grown into the most important trading centre in Western Europe. Its success was based on its port and wool market. In parallel with its economic prosperity, there developed an astonishing cultural and intellectual activity in the city. By the sixteenth century both art and printing had reached unparalleled levels of perfection. Four famous names associated with the history of early English Bibles - William Tyndale, George Joye, Miles Coverdale and John Rogers - are all connected to the city of Antwerp and its printers. The publication of Thomas More's *Utopia* was very much a Flemish affair, with support from Erasmus of Rotterdam.

Cosmopolitan humanism created a mental atmosphere that proved highly conducive to the pursuit of art and science. Antwerp became the most vibrant cultural city in Europe. If the arts were initially stimulated by commissions from the Church and gentry, increasingly works of art were created 'on spec', in oth-

Nicolas Hilliard (after Levina Teerlinc),
Portrait Miniature of Lady Hudson, 1575
Executed on ivory.
Rijksmuseum Amsterdam.

er words, they were produced for sale on the open market. A sophisticated commercial infrastructure gave birth to the so-called *panden* which were specialized sales halls for the arts. That structure made it possible to sell works of art directly to the customer, either at home or abroad. The Guild of St Luke took a pragmatic approach to this commercialization of art.

English market

From the outset, England was a major market to which the Flemish exported their paintings, tapestries, illuminated manuscripts and other works of art. From the eleventh until well into the sixteenth century, for instance, the Meuse Valley was known in England for its *dinanderie* (after Dinant), which included both ecclesiastical and domestic articles in copper, bronze, or pewter. During the sixteenth century paintings and other works of art produced by Flemish masters were shipped from Antwerp to London in quantity. This happened even in a time when Catholic subjects (the bulk of the Flemish output) were *not* appreciated, specifically in the aftermath of Henry VIII's defiance of the Pope. If art could not be imported legally, there were ways and means of getting the product across anyway. The absence of a reliable London port record of art shipments is an indication that many cargos were smuggled into the country.

In 1585 Antwerp was conquered by the troops of Alessandro Farnese, Duke of Parma, and placed under the rule of Philip II. The subsequent Protestant exodus included the industrial and intellectual elite. Of Antwerp's 100,000 inhabitants in 1570, by 1590 no more than about 40,000 remained. Spanish repression reduced the once cosmopolitan city to a Catholic provincial town: stagnant, intolerant, inward-looking. The wealth of Antwerp, the know-how, the expertise, and in many cases even the equipment (printing presses for ex-

Sir Peter Lely, *George Monk, First Duke of Albemarle*, 1700. Oil on canvas, 118 x 96 cm. Rijksmuseum Amsterdam.

ample) - all of that moved to the Northern Netherlands, to Amsterdam, Haarlem, Leiden, and elsewhere.

The mass migration of Flemish talent to the North caused a shift in the balance of power within the Low Countries. Building on the experience of Flemish refugees, the Dutch created a commercial, intellectual and artistic empire that for a considerable time remained unrivalled in Europe. Antwerp had set the example. Amsterdam would follow in its place. Boosted by the dramatic decline in the population of Antwerp after 1585, that of Amsterdam grew in a spectacular manner. It increased from 30,000 to over 100,000 in the course of a single generation. Many of the refugee Flemish industrialists, printers, painters and other professionals settled there. Over 30% of those obtaining citizenship in Amsterdam in the years 1575-1606 were from the South (of whom 50% came from Antwerp). Of the three hundred and twenty biggest account-holders in the Amsterdam Exchange Bank in 1610, over half had immigrated from the South. Of the thirty-eight goldsmiths who became citizens of Amsterdam in 1585, twenty-eight were of Flemish descent. The large-scale immigration of artists into the Netherlands transported a ready-made infrastructure of art education and trade from the South to the North. The development towards an open art market which had started in Antwerp continued in an even more spectacular manner in Holland. That development was accelerated dramatically because of specific socio-economic conditions in the Northern-Netherlands.

Competition

In a time that the notion of nationhood was not a matter of concern, Holland was effectively made up of cities. This city-culture created a society that did not nurture the leading role of an aristocracy as was the case in Britain. Socio-economic life was dominated by well-to-do 'burghers' who lived and worked in the cities. Equality of opportunity in Dutch economic life gave society a competitive edge that at the time had no rival elsewhere in Europe. The Dutch 'Golden Age' was an era of extraordinary vitality, be it in economic, scientific or artistic terms. With the growing prosperity of the Republic, the demand for works of art increased.

The influence of the Church was no longer a dominant force in that society. Calvinism may have left its mark on the age, but it did not enslave people to religion. Christian duty and sharp business practice did not exclude one another. It was an age of prayers and profit. Protestantism also brought about the decay of sacred art. What once had been mere background to a picture - such as landscape, flowers, groups of figures, the face of the donor - now came to the fore. Once the divine element was eliminated, the decoration of houses rather than churches became the main purpose of the pictorial arts. With the discarding of transcendental aims, portraiture and genre painting were to dominate the art market.

In order to satisfy growing demand the artist's studio was rationalized in a remarkable manner. The studio became a kind of early industrialized factory floor, with a proper division of labour amongst specialist employees who worked on a production line of art. The example of Rubens's studio is well documented. Similar ways of working were introduced by Sir Anthony van Dyck (1599-1641) and by Sir Peter Lely (1618-1680) in their London studios. All this, of course, long before the notion of the 'division of labour' was discussed by Scottish economists of the eighteenth century. Dutch painters tended to cultivate the taste of their clients, who did not want large canvasses at home, but rather something modest that was a 'joy to their eyes', a pleasant image decorating the wall. They also wanted value for money. Originally, the price of a work of art was calculated according to the cost of materials added to the working hours spent by the artist.

Intense competition made art cheap. It meant that painters needed to supplement their income in order to keep their families afloat. Jan Steen ran a public house, Jan van de Capelle was a textile merchant, Willem Kalf an antique dealer, Jacob van Ruysdael was a surgeon, and most cruelly of all: Meindert Hobbema stopped painting altogether after marriage. He found a more lucrative job in an Amsterdam tax office. The seventeenth century produced too many artists and not enough clients. The market was too small for such an overwhelming presence of talent. It has been estimated that during the seventeenth century some five to ten million paintings were produced in the Netherlands. Less than 1% survives of this unbelievable output.

To young artists, the presence of so many painters proved inhibiting. For many there was but one solution: *move* - move elsewhere, anywhere. And move they did during the Golden Age. They moved in their hundreds. They headed for Italy, Sweden, Germany, even for Russia - they moved above all to Britain. After all, there was a well-established tradition of English collectors buying art in the Low Countries. From an English point of view it made perfect sense to attract artists to cross the Channel. If Flemish and Dutch art was in high demand, why import just single paintings? Why not employ the painters themselves? It is interesting to note that English ambassadors in the Netherlands - William Temple for instance - regularly functioned as 'scouts' who encouraged artists to move to England with the promise of employment or commissions.

Anthony van Dyck, *Portrait of Sir Thomas Wharton*, 1639. Oil on canvas, 217 x 128,5 cm. The State Hermitage Museum, St. Petersburg.

Artists were invited to England as early as the beginning of the sixteenth century. A reference in 1502 to a 'Mynour, the Inglis payntour' records payments to this figure for bringing portraits of Henry VII, his queen and their children to James IV of Scotland. The painter concerned is Vewicke Maynard (the name appears in different forms). He is one of the few painters from that period whose presence is securely documented in England, although none of his works have survived. He enjoyed a long career at the courts of Henry VII and Henry VIII where in 1506 he is referred to as 'Maynard Waywike Duchman'. In that same year Maynard undertook to produce designs for the tomb effigy of Henry VII's mother Lady Margaret Beaufort (Westminster Abbey) which were carried out by the Italian sculptor Pietro Torrigiani in 1511/2. In around 1540, Henry VIII tempted the Flemish stonemason and sculptor Willem Keur (known as William Cure) to join those working on Nonsuch Palace. William stayed in England. His son Cornelius Cure was appointed master of the Royal works by Elizabeth I. He is best known for his tomb of Mary, Queen of Scots in Westminster Abbey. It was not just men who were invited over. Bruges-born painter Levina Teerlinc (1510-1576), eldest daughter of Simon Benninck (1483-1561), one of the finest Flemish illuminators of his time, was employed by Henry VIII as court painter; she produced a number of fine miniatures of the young Mary I. Her annual salary was higher than that of her illustrious predecessor Hans Holbein.

What was at the time considered of fundamental importance in English socio-religious life seemed to matter little when it came to immigrant artists from the Low Countries. There were Catholic artists at work in Protestant England, there were Protestant artists commissioned to work in Catholic Britain. Anthony van Dyck was one of a number of Flemish Catholics who agreed to work in a Protestant country. Ironically, his most important English patrons were Puritans or Puritan sympathizers, amongst them Philip, the fourth Lord Wharton, who acquired more than twenty paintings by the artist. Aesthetics eclipsed all religious strife.

Some artists arrived under extraordinary circumstances. In 1630 the Amsterdam-born still life painter Jan van der Beeck (1589-1644) - Latinized name: Johannes Torrentius - was released from prison and allowed to travel to England at the request of Charles I. The artist had been tried in 1627 for being involved with the outlawed Rosicrucians. In spite of expectations, Torrentius produced little in England and eventually returned to Holland. Even more remarkable was that in June 1672 Charles II issued a declaration in which he invited Dutch artists to move to England. The Restoration brought about an expanding demand for paintings which could not be satisfied by English artists. Marine painter Willem van de Velde (1611-1693) responded to the call and left Holland to enter the service of the king. He was joined by his son Willem van de Velde the Younger, who was to become a master marine painter. The quality of his work inspired the emergence of an English school of seascape painters. The fact that the English and Dutch were at war with each other at the time (the Third Anglo-Dutch War) did not bother father and son. Soon after arriving they began work on the first of many major commissions for the king, designing a set of tapestries that depict the bloody sea-battle of Sole Bay.

In spite of sporadic tensions, it appears that the immigration policies pursued by the English authorities contributed to the relatively quick integration of immigrants from the Low Countries. Many of them set up workshops and were legally forced to employ local workers. The establishment of the tapestry industry in England is an example of this practice. The same process however did *not* function in the arts. As early as 1444, London goldsmiths complained that alien competitors in Southwark only employed fellow foreigners. In 1570, Jacob Jansen and Jasper Andries, immigrant potters from Antwerp, petitioned Queen Elizabeth for a patent in tin-glazed earthenware. The request was rejected, but they set up a successful business in the liberties of Aldgate. In the following years the workshop attracted potters from Flanders who worked in an establishment known as 'the Rose' close to the Dutch Church of Austin Friars. The potters who ran the studio kept their expertise confined within the circles of men trained in the Low Countries and did not employ English apprentices. Why did immigrant artists ignore the conditions laid down by the authorities? How was it possible that Flemish and Dutch painters in exile - some of whom were of a second or even third generation and born in England - were able to maintain an almost unbroken tradition in art?

Throughout the sixteenth and seventeenth century, artists from the Low Countries may have become socially integrated in their country of refuge; professionally, however, they refused to mix with British artists. The work of these immigrant artists was much sought after, which allowed them to run a 'closed shop'. There were tensions with local artists. In 1627 for example the Painter-Stainers' Company unsuccessfully attempted to prosecute Cornelius de Neve, Daniel Mytens, George Geldorp and Abraham van der Doort for failing to obey the company's ordinances. Artists from the Low Countries did not employ English apprentices. They used fellow countrymen instead. They married each other's daughters or widows. They educated their children in their own workshops and saw to it that they finished their apprenticeship in the Low Countries. They literally kept their art within the family, be it in London, Norwich or Edinburgh.

In 1585, Arnold Bronckhorst was succeeded as court painter to James VI of Scotland by Adriaan van Son. The latter had been a citizen of Edinburgh for some time and was an active member of the Netherlandish community in the city. His son, Adam de Colone (1595-1628), was baptized in Edinburgh on 19 October 1595. Among the witnesses at this baptism was Sir Adrian van Damman, who had been a professor at Leiden University and was now ambassador of the confederate provinces at the Scottish court. The family circle was distinctly Dutch and included merchants, clockmakers, and jewellers. Adam de Colone used his mother's maiden name and was trained in the Netherlands and Flanders. Some thirty portraits by him have survived and both in technique and style his work remained distinctly Dutch.

In his London studio Peter Lely employed predominantly artists from the Low Countries. The Brussels-born portrait painter Jeremiah van der Eyden was one of them. He was employed by Lely to paint the draperies in some of his portraits. Another painter employed by Lely was the Antwerp-born portrait painter John Baptist Gaspars, who had settled in London in 1642. His long-term association with Sir Peter earned him the nickname of 'Lely's Baptist'. He was specifically employed to paint postures and drapery. Joseph Buckshorn

Hendrik Carré (after Gottfried Kneller),
Portrait of the *First Duke of Albemarle*, 1697.
Oil on canvas, 85 x 68 cm.
Rijksmuseum Amsterdam.

[Boxhorn] was a native Dutchman who had settled in London about 1670 and worked there for Lely, whose pupil he had been. He enjoyed the reputation of being one of the last good copiers in England. Amsterdam-born portrait painter Willem Wissing moved to London in 1676. He entered Sir Peter Lely's studio as an assistant. After Lely's death he pursued a successful independent career. Dordrecht-born portrait painter Willem Sonmans [William Sunman] was one of the Dutch artists who had followed Sir Peter Lely to England during the reign of Charles II. After Lely's death he obtained permission to paint the king's portrait, but failed to gain appreciation and subsequently moved to Oxford. Thereafter he spent term-time in Oxford and the rest of the year in London. A number of his portraits are to be found in the Bodleian Library in Oxford.

Trade secrets

Artists from the Low Countries were acutely aware of the distinct contribution they made to the arts in Britain. Protecting their trade secrets was crucial to them maintaining their enduring success. Painters guarded every aspect of their art, be it the mixing of their paints, the make and handling of their brushes, or the intricate matters of style and technique. They grouped together in order to exclude all 'intruders'. Their work remained Flemish or Dutch both in content and in style: even if they had been born in Britain or if they were commissioned to paint typical English subjects. The Thames as depicted in

Willem van de Velde,
*The Taking of the English
Flagship the Royal Prince,*
1666. Oil on canvas,
59 x 81 cm.
Rijksmuseum Amsterdam.

their paintings could very well have been a Dutch river. And those artists who specialized in portraying the grand estates and country houses in Britain - another genre in which they excelled - did so with a Dutch eye for detail. This form of 'protectionism' was not new to these immigrants. In fact, it had been part of their education. Artists in the Low Countries received their training through a long-established master-apprentice relationship that was regulated by local guilds of St Luke. These guilds governed the commercial activities of their members, protected them from outside competition, and assured the high level of technical competence for which Flemish and Dutch painting was renowned.

It was not until the eighteenth century that the Dutch and Flemish artistic presence in Britain began to wane. And once it did, the collapse was spectacular. Lübeck-born Godfrey Kneller (formerly Gottfried Kniller, 1646-1723) had moved to London in order to study the artistic achievements of Anthony van Dyck. Although young Kneller had studied mathematics at the University of Leiden, he was drawn to the arts instead. He learned his trade with Rembrandt and Ferdinand Bol in Amsterdam. Once settled in London, he continued the Van Dyck-Lely tradition with spectacular success. By the mid-1680s he was the most sought-after portrait painter in England. During the reign of William and Mary his position as a court painter was unrivalled. In 1701 he painted the famous equestrian portrait of the king at Hampton Court Palace in which William III is conceived as a modern Hercules delivering England from the despotic rule of James II.

Kneller's reputation suffered during the late eighteenth century. Changes in aesthetic appreciation mixed with elements of xenophobia made critics flatly deny Kneller's contribution to English art. In fact, the attack on the baroque culture was aimed at William III personally. In his influential *Anecdotes of Painting in England* (1762/80 - reprinted in 1826) Horace Walpole rejected any artistic value in the art commissioned by the court, expressing the extraordinary point of view that the Netherlands never had developed any sense of aesthetic refinement at all:

The prince ... contributed nothing to the advancement of the arts. He was born in a country [Holland] where taste never flourished.

Walpole's view was exceptional and controversial. Later historians expressed a more balanced view, and the admiration for art from the Low Countries has to this day never diminished. ■

The Dream in the Reality in the Dream

The Universe of Saskia Olde Wolbers

[DAVID STROBAND]

Quite a phenomenom, the oeuvre of Saskia Olde Wolbers (Breda, 1971). The visual artist, who lives and works in London, is extremely well-known in the art world; her work attracts glowing reviews and she has received several prizes for it. To date, though, this has been based on just nine works with a total viewing-time of fifty-seven minutes. Her first work, *The Mary Hay Room*, appeared in 1997; the most recent, *Pareidolia,* in 2011.

Exploring Saskia Olde Wolbers' work is something of an adventure. Her creations could be called visual artworks. Though they are also stories, and also films. But not just films, not just stories. Is that why we call it visual art? In any case, Olde Wolbers received her Bachelor of Visual Arts from the Rietveld Academy in Amsterdam and her Master of Fine Arts from the Chelsea College of Art & Design in London, and she exhibits at visual arts institutions.

The first time I saw her work remains etched in my memory. The work was called *Day-Glo* and was on show at the end of 2000 in the exhibition *Mindset* of the Stedelijk Museum Bureau in Amsterdam. Even then this artist occupied a position of her own in the visual arts world. An artist who let image and spoken text communicate so freely with each other, who gave such free reign to the imaginative association between literary and visual forms: such an artist was a novelty ten years ago.

Her images, filled with metallic or plastic objects that emit soft colours and have been dipped in liquid, suggest a story, while the spoken texts or voice-overs evoke strong visual associations. Her early images and texts in particular border on science fiction. You never arrive at a concrete interpretation of these narrative and visual elements, but they don't let go of you either.

My first confrontation with *Day-Glo* brought back memories of the trip through the forbidden zone in Andrei Tarkovsky's film *Stalker* (1979). What is shown here is a bare, peculiar world which all real life seems to have fled. In *Stalker*, however, we still have a few characters. In Olde Wolbers' visual world not one is to be seen. Unidentifiable objects float past us in an open and empty universe. There seems to be an infinity of space both inside and outside the frames, but at the same time these worlds have an oppressive look and generate a feeling of claustrophobia. They also evoke associations with the visually stylized worlds of Stanley Kubrick's films from the 1960s and '70s.

Day-Glo, video for projection with sound, 6 minutes (loop), 1999. Courtesy Maureen Paley, London.

Sculptured language

In the above paragraph I put Saskia Olde Wolbers' work in the context of cinema, but that is not really correct. Cinema has a strong tradition of storytelling, a plot that is slowly built up and gets resolved, with images and storyline helping each other out. In Olde Wolbers' work image and voice-over seem at first glance to be at odds with each other. In her English texts, rather monotonously spoken by a male or female voice, a number of characters are introduced. Sometimes it's actors who speak the text, sometimes friends. Often the voice belongs to one of the story's main characters , giving us his or her view of events. Usually the characters are engaged in a battle with life and with themselves. They are victims of unreal events and are imprisoned in certain memories, not knowing whether these are real or imaginary. In fact lies and truth are constantly changing places in these spoken worlds. The voice-over sketches peculiar worlds in which events melt into each other in unpredictable ways. These unfathomable stories are narrated soberly, often in an accent that reveals where the story is taking place.

Art critic Sacha Bronwasser neatly sums up Olde Wolbers' textual world: ` In a language that puts everything so precisely in its place, that is so simple and at the same time so smart - a `sculptured' language.' The tone of the spoken texts has to be sober because the words mustn't overshadow the images. The tales are fictional, stories that have come into existence after a long period of research. While images and text at first seem to lead parallel lives, they soon become interwoven in your mind. They are in constant contact, in fact, but it is hard to pinpoint exactly how that is. The unreal character of both the literary and the visual components undoubtedly plays a big role here.

It is striking that in the above quotation Sacha Bronwasser uses the term ` sculptured' with reference to the *text*. The visual worlds of Olde Wolbers are also created along traditional lines using a wide range of manual procedures. At first glance these visual constructions seem to have been produced using all kinds of digital techniques, but nothing could be further from the truth. For each work a model is built in the studio where with the help of various materials (vacuum-formed plastic, braided nylon, cod liver oil capsules, shapes

Kilowatt Dynasty, video for projection with sound, 6 min. (loop), 2000. Courtesy Maureen Paley, London.

made from wire and fishing line, lots of paint and glue ...) settings are created. They are mostly placed in a pool of water set up in the studio. Recorded at length by small, mobile digital cameras, we are then shown strange, pleasurable liquid worlds full of slowly pulsating dynamics.

Longing and disillusion

Olde Wolbers does her writing and building in parallel. While she is writing, images will occur to her and she will start constructing them right away. Sometimes she has made objects that only later find their place again in a story. In her fantastic settings, visual worlds between dream and reality, stories reverberate that are full of human tragedy and failings, but also of longing.

Cosmos from 1998 (a five-minute film) tells the story of a Russian woman, trying to snare a rich American husband through a dating agency. Eventually an art gallery owner comes to visit her in her hotel room. Afraid that he will discover that she doesn't know anything about art, the Russian woman decides to make a monumental sculpture out of soap bubbles. The sculpture, which is meant eventually to take the form of the Taj Mahal, grows only slowly and the Russian woman lets the soap do the work for her. The result: the whole hotel gets flooded and in the basement car park a huge ice sculpture is formed. This artwork causes the death of several people, among them the gallery owner. The story is told calmly by a woman's voice. The images show spaces where the ice has taken over the concrete and where in the filtered light pillars of ice and long icicles almost appear to be dancing together.

In *Day-Glo* from 1999 (six minutes) a man with a Spanish accent tells an estate agent of his life full of illusions and loss. He had emigrated from Spain to Australia and there met the love of his life. After a failed business growing vegetables the couple returned to Southern Spain, where they built a number of greenhouses to grow cucumbers and tomatoes in. That too is a disastrous failure and Luis Zarzuela, the narrator, decides to turn his greenhouses into a virtual theme park where emigrants who have recently returned to Spain can soak up the Australian atmos-

Placebo, video for projection with sound, 6 minutes (loop), 2002. Courtesy Maureen Paley, London.

Interloper, video for projection with sound, 6 minutes (loop), 2003. Courtesy Maureen Paley, London.

phere once more. At first he has a lot of visitors, but then nobody comes any more, as people become sad when they are reminded of their failed dreams. Zarzuela wants to close the park, but can't because of one visitor who is spending more and more time wandering round the park: his own wife, who has fallen in love again with his former self. He finds himself obliged to distance himself from her and leave her with her new love: the young Luis Zarzuela. I quote a few sentences from the end of the story:

But for Carmen our world was a fantasy amplifier.
She loved being in there,
Taking her early morning walks.
I was pleased she loved my creation so much,
Although I was seeing less and less of her.
The morning walks became day walks ...
And then it happened ...
One night she didn't return home at all,
Which to me meant only one thing.
She was having an affair.
I found out she was flirting with her memories of me.
She was having an affair ..
With the Luis she met twenty years ago.
Her visits to the real world became less frequent,
Not returning home for days on end.
One day I said to her, 'Do you want me now or then?'
She moved in with him, away from the present.

While the story is being told you see a strange landscape with a metallic glow, in which a multitude of small pointed shapes light up and form a rigid pattern. First you move past all kinds of greenish and yellowish branch-like shapes, then a large number of peculiar sculptural forms go by that seem to have been derived from comic books or old science-fiction films. The landscape of this Spanish park, surrounded by an impenetrable blackness, is made from a big curved sheet of metal, with plastic shapes on it that are lit from the inside. The whole contraption was put on a record player and rotated by one of Olde Wolbers' acquaintances. The camera recording the whole was hanging on its side.

The above two stories deal with longing, disillusion, even humiliation. Contemporary phenomena such as a virtual theme park or a dating agency are combined with age-old human tendencies. This work also contains some social criticism: in the part of southern Spain where *Day-Glo* is set, human exploitation is rife.

Under water

In *Kilowatt Dynasty* (2000, seven minutes) a woman with a Chinese accent tells about her upcoming birth in 2016. Her mother will be a presenter on a television shopping programme. The television channel, which promotes washing machines among other things, has its studio under water, close to the great Three Gorges Dam in China. The windows behind the presenter look out on old submerged villages (the actual flooding of hundreds of villages was a much disputed act of the Chinese government). The future father of the narrator is an activist protesting against the dam who has chained himself to the gate of the visitors' centre. At a certain moment he storms into the studio and claims straight to camera that he has taken the female presenter hostage. In reality she's not in the studio at all but wandering around above water in the newly built city on the shores of the reservoir. Then, inexplicably, she is suddenly in the studio after all and reiterates the demand of the hostage-taker. This last element puzzles the not-yet-born narrator. She suspects that her mother has fallen victim to inverted dream syndrome. Because of the great emptiness of the underwater studio and the whole reservoir she is confusing dream and reality. Astronauts often seem to suffer from this syndrome, thinking that their families at home are the reality of that moment and that their space-flight is a dream. This kind of inversion of dream and reality is typical of Olde Wolbers' work.

The spoken text is backed by Chinese gongs and all kinds of electronic sound effects. In *Kilowatt Dynasty* even the images give you little to hold on to. In the beginning the camera glides across water and comes to a lot of little islands made of plastic cylinders and funnels. The camera slips down into one of them and we find ourselves in a magical, weightless, liquid world with soft green lighting. At one point the camera moves between undulating, snake-like forms, made from copper wire braided to look like fish scales. Masses of plastic packaging materials and Italian plastic oil bottles have also been used in this film.

Olde Wolbers loves making things and using different techniques. She is always trying out new procedures. For *Kilowatt Dynasty* she still used a tiny bath standing on a transparent table of synthetic material. The virtually weightless set moved around the camera, which was encased in a kind of bubble. As there were also lamps hanging above the water, it was a risky undertaking. Since then her sets have become more professional. The tiny bath, for example, has been replaced by a big water tank and it's no longer friends and acquaintances who keep her sets moving. And she now orders motorized cameras from a specialist company that will make a special dolly, a little wagon on which the

Trailer, video for projection with sound, 10 minutes (loop), 2005 Courtesy Maureen Paley, London.

camera can ride. Olde Wolbers creates her work on miniature sets, so she also needs small-scale equipment.

The works *Placebo* (2001, six minutes) and *Interloper* (2003, six minutes) are independent of each other, but both are inspired by the true story of the fake French doctor Jean-Claude Romand. For years he made everyone around him believe he was a doctor. When, in the early 1990s he began to suspect that people were on to him, he killed his wife, his two children and himself. *Placebo* and *Interloper* don't actually tell the story of this fake doctor; there is already a feature film that does that. These works create a magical, somewhat sinister atmosphere around such human feelings as longing, surprise and belief. The visual landscape in *Placebo* has been created out of hamster cages with hospital furniture made out of wire inside them. 'Those models were dipped in paint and then filmed under water. The paint, that hangs down like skins from the wire and doesn't mix with the water, attracts bubbles and froth. The walls flutter, the empty rooms look like a living organism out of a nightmare', so Sacha Bronwasser writes.

Red cinema, green jungle

Olde Wolbers' main interest is in literature, more than in visual art. She likes Charles Dickens, Fyodor Dostoevsky, Michel Tournier, David Mitchell, Marcel Proust, Oliver Sachs and Haruki Murakami. But visual art gives her the opportunity to position herself between literature and film. This way she doesn't have to compete with either discipline.

Trailer (2005, ten minutes) is the result of two investigations by Olde Wolbers. She lived for some time in Los Angeles and there became interested in its old, somewhat dilapidated movie houses and also in Kinemacolor, an old technique that used rotating red and green filters to colour black-and-white films. *Trailer* is made up of green images of a jungle and red impressions of the auditorium and foyer of an old cinema. The story arose from her reading of a news item about a love affair between the Hollywood stars Clark Gable and Loretta Young. It resulted in a child, Judy Lewis, who was told throughout her life that she had been adopted by her mother. Lewis did not discover the truth until she was an old woman and so could only admire her parents on screen. The narrator of *Trailer* is Alfgar Dalio. While watching an old movie trailer, he notices that he shares his name with a moth, a parasite that lives in the Amazon jungle. From his father he learns that he is adopted and a product of Hollywood's glamour years. The story also features two actors who played small roles in the 1930s, Ring Kittle and Elmore Vella. Dalio decides to watch all their old films at a cinema. The images seem familiar and give him a warm feeling. He goes to the old woman at the box-office and asks for information. She turns out to know everything about Kittle and Vella. While flying over the Amazon for their first film in Kinemacolor, they had crashed. Through this a hallucinogenic plant, the Coxocotl, was reanimated and named after Vella. The only enemy of this plant was the moth Alfgar Dalio. The couple lived among the plants for some time and were completely forgotten by the film world. Their films were not issued in Kinemacolor and were therefore dated. In a last attempt to achieve some renown they had set up a cinema that showed many of their films. In black-and-white only.

I quote the beautiful start of the story: `Somewhere in the vast Amazonian forest ... among plants whose indigenous, Spanish and Latin names ... compete with one another outside of their awareness.' The camera very leisurely explores the sparkling red interior of the cinema and the watery green of the jungle. Slowly the story unfolds with all its amazing disclosures, both visual and spoken.

Above water

In *Deadline* (2007, eighteen minutes) a woman, Salingding, recounts fragments of traditional stories from a fishing village in Gambia. She does so during a sixteen-month journey in a primitive vehicle (which has the word `Deadline' on it) from Gambia to Nigeria, where she has to catch a plane. Mythical stories about the snake Ninki Nanka and a confused grandmother play a part here. At the airport at the end of the story Salingding sees a stranger who is holding a book that has on its cover a photo of the vehicle `Deadline'. The images show a strange, round rabbit made out of fishing line and filled with a mobile yellow fluid that seems to be slowly dripping from its extremely long ears. The fluid defies gravity and moves from bottom to top. Meanwhile the camera wanders slowly between oval stone shapes that evoke associations with modernist African architecture. It also follows the movements of two silver-coloured snakes. Alongside the text you hear soft African drumming.

In this work there is a difference in the experience of time between image and text: the narrator talks rather quickly of all kinds of traditions and events, while the images move very slowly. In this way image and text interact even more intensively.

According to Sacha Bronwasser, whom I quoted earlier, *Deadline* is more rooted in reality than the earlier works. On a trip through Africa Olde Wolbers took many photographs of modernist African architecture of the 1970s. Motifs from these photos can be seen in the film. In an interview the artist said that her main character Salingding could be carrying those photos with her. Africa has an exceptionally rich oral culture and Olde Wolbers has made use of that too; for instance, she heard a story about a taxi driver who had driven through eight different countries to catch a plane. *Deadline* is also the first work that to a great extent was not filmed under water.

Zen and archery

At the beginning of 2011 Olde Wolbers told Sacha Bronwasser: `For a year and a half I've been working on a robot and now it's finished. It is a bird that can spread its wings and move its head. It's a kind of puppetry. It is a very simple robot, but it looks very good. It is made from Nitinol, a kind of wire that has `memory' and reverts to a certain form.'

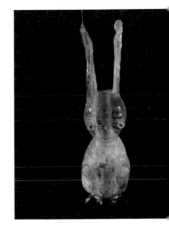

This creation can be admired in *Pareidolia* (2011, twelve minutes), that had its premiere at *A Shot in the Dark*, a retrospective of Olde Wolbers' work at the Secession arts centre in Vienna. The `movable' bird plays a part in it, together with a fictional story about a Japanese archer in the 1920s. In his book *Zen and the Art of Archery* the German professor Eugen Herrigel uses an eye-witness report about the Japanese archery master, Awa Kenzo, who shot two arrows in complete darkness. The amazing thing was that the second arrow split the first. Kenzo attributed this to external, even spiritual powers that had taken possession of him at the time. Herrigel's description of traditional Japanese archery and the spiritually-coloured interpretation of it contributed to the greatly increased awareness of Zen Buddhism in the western world in the mid-20th century.

The title *Pareidolia* refers to a psychological phenomenon, a form of illusion in which people attribute specific meanings to vague, arbitrary observations. In this work Olde Wolders shows again how she remains fascinated by the impossibility of a clear divide between reality and imagination. In the end not even the scientific gloss of a publication by a German professor can hide the fact that his conclusions are based on vague assumptions. In this work, with its very specific title, Saskia Olde Wolbers seems to be pointing to the highly subjective content of historic tales. They are rarely based solely on objective research or on pure fiction, but float somewhere between the two and remain caught in illusion or confusion.

The interesting thing about Olbe Wolbers' work is that for her this conclusion isn't so much a goal as a means. That is what keeps her work alive. ∎

Deadline, video for projection with sound (loop), 18 minutes, 2007. Courtesy Maureen Paley, London.

FURTHER READING

Stijn huijts, Gianni Jetzer, Patricia Ellis, Saskia Olde Wolbers: *now that part of me has become fiction,* Artimo Amsterdam, 2003

Rainald Schumacher, *Saskia Olde Wolbers*, sammlung goetz, Munchen 2010

http://curatingdiscourse.blogspot.com/2007/11/saskia-olde-wolbers-deadline-maureen.html
http://www.Secession.At/art/2011 –olde-wolbers-d.Html
http://www.Reisereport.At/oe-reportagen/redaktion.Php?Nr=307

Translated by Pleuke Boyce

Raoul De Keyser, *Lines*, 1972.
Acrylic on canvas, 188 x 140 cm.
MuZEE, Ostend.

Chronicle

A Big Friendly Giant
Contrasts and Extremes in
Walter Van Beirendonck's Clothing

Walter Van Beirendonck,
1996 © Jean-Baptiste
Mondino.

King Kong Kooks, *SexClown*, *Cosmic Culture Clash* and *Weird*: these are all collections by fashion designer Walter Van Beirendonck. With his sensational clothing full of radical statements he pushes the boundaries of conventional values. His idiosyncratic fashion touches on sensitive themes leaving a trail of bewilderment behind it. Is it provocative work by an artistic genius or the creative chaos of a rebel? Who is this designer, and why is he so famous?

Walter Van Beirendonck (Brecht,1957) grew up in Flanders, the son of a garage proprietor. That he was bursting with creativity was obvious at an early age. Whereas the fashion at his boarding school was short trousers, Van Beirendonck went around in platform soles. It was the era of glam rock and he was beginning to associate himself with the extravagant pop star, David Bowie, who was forever reinventing himself. After doing a preparatory year at the Royal Academy for Fine Arts in Antwerp, he began a four year intensive course in Fashion and Stage Costume. The end of the seventies was an inspirational period for a fashion student: Gianni Versace, Jean-Paul Gaultier, Comme des Garçons and Thierry Mugler were beginning to make their mark and their approach to fashion must have worked like an aphrodisiac on the young Van Beirendonck. In 1980 he graduated with distinction, alongside Martin Margiela,

and two years later was responsible for causing ructions in Belgium. The controversy surrounding his first show, *Sado*, in which he displayed women with whips and muzzles, seems to have set the tone for the rest of his career.

Van Beirendonck designs mainly men's clothing, but introduces a female silhouette from time to time. He sees the tenuous boundaries within which fashion designers manoeuvre as a challenge. By questioning these conventions he has regularly succeeded in stretching the boundaries. The characteristiscs that would distinguish Walter Van Beirendonck were evident already after his first couple of seasons: the combination of contrasting materials and colours, unusual proportions, the naïve alongside the aggressive, fantasy and frequent allusions to sex. His work demonstrates his social engagement and shows him to be an innovative storyteller. In *Bad Baby's Boys* and *Let's Tell a Fairy Tale*, his two fairy-tale collections, he combines teddy-bear sweaters and pompoms with the harsh reality of the gay scene halfway through the eighties. With the slogan *Safe Sex* he is referring to the disease of AIDS – one of his models had died from it.

As a result of the success of their first shows in Antwerp in the mid-eighties, Van Beirendonck formed the much acclaimed group, *The Antwerp Six*, with fellow-students Marina Yee, Dirk Van Saene, Dirk Bikkembergs, Dries Van Noten and Ann Demeulemeester. They made an overwhelming impression on the international press during a London fashion fair and put Belgium on the fashion map for all time. Once Van Beirendonck's talent had gained international recognition, his business acumen ensured him financial independence, a great bonus for a novice fashion designer. Following his appointment as a lecturer at the Antwerp Academy in 1985, Van Beirendonck was assured a regular income that he could combine with commercial commissions. He invested the money he earned straight into his own business.

This meant he could experiment freely with materials, proportions, symbols, bright colours,

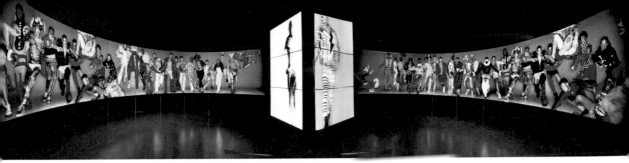

Walter Van Beirendonck's Wild Knights at the exhibition Dream The World Awake © Ronald Stoops.

cyber pop and internet – continually improving himself. Because of the way he brought innovation to fashion design he became an extremely influential fashion designer. In the booming nineties, in addition to his main *Walter Van Beirendonck* line he had the label *W&L.T. (Wild & Lethal Trash)*, a huge commercial success that catapulted Van Beirendonck to stardom in the world of fashion. His spectacular Parisian shows were the *must see* of fashion week and had an international following. The German jeans manufacturer Mustang was also partly responsible for the worldwide spread of Van Beirendonck's label and gave the Belgian carte blanche for years. He caught the eye of the rock band U2 and designed the costumes for their *Popmart* tour (1997-1998).

When Mustang suddenly started to interfere in the design process, and because of the changing spirit of the times at the end of the nineties, which suited Van Beirendonck less well from the aesthetic point of view, his artistry began to suffer. In 1999 he opted for artistic independence and continued only with his top line, which he sold in his shop-cum-gallery, *Walter*, in Antwerp, a joint venture with his partner Dirk Van Saene. To give vent to his feelings about the disagreement with Mustang, and to be able to follow his own passion for design, he started the *aestheticterrorists* line. But this was granted only a short life following the events of 9/11 and the changes in the world of fashion that came with them. In 2011 he was appointed as artistic leader of four exhibitions under the name of *Mode 2001 Landed/Geland*, which were meant to draw attention to Antwerp as a city of fashion.

After that all was quiet around the Belgian designer for a while until about the middle of the last decade when, thanks to commercial commissions, he had acquired sufficient financial re-

sources to put on a show again, the first for years. His fans relived the old days. Van Beirendonck gloried once more in his extreme statements with his collection *SexClown* (Summer 2008). Taking a fetishist approach, he designed shocking pieces of clothing with an almost militant theatricality. He showed his mastery of his trade by communicating things that fascinated him personally in his fashions. Couturier Azzedine Alaïa: "A Walter-shirt expresses more than what others are expressing in a whole collection."

His interest in architecture, ethnic rituals, decoration, sex and innovation works as a source of inspiration. Concealed within the good-natured Flemish giant is an unfettered hunger for knowledge. This hunger, together with inspirational artists such as Roy Liechtenstein, Marc Newson and Leigh Bowery, feeds the design machine that is Van Beirendonck. He has a multidisciplinary vision of fashion, and a general exhibition, *Dream the World Awake*, with an accompanying catalogue, has been organized to demonstrate this.

At the moment he has his own ladies' and gents' collections, he is the artistic director of Scapa Sports, he designs the children's collection *Zulupapuwa* for the Belgian fashion chain JBC and he is head of the Fashion department at the Royal Academy for Fine Arts in Antwerp. Here Walter Van Beirendonck teaches his students, who come from all over the world, to communicate by means of their work and he introduces them to his own marvellous world of fantasy.

Martino Bidotti
Translated by Sheila M. Dale

www.waltervanbeirendonck.com
Walter Van Beirendonck, Dream the World Awake, Lannoo, Tielt, 2011, 240 p.

Film and theatre

Bullhead
Illegal Hormones for the Mass Market

Right from the start *Bullhead*, the debut film by the Flemish director Michaël R. Roskam, received the equivalent of a standing ovation in the press. It began in February 2010 when the film was selected for the Berlin Film Festival; by the end of 2011 more than 450,000 Flemings had paid to see it. Virtually all the reviews, both in Belgium and abroad, began by referring to the powerful acting of Matthias Schoenaerts, who fattened himself up so as to play the role of hormone farmer Jacky Vanmarsenille with the necessary precision. This recognition gave Schoenaerts' career an immediate boost on the international stage. The film has since won awards at Beaune, Motovun, Austin, Montreal and Moscow, and *Bullhead* was selected as the Belgian entry for a Foreign Language Oscar. Good news for the Flemish film industry and for Michaël Roskam, but what kind of film is *Bullhead* actually, and is all the hype really justified?

Bullhead has often been described as a tragedy, with touches of Shakespeare and Martin Scorsese. This is an accurate description: the main character is a thoroughly tragic hero. He is predestined to go under in a cloud of dark fatality. His problem is the flesh, even more so than Hamlet, who in his day expressed the wish "O that this too, too solid flesh would melt". Jacky Vanmarsenille's spirit literally disappears under a gigantic pile of flesh. Jacky swallows huge quantities of testosterone, with the result that his flesh keeps growing and like a pernicious weed threatens to choke the plant. We only discover why he is taking testosterone later, in the course of two beautifully integrated flashbacks. We see how, as a child, Jacky was the victim of a dramatic act of violence that scarred him for the rest of his life. No matter how hard the adult Jacky tries to follow his finer instincts, the mass of flesh and the overdose of male hormones prevent him. For example, he's completely clueless as to how to go about winning the girl of his dreams.

The flash of brilliance that made *Bullhead* into such an extraordinary film is that Michaël R. Roskam set the subject of 'too-much-flesh' in the world of cattle farmers, cattle fatteners and hormone traders. The metaphor of the flesh works on more than one level, and usually in a very dramatic way. *Bullhead* is the story of a male culture of red meat, machismo, honour and violence. In the course of his career, Martin Scorsese made a lot of films on this theme. The resulting movies were often hard, just like *Bullhead*. However, Bullhead is not a testosterone film, but a film about testosterone. Most of the Flemish crime films that have been so popular with the public in recent years have been injected with far higher doses.

The story within which the central plot is played out has all the seeming hallmarks of a genre film, except that it isn't one. It could have been a crime film about the hormone mafia, or even a mafia film about rival clans fighting over territory. The reference to real-life criminal events, for example the murder of the veterinary inspector Karel Van Noppen in 1995, is equally misleading. We take note of it, and it connects the film to Flemish society, but it is not an essential part of the film.

In its less inspired moments, *Bullhead* slips up on the genre theme. For instance, the intrigue involving the police commissioner is clearly one of the film's less successful episodes. It seems to me that Roskam has made the film more complex in structure than it needed to be. As a viewer you don't need the tiny little pieces of the puzzle, since they merely divert your attention from the overall picture to the way it is put together.

There are also a few moments of comedy, to which a few critics took offence, more specifically the scenes involving the two Walloon garage mechanics working on the car used to commit the murder in question. There's a lot of blood and guts on screen here, but it also provides a cheerful if marginal commentary on Belgian society with its warring French- and Dutch-speaking communities.

Matthias Schoenaerts,
Photo by Nicolas Karakatsanis.

Strangely enough, these grotesque intermezzos don't really detract from the tragic tenor of the work, any more than they do in Shakespeare's tragedies. He too was not averse to this sort of comic contrast. Moreover, alongside the pitch-black fatalist tone there is a subtle element of expressionist distortion running through the narrative. In the way Schoenaerts' fattened-up body is portrayed, in the desolate Flemish exteriors, the sombre landscapes, the aesthetics of the provincial highways, the roadside brothels, and the Flemish *faux chic*. Seldom has the countryside with its small farms and untidy farmsteads felt so cold and damp as in this film.

What makes *Bullhead* an important Flemish film is that the director has developed a universe of his own, a world with its own smell, in terms both of style and content. In Flanders a lot of work has been done in recent years in existing genres, formats and models. Bullhead bucks that trend. There are obviously film directors and films that have defined his vision, but the film is not simply a carbon copy of an existing original.

Roskam has also deliberately opted for a restrained directing style. With the testosterone theme as starting point that is not an obvious choice, but it is this decision that makes Schoenaerts' role so powerful. His fellow hormone farmers are also portrayed in a calm, somewhat sedate fashion. There are no cold killers. Instead they are the prototype of the fun-loving, unthinking Fleming who likes to earn a bit on the side. They too belong to a clearly patriarchal culture, where the women might wear the pearls but definitely not the trousers. Both the men and the women speak a language that is completely turned in on itself: a dialect (both from the far east and the far west of the country) that is only understood in their own hamlet.

A second notable directing choice is the slow, contemplative pace which utterly precludes any vestige of an 'adrenaline film' approach. Roskam frequently has recourse to very slow-motion shots, which suggest that the characters' consciousness too is only working at half speed. The dark, wide-screen photography by Nicolas Karakatsanis, with its stark contrasts, fits nicely with the director's vision; Raf Keunen's score looms large and underlines the omnipresent feeling of deadly menace.

This decision to go slowly rather than opt for the classic fast-paced performance makes it all the more surprising that *Bullhead* has achieved audience figures that far more mass-market pictures could only dream of.

Since the *New Wave*, outstanding directors who are also outstanding scriptwriters have been referred to as auteurs. Bullhead shows that just such a one has been born in Flanders.

ERIK MARTENS
Translated by Gregory Ball

www.rundskop.be
Bullhead has been nominated for the 2012 Oscar Academy Awards in the Best Foreign Language Film category.

Eccentric, Venomous, Topical
Wunderbaum Theatre

On Sunday 21 November 2010 a small group of actors from Holland and Belgium performed *Looking for Paul* in the Redcat Theater in Los Angeles. The perspective in this production is set in the first instance by a female character from Rotterdam who finds herself confronted, against her will, by a work of art. To be precise, the woman's house stands right opposite the metre high Santa Claus, ("Gnome Buttplug", as it has been dubbed), by the American artist Paul McCarthy. She is of the opinion that this offensive work of art has seriously damaged her outlook and she travels to Los Angeles to meet McCarthy in person and wreak revenge.

Fiction and reality are beautifully intertwined here. The purchase of Santa Claus ten years ago by the municipality of Rotterdam did indeed cause quite a commotion and the work of art is still a topic of discussion today. Those for and against argue with each other about art in general and about the merit of this work in particular. At the very time that financial backing for art is a hot item and local and state subsidies are running into increasing difficulties, *Looking for Paul* meets the demand for engaged theatre that provides a commentary on the spirit of the age.

Their stay in Los Angeles also gave the actors from Wunderbaum the opportunity to do some research into the subsidy system in the United States. The discovery that the state of California hands out two million dollars a year to culture came as a shock to them. Wunderbaum alone receives that much in four years in the Netherlands. Up to now, that is, one should add, because in times of crisis the present government is certainly not inclined to subsidize art in general and theatre in particular as generously as before.

Discoveries like these were given a place in the production that ended with a twenty minute long tumultuous performance in the style of McCarthy, whom Wunderbaum greatly admire – indeed, McCarthy himself and his wife and daughter came to see the show. Documentary theatre that runs wild into chaotic slapstick and leaves the audience thunderstruck that is typical of Wunderbaum's work. Back in the Netherlands the group organized two theme-evenings on the topic of Paul McCarthy, with the showing of his video work, the performance of *Looking for Paul* and discussions afterwards on art and politics with different people involved in the field.

The name Wunderbaum is borrowed from a pine tree shaped air-freshener from Germany. Maybe it was the slogan, "Wunderbaum erfrischt die Luft in jeden Raum" [Wunderbaum freshens the air in every room], that gave the actors the idea of taking their name from the tree, because freshening the air and giving a new impulse to the theatre establishment is what the collective aims to do. Moreover, the Dutch word 'wonder-boom' is the name for the castor oil plant (ricinus communis), an extremely poisonous plant, and Wunderbaum's productions are characterized by a certain degree of venom.

The exceptional talents of these actors who graduated from the theatre academy in Maastricht in 2001 were spotted by Johan Simons, probably the most important Dutch producer of the last decade. He took the group under the wing of his company ZT Hollandia, in Eindhoven, and when he moved to Belgium he took the actors with him as a sub-group of the prestigious NTGent where he was artistic director. Since 2009 Wunderbaum has been an independent company that produces shows under the supervision of the Rotterdam Schouwburg production house.

Apart from being extremely unusual and venomous – as *Looking for Paul* also demonstrates – Wunderbaum is highly engaged with what is going on in the world. The actors frequently research a sub-culture in modern society, they play reformed shopaholics (*Magna Plaza*, 2007), pseudo religious drifters (*Camp Jesus*, 2008), British football fans on a boozing trip (*Beer Tourist*, 2008) or the harassed inhabitants of a demolition area

Wunderbaum, Our Pope, 2011 © Fred Debrock.

(*Natives*, 2010). In order to get as close as possible to the realities of life, the group prefer to act on location. So Magna Plaza could be seen not only in various shopping centres in Europe, but also, in a censored version, on a city square in Teheran.

For the 2011-2012 season the group is staying close to base with two productions for small auditoriums: *Our Pope* and *Flow my tears*. No production shows what a powerful collective Wunderbaum is better than *Our Pope*, based on a dramatic text by author and journalist Arnon Grunberg. Grunberg wrote the text at the request of the Teatr Wspólczesny from Wroclaw in Poland. After reading it, the artistic director decided to abandon the planned cooperation. In a rejection letter that left no room for misunderstanding – published in the programme for the Wunderbaum performance - she mercilessly exposed the shortcomings of this undramatic text. Subsequently Grunberg handed the text over to the Wunderbaum actors, who are wholehearted fans of his contrary work.

Our Pope is both a kaleidoscopic farce and an evening's worth of provocation, not so much on account of the scornful treatment of the Catholic clergy, but because the text – certainly not a well made play – places a huge burden on the players' talent and the public's leniency. The energy and verve with which the actors handle the coarse clichés and silly associative jokes command deep respect. It is definitely the bewitching power of the actors rather than the dramatic force of the original text that earns applause.

Flow my Tears, which had its première in January 2012, is a co-production with De Veenfabriek, a company from Leiden that specializes in musical theatre. Only a single actress from Wunderbaum plays alongside the famous actor Jeroen Willems in the production. This performance is based on the music of the seventeenth century composer John Downland, and in it two actors imagine they are Indians who have got lost in a world where music is the only thing that can still provide comfort.

Both *Our Pope* and *Flow my Tears* are a deviation from the successful path Wunderbaum has trodden so far – 'location' theatre, eccentric, sharp and never far removed from commentary on subcultures. It is good that the group is exploring new ways and trying to attract a new public, but at the same time there is already a gnawing nostalgia for the earlier productions that gave Wunderbaum an ineradicable place in the landscape of Dutch and Flemish theatre.

Jos Nijhof
Translated by Sheila M. Dale

www.wunderbaum.nl

How *Ontroerend Goed* Widened Its International Circuit.

In the last few years the performance theatre company *Ontroerend Goed*, from Ghent, have built up a remarkable circuit abroad, with exotic repertoires and ecstatic reviews. What's their secret?

Let's take a step back in time. At the end of the nineties the company consists of a pupils' club (Alexander Devriendt, David Bauwens, Sophie de Somere, Joeri Smet) giving poetry performances in cafés in Ghent. The live aspect is crucial from the beginning. The presence of an audience determines the form and, with it, the content, the search for the relationship between performer and public, in the here and now. In 2001 it is time to make professional choices. Poetry recedes into the background in favour of performance, and the *PORROR* trilogy (an absurd review of porn, poetry and horror) is a first step in the direction of "seriousness". When *PORROR* receives an important award, *Ontroerend Goed* enters the (new to them) landscape of Flemish theatre, and has to adapt to it. The company is picked up by the arts centres and granted their first project subsidy for *Exsimplicity* (2004), and the crazy club suddenly has to produce "real theatre". The fact of having to face these expectations leads to productions such as *Exsimplicity* and a sequel *Killusion* (2005) which fail to make much of a stir. As if the lack of self-confidence is also reflected in what they produce, *Ontroerend Goed* continues to examine the medium itself and the extent of its own imagination – "what is theatre, actually?" Typically the "fringe project" *The Smile Off Your Face* (2004), a performance given on the margins of a festival, is more successful. Members of the audience are put in a wheelchair and taken on an intimate sensory tour – a mad idea that could only occur because of the total lack of expectations. It's gradually dawning on them, *Ontroerend Goed* seems to function best under the motto of "nothing obligatory, anything possible". But how do you keep that freedom when, as a young com-

pany, following two project subsidies, you are given a state grant (2006-2008)? The government money puts considerable pressure on the theatre group in addition to the artistic pressure.

The result is *Soap* (2006), a series of five shows that have to be produced within the space of three months. The spectacular, but unachievable, idea is a huge flop, and *Ontroerend Goed* collapses in a crisis that in two respects will lead to an impressive restart on the international circuit. First of all the failure leads to a somewhat paradoxical decision to go to the Edinburgh Festival with *The Smile Off Your Face*, because "in times of crisis you need to invest". Maybe it's also a psychological flight from Flanders, where the four untrained dramatists had been received with some reserve and Soap had proved the criticasters right. The Edinburgh Festival proves to be a good bet. The fringe project wins the Total Theatre Award there in 2007 and in 2008 the Adelaide Fringe in Australia too. A chain reaction is set in motion, the Sydney Festival and the New Zealand Festival can't follow fast enough. Unlike Flanders foreign countries seem to take *Ontroerend Goed* to their hearts straightaway.

There's another consequence of the failure of *Soap*, it obliges *Ontroerend Goed* to redefine themselves artistically. *Soap* had brought a latent feeling of doubt into focus: were the attempts at "real theatre", with a written script and professional actors really authentic? Alexander Devriendt decides to change tactics and does his next production with thirteen teenagers from the youth theatre company KOPERGIETERY. Once again it's the freedom of free verse that leads to success: *Pubers Bestaan Niet* (2007) – English title *Once And For All We're Gonna Tell You Who We Are So Shut Up And Listen* - is a rough ride during which the youngsters examine clichés about themselves. Thanks to their earlier production **The Smile, Once And For All** had it made on the international scene, and in 2008 this performance also carries off the Total Theatre Award in Edinburgh. Two triumphs in a row, and with two very different performances *Ontroerend Goed*

Ontroerend Goed, *Once And For All We're Gonna Tell You Who We Are So Shut Up And Listen*, 2004 © Phile Deprez.

couldn't wish for a better visiting-card. The merry-go-round has taken off and, after the English-speaking countries, Morocco, Japan, Jerusalem, Singapore, Italy, Germany, The Netherlands and France succumb.

What's to explain the brilliant success of *Ontroerend Goed* abroad while the reactions in Flanders are much less hysterical? Let's put things in perspective, the big festivals in the English-speaking world set the tone abroad. Performances such as *The Smile* and *Once And For All* were acclaimed enthusiastically at these festivals, and more recent performances such as *Teenage Riot* (2010) and *Audience* (2011) even cause a stir, with incensed reviews and people leaving the auditorium shocked. To understand how these performances "push the boundaries" we need to go back to the beginning, *Ontroerend Goed's* research into its relationship with the audience. In the context of the theatre in the English-speaking countries this relationship has the value of a contract, the spectator is safe. The spectators of a comedy show know that they're not safe, the participants in reality TV know they'll be put under scrutiny – but they've opted for this. However, don't do to the unsuspecting public what you do to the comedy audience, remove it from its safe and comfortable seat.

And that's precisely what *Ontroerend Goed* does. In *Intern* (2009) the audience's trust is won and then abused; in *Audience* the public is caught on camera. In *Teenage Riot*, in which teenagers jeer at the audience, yet another power relationship is overturned, that between youngster and adult. Even Lyn Gardner, a leading critic on *The Guardian* and an *Ontroerend Goed* fan from the very first moment, found it unheard of for youngsters to be telling adults what they ought to do. In a vertical society like in Britain such a thing's apparently *not done*.

Ontroerend Goed has found its track. But doesn't that carry a risk too? In the past *Soap* forced them to stop and think. Will they stop and think again now *Ontroerend Goed* is on an international high? Business leader David Bauwens: "It's part of theatre that you fail from time to time. I think there'll always be crises that mean we have to redefine ourselves." Another risk is the organizational structure. In the coming round of subsidies (2013-2016) Alexander Devriendt bears sole responsibility for all the projects. Devriendt is surrounded by a network of almost lifelong friends, sympathizers, fans, fathers and girlfriends – even the board is a friends' club. Something that's developed historically and that's understandable, but isn't that in-crowd in need of a bit of critical opposition? Isn't an organization with such a narrow base extremely vulnerable? According to Bauwens the company is working on broadening its base via *"Ontroerend Goed Supports"*, a new track which will give young authors an opportunity. The first project under this banner was a show by two very young women who also took part in *Once And For All*. They've grown up in the Ontroerend Goed school. Are they likely to come up with an alternative form of artistic expression?

Maybe these objections are premature. *Ontroerend Goed* has been able to rediscover itself in the past. The secret of their international success? The courage to change track, a stubborn instinct for doing their own thing mainly, a mad passion for work and a certain amount of luck in timing. If *Ontroerend Goed* can keep their feet on the ground in the years to come, the sky may well be the limit.

EVELYNE COUSSENS
Translated by Sheila M. Dale

www.ontroerendgoed.be

History

The Oldest Share Certificate in the World

In 2010, while doing research in the West Frie-sian Archive for my master's degree in History, I came across 'the oldest share certificate in the world'. The document was tucked away in a collection of loose archive papers entitled *Finances of the Dutch East India Company (VOC)*. This national trading company, which consisted of six local 'chambers' and continued in existence until 1795, was set up in 1602 with the support of the Estates General, the central government of the United Provinces, in an attempt to suppress the fierce competition between many different local companies. This share certificate could easily have been discovered long ago, but nobody realised what kind of document it was. At first sight it looks like payment for a VOC bond, such as the company issued regularly to deal with short-term liquidity problems.

However, the VOC was also the first trading organisation to be financed by the large-scale issue of transferable shares. This method of financing was innovative because, for the first time in history, virtually anybody could buy such shares and the capital so raised was committed for an unprecedented length of time (originally ten years). The shareholders were compensated for this lengthy period by being allowed to trade their shares freely. This laid the basis for modern share dealings and speculation, which actually began soon after 1602.

The document I discovered is therefore not a bond but in fact a VOC share certificate. And it is not really so strange that this scrap of paper had not been noticed earlier. Firstly, until then only three such pieces of paper were known and all

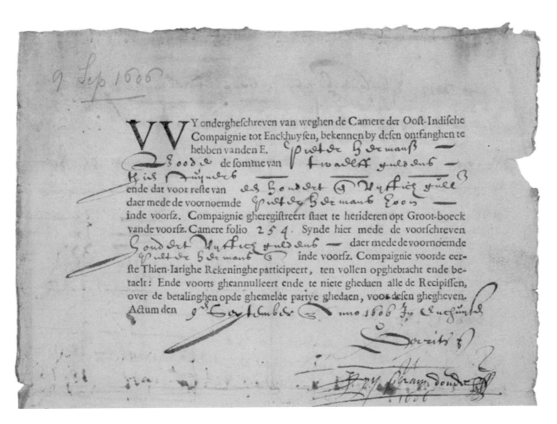

were from a later date[1]. Secondly, the 'share' is actually a quittance, a receipt for the final payment for a share. To persuade investors to put their money into the VOC they were allowed to pay for their shares in four instalments. This particular 'share' certifies that the shareholder concerned had paid his final instalment of twelve guilders and fifty cents. He did this on 9 September 1606, four years after he had bought the share for 150 guilders from the VOC chamber in Enkhuizen, a town now situated in the province of North Holland.

Although in strictly legal terms the document is not a share but a receipt, it comes very close to what we now consider to be a share. The VOC itself did not issue share certificates. A shareholder's only proof of ownership was the entry of his name in the bulky registers of the VOC chambers. Apart from receipts for payment such as this document, a shareholder would have no other evidence to take home with him. This quittance is the oldest printed proof of share ownership.

The holder of this share, the Enkhuizen town messenger Pieter Harmensz, seems to have considered his quittance to be a form of share certificate. Another feature which adds to the unique character of the document is the notes on the reverse. These are records of the dividend payments that Pieter Harmensz received on his share. The other three surviving quittances do not have such notes. Every time that Pieter Harmensz was paid a dividend, the VOC clerk made a note of it on the back of the quittance. His widow also continued to receive dividends, and the annotations show us exactly how many dividends an individual shareholder of the Enkhuizen chamber received between 1602 and 1650.

The annotations reveal that Pieter Harmensz had to wait a long time for his first dividend. It was only in 1612 that he received a payment of 57.5%. More striking still is that the annotations reveal that until about 1620 the average annual return on his shareholding was no higher than 6.25%. That was the same interest paid on gov-

ernment bonds, which were relatively much safer. Although the VOC became more profitable from about the mid-17th century, this particular shareholder had to wait a long time before his share gave him a decent return.

The impression left by these annotations supports recent research into the VOC[2] which has shown that shareholders were not well treated by the directors of the company or by the government. Continuous warfare against the Spanish in Asia required so many investments that the shareholders were pushed to the back of the queue. Presumably the VOC did not have enough money to compensate its investors. This picture is reflected in the finances of the local Enkhuizen chamber of the VOC which I researched for my master's thesis[3]. In 1612 the Enkhuizen chamber almost went bankrupt and had to appeal to the other chambers in order to survive. This 'oldest share certificate' not only brings to life the origins of the modern day stock market but also throws light on the difficult first two decades of the VOC.

Ruben Schalk
Translated by Chris Emery

The share can be viewed interactively on www.worldsoldestshare.com.

1 They are in the possession of the University of Leiden, the Amsterdam Stock Exchange and a private consortium in Germany.

2 See Oscar Gelderblom, Abe de Jong & Joost Jonker, 'An Admiralty for Asia: Isaac le Maire and conflicting conceptions about the corporate governance of the VOC', in ERIM Report Series in Management, June 2010, pp. 1-52.

3 R. Schalk, Financing the Dutch Golden Age: the Credit Market of Enkhuizen, 1580-1700 (MA thesis, Utrecht University, 2010). Viewable on http://igitur-archive.library.uu.nl/student-theses/2010-0826-200318/UUindex.html

The 'Pirenne Phenomenon'

It is hard to imagine an academic historian to-day receiving the kind of public acclaim that befell the Belgian Henri Pirenne (1862-1935). Along with fifteen honorary doctorates and the presidencies of the Carnegie Endowment for International Peace and the International Union of Academies, he received the Belgian Grand Cross of the Order of the Crown, became a *Commandeur de la Légion d'Honneur* in France and was honoured by President Warren Harding at the White House during his tour of the United States in 1922. As Sarah Keymeulen and Jo Tollebeek explain in this short but entertaining biography, Pirenne was of course no ordinary historian. Contemporaries lauded his seven-volume *History of Belgium (Histoire de Belgique)*, which presented modern Belgium as the natural outcome of a historical process reaching back to the Middle Ages and forged by the relatively harmonious coexistence of Latin (Walloon) and Germanic (Flemish) populations. As the first scholarly history of the young nation, the work legitimized Belgium's existence and raised it up as a model for peaceful international relations after the carnage of the First World War. In fact, that war was primarily responsible for Pirenne's international fame. When the German authorities attempted to re-open Ghent University as a Dutch-language institution in 1916, Pirenne (a Walloon) led academic resistance to those plans. His arrest and deportation to German prison camps, reviving the image of "plucky little Belgium" brutalized by German aggression, turned him into a celebrity for the cause of democratic civilization on the world stage.

Pirenne's current reputation as a historian does not rest so much on his *History of Belgium* as on his innovative work on the history of early capitalism, the medieval origins of European cities, and on the daring "Pirenne" thesis, which identified the rise of Islam in the seventh century as the crucial moment in the transition from classical Antiquity to the Middle Ages, ending an

economic system centred on the Mediterranean and forcing new networks of trade to develop that oriented Europe decisively toward the Atlantic. Even though about 75 years of new historical research have undermined most if not all of his theories, his brilliance at historical synthesis and his talents as a speaker and writer are not in doubt.

He is most certainly a fascinating figure, the subject of one full-length, largely adulatory biography by the American medievalist Bryce Lyon (1974) and several assessments since then, some hostile. Keymeulen and Tollebeek have distilled the essence of these debates in a respectful but critical essay written for a large audience. Their great contribution lies in the rich visual documentation drawn from the Pirenne records at the *Université Libre de Bruxelles*. Conscious of Pirenne's significance as an academic and national icon, his family preserved even the most minute mementos of his life and career, from his wife's scribbled note to the maid, asking her to fetch Pirenne's umbrella upon his imminent deportation in 1916, to images of the *deuil national* proclaimed by the press upon his death in 1935. They document Pirenne's earliest reflections on his historical plans in 1882-88, when he

Although most of their book naturally deals with the war experience and the later years, Keymeulen and Tollebeek rightly call attention to Pirenne's meteoric rise earlier in his career. The "Pirenne phenomenon," as they call it, owes much to the 1880s-90s, when internal political tensions and the emerging Flemish movement weakened the young Belgian nation. This talented son of a liberal industrialist freemason and a pious Catholic mother seemed the right person to provide the nation with a common past in which trade and manufacturing brought people together, regardless of ideological or linguistic differences. It is a reminder that, although Pirenne's great fame came after the First World War, he really was a man of the nineteenth century, for whom Walloons and Flemings were destined to prosper united under the leadership of an enterprising bourgeoisie.

WALTER SIMONS

envisaged, curiously, a history of "the Low Countries" (les Pays Bas, translated here as "the Netherlands", p. 25) rather than of Belgium. They illustrate his influence abroad in unexpected ways, as in the wonderful photograph of Pirenne relaxing on a terrasse in Cairo in 1933, with his notes for a lecture on Europe and Islam jotted down on Continental Savoy hotel stationary. To retrieve the precise historical context of these images is no easy task and there are a few slips. A rather enigmatic cartoon in Le Clarion Hardy of January 1922, showing Pirenne "as a painter of Belgian history" with the "captured âme belge (Belgian soul)" in a cage, as the authors suggest (p. 70), must be an allusion to Armand du Plessy's 1921 film of the same title (L'Âme Belge), one of several patriotic silent movies circulating in those days. The devastated city printed on the menu for the Pirenne banquet organized by the Ligue National du Souvenir in 1921 does not depict "the burning [of] Ghent" (p. 69) but the "Fire of the Ypres Cloth Hall in 1914" by Alfred Bastien, part of his famous "Panoramic View of the Yser", completed in 1921 and exhibited in Ostend in the 1920s to cash in on the lucrative tourist trade in "Flanders Fields". Pirenne was indeed a "national treasure" comparable to the Ypres town hall.

Sarah Keymeulen and Jo Tollebeek, Henri Pirenne, Historian: A Life in Pictures, Lipsius, Louvain, 2011, 123 p., 108 colour and b/w illustrations (ISBN 978 90 5867 885 0).

Language

Principles for the Linguistic Future of Europe

Philippe Van Parijs on Justice, Fairness and Respect among Languages

Europe is a continent where more than 300 languages are in use. Its language situation is nothing if not complicated. The 23 national languages of the EU member states have been recognized as official languages of the Union. A further 40 are recognized by the Council of Europe under its *Charter for Regional Minority Languages*. Another 120 languages - ranging from Alderney French, Basque and Breton to Welsh, West Flemish, West Frisian, Yiddish, Yurt Tatar and Zenatiya - are listed in the *UNESCO Atlas of Endangered Languages* (2010) as 'endangered'. In recent decades large numbers of immigrant languages have arrived and established themselves: London alone has over 300 immigrant languages in its schools, and so has Barcelona; but these immigrant languages, which range from Arabic, Berber/Tamazight and Bengali/Sylheti through Chinese, Kurdish and Lingala to Turkish, have no status of any kind. And everywhere today, alongside all the languages mentioned, we find English as the global *lingua franca* and the ever more common vehicle for communication across language barriers.

The complexity becomes even greater when we note the many competing views in the European-wide debate on this issue – not just those of political economists (De Swaan, Grin), but also of writers and intellectuals (Amin Maalouf, Devoldere), human rights advocates and educationalists (Skuttnab-Kangas), UNESCO specialists in language endangerment (Harrison, Moseley), language policy analysts (Spolsky) and historians of the linguistic legacy of colonialism and imperialism (Calvet, Ostler).

And actually, when we ask how Europe handles all this diversity and multilingualism, the fact is that the EU constitution officially acknowledges only two basic principles: on the one hand it recognizes linguistic diversity as one of the cornerstones of European civilization, while on the other it bans language discrimination. That is to say, in actual practice linguistic policy-making often amounts to an agreement to disagree, or simply embodies the lowest common denominator across the European political spectrum – between, for example, on the one hand France's constitutional monopoly on the French language (a model also followed by Greece and by Belgium, where the use of the three national languages is linked to territories), and on the other the more pluralistic practice in countries like Spain, the Netherlands and Britain, where at least the traditional indigenous linguistic minorities have been granted some degree of language rights and protection.

Understandably, therefore, people often regard European multilingualism as an issue of power, of might is right. Not so Van Parijs. It is not that he denies these power-political realities or the existing inequalities in the field of languages. On the contrary, he is very well aware of them, and his starting point is actually the unjustness of it all. Global democracy, issues of social and economic justice, and the need for a basic income have long been central themes in his work as a philosopher at the Catholic University of Louvain (UCL in Louvain-la-Neuve), where he holds the Hoover chair of economic and social ethics, while at the same time he also has long-standing connections with Oxford and its Political Theory project. Consequently, it now comes naturally to him to address the inequalities that exist in the field of languages, and to ask: What can we do about this, from the perspective of a general theory of justice? And what should we do to reduce the injustices we encounter in this domain?

Here, right at the outset, one might object: but is this actually a feasible prospect? After all, in the real world in which we are living, the free play of market forces can only exacerbate existing inequalities between people, including inequalities of language. So what about justice, fairness and equality – how could these ever be applied to the domain of language?

Pieter Bruegel,
*The Construction of the Tower
of Babel*, 1563.
Oil on oak panel,
114 x 155 cm.
Detail. Kunsthistorisches Museum,
Vienna.

Again, Van Parijs begs to differ. Here we have a political philosopher who raises many important questions while he reflects on the principles of justice involved . For in all this linguistic diversity – with its attendant historical, social, cultural, psychological, collective, individual, economic and political ramifications – what rights do speakers actually have? What principles of justice, fairness, cooperation and respect apply here? What theory of justice can underpin those principles and how would this work out in actual practice?

There are many important issues that arise here. But three elements in particular mark out his position. The first of these is his conclusion – arrived at through a series of political-economic cost-benefit analyses of language-learning situations - that interventions will always be necessary in this domain, if our aim is to ensure some sort of fairness and a reduction of inequality and injustice between the languages involved.

Secondly, and again a very important achievement, there is the set of working principles he develops for the actual reduction of unfairness - principles of cooperation, fair distribution, parity of esteem, respect, democracy and territoriality. As he makes very clear, especially in chapter 5 on the territoriality principle, these principles are directly relevant to an understanding of the Belgian language question. And as a French-speaking Belgian with an excellent command of Dutch, Van Parijs certainly knows what he is talking about when he advocates the territorial principle ('in France one speaks French') as the most important and necessary safeguard a language can have: 'language survival requires a territorially differentiated coercive linguistic regime'. In Belgium people know this from history and experience; in the Netherlands English is already everywhere.

Thirdly, there is his advocacy – on grounds of democracy, access, fair distribution and egalitarianism – of an acceleration of the spread of English as *lingua franca* everywhere. Yet at the same time, as a corollary, he also proposes a language tax on all the world's Anglophones, to compensate speakers of other, less widely-used languages both when they are using those other languages and when they are learning English, for the unfair advantage and privileged position that mother-tongue speakers of this global lingua franca enjoy in the globalised world of today. This may be a thought experiment of a philosopher, and one may initially be inclined to dismiss it as unworldly – a bit like taxing the Italians for their overabundance of sunshine so as to compensate the Finns for their three months of polar darkness in winter – but on further examination Van Parijs actually makes a strong case, and one that will be very hard to refute. In that sense it could be said that Van Parijs is now doing for language rights what others over the past decades have been doing for animal rights.

There are many other thoughtful, well-developed and densely structured arguments in the two hundred pages of this book, supported by a further 60 pages of notes and a 15-page bibliography. Van Parijs's critical scrutiny of the principles and interests at stake here, his cogent reasoning, the high standards he sets and his forceful conclusions will make this book especially relevant to the future development of European language policy.

REINIER SALVERDA

Van Parijs, Philippe (2011). *Linguistic Justice, for Europe and for the World*. Oxford: Oxford University Press [Oxford Political Theory Series].

Further reading

Calvet, Louis-Jean (2011). *Il était une fois 7000 langues*. Paris: Fayard.

Denis, Jean-Pierre & Franck Nouchi (eds.) (2011). *L'Atlas des Minorités*. Paris. La Vie-Le Monde.

Devoldere, Luc (ed.) (2007). *Standing Tall in Babel. Languages in Europe*. Rekkem, Flanders: Stichting Ons Erfdeel.

Council of Europe, *European Charter for Regional Minority Languages*. At:

http://conventions.coe.int/treaty/en/Treaties/Html/148.htm

Harrison, K.D. (2008). *When Languages Die: the Extinction of the World's Languages and the Erosion of Human Knowledge*. Oxford: OUP.

Ostler, Nick (2010). *The Last Lingua Franca. English until the Return of Babel*. London: Allan Lane.

Moseley, Christopher (ed.) (2010). *UNESCO Atlas des langues en danger dans le monde*. Paris: UNESCO. See also: atlas@unesco.org.

Spolsky, Bernard (2009). Language Management. Cambridge: Cambridge University Press.

Literature

Sex, Death and Rock 'n' Roll in Peter Pontiac's Cartoons

When Peter Pontiac was ten years old, his aunt took him to a music shop to look for a guitar. At last it was all going to happen. But the shop-keeper gave him a disparaging look and told him to come back when his hands were bigger. He left the guitar shop disappointed. Before his hands were big enough, his aunt committed suicide. Pontiac became not a musician but a cartoon artist.

Peter Pontiac (Peter Pollmann, b. 1951 in the Netherlands) would still rather be a musician. He has been drawing now for more than forty years, but he would still like to strike a bargain with the devil and swap his pencil for a guitar. Speaking of the devil – he doesn't exist in 2012, but in Pontiac's Catholic childhood he was all over the place. Now the lord of darkness appears only in his comic strips, with a swishing tail and usually in the company of a group of pretty girls. It's a good thing the devil has disappeared because otherwise Holland would have had to do without one of its finest draughtsmen. Pontiac creates strip cartoons, graphic novels and illustrations for newspapers, books and record sleeves. He has added something to the Dutch comic strip that was not there before: a combination of authorship skills and artistry. For this he was awarded the Marten Toonder Prize in 2011, the most important Dutch prize for comic strips (worth 25,000 euro) and intended for strip cartoonists who have made a contribution to Dutch heritage with their work.

For Pontiac, who had never had any training, the deciding factor was the record sleeve Cheap Thrills, which the American strip cartoonist Robert Crumb drew in 1968 for Big Brother & the Holding Company (which Janis Joplin once sang with). "A sign, a revelation. That you could have something like that on a record sleeve!" It was a sleeve, but at the same time a strip cartoon. Every number was depicted visually. He wanted to do that too. He wanted to draw like Crumb,

as an underground artist. The underground was unashamedly autobiographical and critical of society. In his early years Pontiac focussed on the themes to which he is still faithful: sex, death and music. In his opinion art has little do with anything other than sex and death. And in his case there is music too, or rather rock'n' roll. Rebellious and mutinous music that really took hold of the general public in the sixties and is, of course, about sex and death. The Rolling Stones, Jimi Hendrix and later the Ramones: lots of lovely noise. Just as the rockers and punkers were doing their own thing without giving a damn about anybody else, that was how he wanted to draw. "If you're not living on the edge, you're taking too much space", says Pontiac.

He drew his own lonely path. And that provided him with a multitude of faithful fans and national and international admiration. The Marten Toonder Prize is not the first accolade for Pontiac. He exhibited in Amsterdam, Angoulême, Brussels, Barcelona, Beijing and Rio de Janeiro. In October 2011 the collection *1001 Comics You Must Read Before You Die* by Paul Gravett, was published (with a preface by Terry Gilliam). Pontiac is one of the seven Dutch cartoonists in it. Gravett recommends that everyone should be sure to read Kraut.

Kraut isn't a strip cartoon in the classical sense of the word, with text balloons, but it is certainly a graphic novel. It's designed in the same way as one of the very greatest of graphic novels, *A Contract With God*, by the American Will Eisner, who coined the term 'graphic novel'. The drawings are no longer constantly imprisoned in frames, as in the usual strips, but can also stand free of the text. In this way Eisner demonstrated that text is an extension of image, a narrative bridge. The lettering is an important medium for the artist to give a page atmosphere, depth and dynamic. Therefore it is important that the lettering is not computer-originated but that the text is written in the hand of the artist. Pontiac took this advice of Eisner's to heart. For *Kraut* he was even urged on by Eisner, who scribbled on

Peter Pontiac, *Iron Cross 2nd Class.*
Paternal Heroics, illustration for a
limited edition of *Kraut*, 2005.

a packet of cigarettes: "Please keep going. Do a graphic novel too... I need company it's too lonely out there." Pontiac had already carried the idea in his head for a long time. He speaks about it an interview in 1983. Even strip cartoons need time to incubate. *Kraut* did not appear until 2000.

Kraut is a letter to his father, a biographical work, as he himself says. It's a long letter because he has an awful lot of questions. To begin with: where is his father? He disappeared in 1978 in Daaibooi Beach, on Curaçao. Only the car he had hired was found, along with all his personal belongings. The key was still in the ignition. If he deliberately wanted to disappear why? Was it a staged vanishing trick? Had he become unwell while swimming? And there are other unanswered questions. His father was an SS Storm trooper in the Second World War. He worked as a War Reporter for the Waffen-SS. What did he find so attractive in national socialism? Why was he a fascist? In *Kraut* Pontiac provides himself and his readers with pictorial answers. In *Kraut*

we see the answers to the questions we read. We see his father walking into the sea, though whether that is exactly how it happened we don't know. There are witnesses who saw someone walking into the sea. But Pontiac is a master in the art of asking questions. Was it *his* father they saw, or was it a different middle-aged white man? Beneath a fragment from the police report ("It is not known whether Mr J.J.A. Pollmann could swim") we see the skeleton of Mr Pollmann stuck between the rocks. He still has his glasses on. Image and text vie with each other and that is what makes *Kraut* so exceptional. The tension between the questions and the answers, between text and image increases enormously. This design makes *Kraut* a masterpiece, a book that you must indeed read before you die, the best *graphic novel* in Dutch. Drawings and text complement each other and contradict each other at the same time. Pontiac tests the limits of his story and the story of his father as well as the limits of the comic strip medium.

Pontiac's style of writing and drawing is baroque. Almost every plate is a treasure chest which he fills with as much information as possible. "Nothing's lovelier than a drawing where there's a lot to see", he says. What distinguishes this book from most graphic novels is that the text is equally ambitious and baroque. Pontiac is not content just to write. His father is neither a drowned person nor a drunkard, but a victim of the sea 'a prey of Poseidon'. The book is mercilessly frank. Every aspect of his father's life is touched on. Pontiac quotes from his diaries and does not hide his affairs with other women. Pontiac waited for publication until after the death of his mother. "It also had something to do with her 'feeling for Germany'."

When Pontiac started to create comic strips in the late sixties they were open-hearted stories, but mainly about his own life, his addiction and his relationships. He observes and questions himself and the world at large. Why do we do what we do? The world could come to an end at any time. Pontiac doesn't see any horsemen of the Apocalypse, but tanks of destruction. "I am sailing on the Styx." His longer story *Requiem Fortissimo,* from 1985, is exquisite and taut but far from joyful. It is jet black romantic, which indicates a preference for the sublime wherein desire and suffering, pleasure and pain, blend into shivering enjoyment. It is pain of the world, pain about the world. Just like Nescio's *Young Titans,* Pontiac wants to do everything differently. He wants to use not only reason but also his feelings and imagination as the norm. To that principle he has remained true. He is lord of a rainy kingdom, where the sun shines now and then. "I'm pessimistic about the world, but not about life."

Peter Pontiac,
Self-portrait on the occasion of
the Marten Toonder Award, 2011.

GERT JAN POS
Translated by Sheila M. Dale

www.peterpontiac.nl

An Open Book in an Open Landscape
Dutch Writers in Beijing

From 31 August to 4 September 2011 the Chinese capital, Beijing, took on a somewhat orange hue. During that period the Netherlands was playing host to the eighteenth edition of the Beijing Book Fair, one of the largest and most rapidly expanding book fairs in the world. After such major powers as Germany, France, Russia and India, the Netherlands was the first 'smaller' country to be given the opportunity of presenting its writers and literature to the Chinese. The host country's stand covered an area of over 1,500m², and in its form and imagery it symbolised the theme 'Open Landscape - Open Book'. In this way, the intention was to draw people's attention to specific elements of the Dutch way of thinking: openness, transparency and a desire for practicability.

Just over twenty authors travelled to Beijing and sixteen publishers were present on the host country's stand. During the varied writers' programme, the Dutch authors were able to forge contacts with their Chinese colleagues, both at the fair and in the city. In beautifully presented exhibitions one could become acquainted with Vincent van Gogh's correspondence, with books with the finest of layouts, with illustrations for children's books and literary strip cartoons.

Immediately after the fair ended the Dutch Foundation for Literature, which was ultimately responsible for the host country's presentation, spoke of its having been a success. It pointed out that this eighteenth edition of the Beijing Book Fair had attracted more visitors than ever before (half a million). The attraction of the host country's stand was reportedly so great that the other stands had on average to make do with fewer visitors than previously. The press too showed a real interest - and that was absolutely not restricted to the Dutch media. The folder compiled by the Dutch Foundation for Literature with articles from the Chinese press is most impressive.

As a native of Flanders, the writer of this article has to regret that no writers from the Dutch-speaking part of Belgium were present in Beijing. The host stand had just only one small table on which lay books by Flemish writers - no more than that. During the host country's lengthy preparations for the fair, Flanders ought really to have been invited by the head of the Dutch Foundation for Literature to make an appropriate contribution to the stand. Apparently, in the end this was not possible. As a result, however, the Chinese were left with the mistaken impression that Dutch-language literature extends no further south than the border between the Netherlands and Belgium. In the past, such joint presentations had indeed been possible. For example, the Netherlands and Flanders were able to put on a joint exhibit at the *Frankfurter Buchmesse* in 1993. This experience had positive spin-off, since at other international book fairs the Netherlands and Flanders also combined to be 'the host country', as at Barcelona (1995), Göteborg (1997) and Paris (2003) – and each time the Dutch-language literature as a whole made a good impression.

A grouchy type might well ask himself if a book fair in Beijing, so far from home, could be of any possible use to Dutch literature. But that would be to ignore the vast market that can (admittedly theoretically) be tapped. Billions of potential readers at the other end of the Silk Road are maybe just waiting for the chance to get to know Dutch writers.

Criticism was much more vociferous regarding the political and general social context within which the Beijing book fair was organised. China is not exactly a country where intellectual broad-mindedness and the free expression of opinion are self-evident concepts. Furthermore, the Chinese authorities seemed to adopt an even tougher attitude than before in the months leading up to the fair. Fear that the Arab Spring might have an inspiriting effect on the Chinese intelligentsia could well have been a part of this. Many people also wondered if the Dutch literary world, which is often so concerned about freedom and democracy, would really find it easy to present itself in its Sunday best in the Chinese capital. The Dutch Foundation for Literature parried this criticism by pointing out that during the long preparations for hosting the fair a great many contacts had been established between Dutch and Chinese writers and publishers. This had given rise to an intellectual climate based on the mutual exchange of ideas. The fact that Chinese writers were able to share thoughts with their Dutch colleagues during the period of the fair was also extremely important and could well lead to lasting contacts. Actually, it is possible to draw a parallel with the Olympic Games held in Beijing in 2008, and the World Exposition organised in Shanghai in 2010. Very much the same discussion took place on both occasions. As to whether the Land of the Dragon has shown greater openness since these events - the answer to that depends on who you ask.

But let us return to the literature. Now that the spotlights and microphones have long since been switched off, it will be interesting to see if the Chinese publishers retain their interest in Dutch books. If they do, which genres will they prefer, and will they invest appropriately in promoting their translations from the Dutch? Will the contacts established before and during the fair result in long-lasting cooperation? In any case, if Dutch literature wishes to keep a foot in the door in China, some form of permanent follow-up is essential. In short, the work is only just beginning.

Hans Vanacker
Translated by John Irons

www.letterenfonds.nl/en/
www.bibf.net

Why Hella S. Haasse's Work Does Not Need Introduction Abroad

The sad news of the death of Hélène Serafia Haasse in September 2011 is – once more – an occasion to underline Haasse's literary significance, not only as a nationally and internationally recognised literary writer, but also as an author who has always embedded her work in a global context. This article aims to give a short overview of the reception of Haasse's work outside the Netherlands.

Most records of Hella S. Haasse's work emphasize her historical work, but Haasse wrote *across* genres: besides creatively "assembling" historical novels, she wrote experimental (auto)biographies, plays, essays, literary criticism, travel writing, contemporary novels and short stories. This is not an exhaustive list. Her work is diverse, it discusses a wide range of topics and is often hard to capture in traditional genre categories.

Haasse was a productive author who wrote throughout her life with a remarkable consistency: her oeuvre consists of around 30 titles that were published in the Netherlands with timely intervals of two to three years in between – from her literary debut, the short novel *Oeroeg* (1948, translated into English as *Forever a Stranger*), until her last novel *Sleuteloog* in 2002 *(The Eye of the Key)*. The latter mirrors and expands on *Oeroeg*'s theme in its description of an interracial friendship in the Dutch East Indies affected by colonial hierarchy. Born in 1918 in what is now Jakarta (then Batavia, capital of the former Dutch East Indies), Indonesia became a thread throughout Haasse's work. However, the author herself never referred to Indonesia as a "theme", for her the country simply meant "fertile soil for my imagination".

Ten years of Haasse's life were spent in France. Queen Beatrix of the Netherlands once described her as a writer with three countries of origin: the Netherlands, Indonesia and France. These three origins are thematically represented in Haasse's

Hella Haasse.
© David Samyn.

work: fictional returns to colonial and postcolo-
nial Indonesia, French settings, characters and
historical figures of several (double) nationalities. Yet the global background of Haasse also
shows in the acceptance of her work by readers
around the world. One of many examples is that
the Chilean government awarded her work the
Gabriela Mistral prize in 1996. Haasse's oeuvre is, indeed, widespread and widely read. The
translations database of the Dutch Foundation
for Literature mentions 136 translations of circa
28 individual titles into more than 20 languages,
not taking into account the numerous reprints of
her books abroad. As a result Vietnamese can
read *The Tea Lords* in their mother tongue (published in 2002), and there are two Haasse novels
in Welsh.

Haasse's popularity in France particularly
deserves mentioning. Compared to, for example, the small selection translated into Indonesian (four titles), the French embraced Haasse's
novels with 32 translations. The author received
several French honours and awards, of which
the title of *Officier de la Légion d'honneur* in 2000
is probably the most important. Where literary
critic Margot Dijkgraaf indicates that a more intellectual French reading climate is the reason
for this popularity, we might also consider factors such as Haasse's extended stay in France,
which enabled her to build strong relations with
publishers and two outstanding translators, An-
nie Kroon and Anne-Marie de Both-Diez.

At the start of Haasse's career, in 1954, *The
Scarlet City* was reviewed in the *Times Literary Supplement*. The critic Alfred Duggan also
mentions in passing the positive effect of an
"excellent translation". He further describes
the novel's main character, Giovanni Borgia, as
"cultivated and observant", and the storyline as
simply "moving". By framing Haasse's novel with
three Anglo-Saxon historical novels and without
explicitly introducing the young author, this early

reviewer elegantly accepted Haasse as an actor to watch on the global literary stage. Haasse's broad cultural interests, her insightful yet subtle psychological and political awareness travelled easily from the very start.

Haasse's poetical essay titled 'Parang Sa-wat' – meaning "elaborate, stylised pattern on a traditional Indonesian *batik* fabric" – starts with: "Sometimes I wander in thoughts through all the houses, the gardens, I have lived in on Java. I relive situations and events; I re-imagine landscapes." I believe that it is mostly Haasse's capacity to transgress temporal and national boundaries in her imagination that explains why her novels have always found international readership, without need for introduction. Maybe now is the time to open up the online Hella S. Haasse museum to the international reader? Not as a necessary introduction, but as an optional afterword to an impressive universal and diverse oeuvre.

STEFANIE VAN GEMERT

See also: JANE FENOULHET, "Hella S. Haasse and the Historical Novel or: The Triumph of Fact over Fiction", *The Low Countries* no 4 (1996), pp. 110-120.

www.hellahaasse.nl
www.hellahaassemuseum.nl

Hella Haasse in English

- *The Black Lake* (Original title: *Oeroeg*), translation by Ina Rilke, Portobello Books, in preparation since 2010.
- *The Tea Lords* (Original title: *Heren van de thee*), translated from the Dutch by Ina Rilke, Portobello Books, 2011.
- *In a Dark Wood Wandering* (Original title: *Het woud der verwachting*), translated by Lewis C. Kaplan, Academy Chicago Publishers, 1997.
- *The Scarlet City* (Original title: *De scharlaken stad*), translated by Anita Miller, Academy Chicago Publishers, 1997 / Allison & Busby, London, 1997. First published by McGraw Hill Publishing Company Limited, 1954.
- *Threshold of Fire* (Original title: *Een nieuwer testament*), translated by Nini Blinstrub - Anita Miller, Academy Chicago Publishers, 1996 / Allison & Busby, London, 1997.
- *Forever a Stranger and Other Stories* (Original title: *Oeroeg*), translated by Margaret M. Alibasah, Oxford University Press, 1996. (Contains stories by other authors too).

Imagination Takes You Everywhere
dEUS and the Rest of the World

September 2011, the Antwerp rock group dEUS brings out its sixth CD, *Keep You Close*. As with the band's previous releases, that's a major event for the Flemish press. That month newspapers and weeklies publish full-page – positive – reviews and interviews with front man Tom Barman that fill several pages, you can hear talks with him on various radio stations, you can read profiles about him and the other members of the group, and background stories about the history of dEUS... Under the motto 'What's left to do?' one magazine even makes a strip cartoon about dEUS. In the slipstream of the enormous press interest there also appears a series of columns that have that very media exposure as their subject. Worth noting: this time Holland joins, for one day Tom Barman is the editor of de Volkskrant's cultural section.

An exaggeration? Maybe a slight one, but, after the rather distant and unbalanced *Vantage Point* (2008), *Keep You Close* is another exceptionally good dEUS album – the comeback that fans had hoped for. In addition, Barman again shows himself to be the interviewee of everyone's dreams – a rarity among pop musicians. In his enthusiasm he regularly makes frank, pithy and well structured statements about himself and the world around him, like: "People in permanent relationships don't like sex". Moreover, the background of the other group members is more relevant now than ever before. Unlike the previous CDs, *Keep You Close* is a collective achievement in which Tom Barman played the part of director rather than commander.

But most likely the chief explanation for the benevolence of the journalists is the credit dEUS has been living off ever since its debut with *Worst Case Scenario* (1994). With that disc the group smoothed the path for more or less all the Flemish rock and pop bands that came after it. Suddenly it seemed possible to make exciting and fresh music in little Flanders, and to be suc-

cessful with it. dEUS inspired groups all over Europe to have a shot at fame in the predominantly English-speaking pop world. In Belgium the band was not only at the origin of a generation of musicians that can live from its music (Daan, Hooverphonic etc.), but since the middle of the nineties the flow of new, extremely talented and successful groups has been almost incessant. In short, thanks to dEUS Belgian pop has come of age. And that despite the fact that the group itself has had anything but a steady course since its debut.

The eventful history of dEUS – in 2012 the group will be twenty years old – means it also provides material for a great many fascinating stories. During this period the group got off to a lightning start, but then important opportunities were missed; important group members left and others came along in their place; the group was once almost at its last gasp and then they achieved artistic triumphs again. *"And I was a rollercoaster of the kind / That needs to ride so high / to dive so low"*, sings Barman in the title number from *Keep You Close*. It's about a failed relationship, but could equally well be about the career of his group.

Reading the above, you might think that dEUS and front man Tom Barman have got it all nicely under control, recognized for their past achievements, praised for their new disc. Certainly if you also know that *Keep You Close* rapidly became a best seller in Belgium, that the dEUS concerts in the country's largest halls were sold out in 2011 and that in 2012 the group will be at the internationally renowned Belgian rock festival Rock Werchter. Moreover the group is also playing in Holland, France and Southern and Eastern Europe in 2012, always to a full house.

And yet something still niggles. Barman wants more, recognition and success in Great Britain and even more in the United States, the Valhalla of pop music. Granted, dEUS has already played there and even made an impression, certainly in the United Kingdom. Gary Lightbody and Guy Garvey, the front men for the great British pop

dEUS with (left to right) Stephane Misseghers, Klaas Janzoons, Mauro Pawlowski, Tom Barman and Alan Gevaert © PIAS.

groups Snow Patrol and Elbow, take their hats off to Barman and his band. But this isn't enough to satisfy the restless and ambitious front man. A breakthrough in America remains an issue for him. He even wrote a song on the CD *Vantage Point* about his wrestling with this, 'Popular Culture': *"Cause now you know it's not great / if you don't come from the States / you will always be late to be in popular culture."*

The recent media storm over the new dEUS record leaves a murky picture behind on this subject. On the one hand the group members swear in interviews that they have given America up and that extensive touring in foreign parts isn't a foregone conclusion with the young fathers in the group. On the other hand you read in reviews that *Keep You Close* is being promoted internationally and that it will even be the make or break CD for the group abroad. And isn't the American, Greg Dulli, from the Afghan Whigs and the Twilight Singers, singing with them on *Keep You Close* to attract the attention of the music press

in the USA? And especially, doesn't Tom Barman continually keep the door ajar in interviews when he talks about going international, knowing full well that it will make the group uneasy again while at the moment it's more stable than ever before? "If something nice comes up, then we must go, and that'll mean we have to discuss it and then there may be fireworks, yeah", was to be heard recently in a newspaper.

What the future has in store for dEUS seems to depend above all on the opportunities the group gets to play abroad. We shall just have to wait and see what choices dEUS makes. In any case it's clear for Barman. *"Imagination if you dare / can take you almost anywhere"*, as he sings in 'Dark Sets In'.

PIETER COUPÉ
Translated by Sheila M. Dale

www.deus.com

Science

Douwe Draaisma and the Mysteries of Autobiographical Memory

In the opening lines of the blurb on the back cover of his first book *De geest in getal (Mind in Numbers, 1988)* Douwe Draaisma (1953) listed the questions with which the founders of psychology wrestled. "Why does time seem to speed up as we get older? What causes déjà vu experiences? Can you think without images? How do the memories of mathematical prodigies function?" It is fascinating to revisit that list, since they are precisely the problems into which the Groningen professor in the history of psychology has sunk his teeth in the past quarter of a century. In his discerning, sometimes slightly melancholy publications, he explores the mysteries of autobiographical memory, always returning to the original questions that the founding fathers asked themselves back in the nineteenth century.

A fundamental notion in Draaisma's historical approach to psychology is that scientific views are always embedded in a time, a culture and a mentality. In his doctoral thesis *De metaforenmachine. Een geschiedenis van het geheugen (Metaphors of Memory. A History of Ideas about the Mind, 1995)* he shows how our thinking about memory is influenced by the metaphors in which we try to capture it. Those metaphors in turn are a reflection of the spirit of the age and the available technology – from wax tablet to computer. "The history of memory is slightly reminiscent of a tour through the storage areas of a museum of technology", he notes tellingly.

In *Ontregelde geesten (Disturbances of the Mind, 2006)*, too, he demonstrates convincingly how ideas about mental illnesses are leavened by zeitgeist and ideology. At present it is fashionable to see mental afflictions as neurological diseases and to assign psychological and environmental factors a minimal role. But whereas people like the neurologist Dick Swaab act as if we have already precisely located the causes of conditions such as schizophrenia and autism, Draaisma stresses the imperfect and provisional nature of our knowledge and refutes claims that we know the causes of mental illnesses and can locate them in the brain.

One unceasing fascination for this psychologist and philosopher is the vulnerability of memory and the ubiquity of forgetting. The full story of the beginning of our lives has been wiped at the outset from our autobiographical memory. The opening chapter of his best-known book *Waarom het leven sneller gaat als je ouder wordt (Why Life Speeds Up As You Get Older, 2001)* has the title: 'Flashes in the dark: first memories'. Almost ten years later *Vergeetboek (Oblivion, 2010)* contains an essay on the same theme entitled 'Surrounded by a sea of oblivion: the first memory'. Is Draaisma himself perhaps forgetting what he has written? Are these exercises in

Douwe Draaisma.

repetition? Of course, some insights remain valid. In both books he shows that our first memories are almost always described as visual representations. The statements about why forgetting dominates our first years of life also run parallel. It has something to do with language: being able to talk about what you experience has a repetitive effect and increases the chances of your remembering it. And something to do with self-awareness. "As long as there is no 'I' or 'self' experiences cannot be stored as personal memories," explains Draaisma in *Why Life Speeds Up As You Get Older.* "What we call 'forgetting' is the loss of memories unclaimed by anyone," he adds in *Oblivion.* Fortunately, however, this is not just a case of old wine in new bottles, illustrated with different examples. Recent psychological research has deepened his understanding. American researchers gave children a "Magic Shrinking Machine" to play with. If you put toys in it and turned the handle, it produced cheerful sounds and a miniature version of the same toys came out. The researchers visited the toddlers at intervals to hear what they remembered about it, but especially to hear the kind of language they used. They discovered that the children never used words that they did not know at the time of the experiment, but had since learned. That brings Draaisma the following elegant explanation for the scale of forgetting: "In growing up child brains obviously don't bother to give old memories a new code and thus to keep them accessible. As obsolete files they disappear from sight and eventually can no longer be consulted."

In his search for explanations for phenomena that intrigue him, Draaisma does not limit himself to contemporary psychological research. He combs all conceivable forms of knowledge, from literature to philosophy and from psychology to neurology. He confronts the insights of many disciplines and areas of thought with each other. Often the various theories clash and he has to give the verdict 'not proven'. But sometimes insights from different disciplines embrace and the miracle of cross-fertilisation takes place. Draaisma

rebels against the present imperialism of neurology. His scientific ideal is not the world hegemony of one's own favourite scientific field, but the open and non-power based dialogue between the United Nations of Science.

Tomas Vanheste
Translated by Paul Vincent

www.douwedraaisma.nl

Books by Douwe Draaisma available in English translation:

- The Nostalgia Factory (Original title: De heimweefabriek), Yale University Press, in preparation since 2011.
- Disturbances of the mind (Original title: Ontregelde geesten), translated by Barbara Fasting, Cambridge University Press, 2009.
- Why Life Speeds Up As You Get Older (Original title: Waarom het leven sneller gaat als je ouder wordt), translated by Erica Pomerans - Arnold J. Pomerans, Cambridge University Press, 2006.
- Metaphors of memory (Original title: De metaforenmachine. Een geschiedenis van het geheugen), translated by Paul Vincent, Cambridge University Press, 2000.

Politics

The Netherlands Turns Eurosceptic

After the Second World War, Belgium and the Netherlands stood together at the cradle of European integration. For both countries it was important not only that lasting peace should come to Europe but also that there should be intense economic cooperation. As exporting economies they were extremely interested in the development of an internal market. For many decades, Belgium and the Netherlands also worked together in their attempts to strengthen Europe. In addition, robust European institutions were needed if the major member countries were to be prevented from becoming too dominant. Naturally, there were a number of differences of opinion between Belgium and the Netherlands. The Dutch, for example, have always strongly emphasised Atlantic solidarity, while Belgium, following France's example, has begun to adopt a more critical attitude over the years - including towards NATO. Essentially, however, there was a strong pro-European attitude in Belgium and the Netherlands.

In the Belgian European doctrine, the construction of a powerful supranational Europe is as central a feature as ever. To talk about a federal Europe is not even a taboo in Belgium. In the Netherlands, however, the debate on Europe has taken a very different course in recent years. In an increasing number of spheres Dutch politicians as well as public opinion have adopted a more Eurosceptic stance.

In the course of the 1990s, it became clear that the European Union was acquiring quite a concrete influence on people's lives. Numerous regulations were European in origin. Europe came closer, and seemed to be eroding the power of the separate member countries. In Belgium, where a process of state reform has been taking place for decades and the federal state is dissolving anyhow, that is apparently viewed as less problematic. In the Netherlands, the steadily increasing impact of Europe led to incomprehension and evidently to a basic distrust as well.

In an increasing number of specific dossiers, the Netherlands started to question things. In negotiations on the long-term budget, the Netherlands argued the case for a cutback on European expenditure. The European agricultural policy was questioned, as was solidarity with disadvantaged regions. Belgian attempts to further develop Europe, within the field of defence for instance, could no longer count on Dutch support. That became obvious, for example, when during the Iraq crisis an initiative was taken to expand the European headquarters. The Netherlands followed Great Britain's line on the issue completely, rejecting all proposals for a stronger European defence. Populist politicians, such as Pim Fortuyn, adopted a steadily more hostile tone when talking about Europe.

A crucial watershed was the referendum on the European Constitution that took place in June 2005. The Dutch population was for the first time able to express its opinion on the direction of European integration. A good 60% rejected this Constitution. At that moment, it became clear that the permissive consensus on Europe had completely crumbled. The politicians' reticence had a basis amongst the population, which had become far more critical towards the European Union. The result was that political parties started to steer an even more Eurosceptic course. Populist parties in particular, such as Geert Wilders' Party for Freedom (PVV), started a veritable crusade against European involvement and the entire European apparatus, one in which the added value of European attitudes was simply questioned. The more firmly established parties rarely expressed contrary views - and actually took over some of the sceptical discourse.

And the Netherlands is becoming increasingly less hesitant about being the sole member country to be contrary if necessary. The entry of Bulgaria and Romania to the Schengen zone is - at the end of 2011 - only being blocked by the Netherlands. And it was also the Netherlands which, as the sole country, spoke in favour of delaying the approach to Serbia until the latter clearly indicated that it was willing to cooperate more intensively with the International Criminal Tribunal for the former Yugoslavia in The Hague.

During the Euro crisis, the Netherlands ranged alongside the countries that wished to keep solidarity with the peripheral countries to an absolute minimum. Proposals to introduce Eurobonds, for example, could count on little sympathy from the Netherlands. More discussions will have to take place in the months ahead on saving the European economy, with concerted measures presumably being decided on. It must be expected that these debates will be followed with keen interest in the Netherlands. Also when it comes to the discussion on the following European long-term budget (2014–2021), the Netherlands will adopt clear standpoints that differ to a significant extent from the pro-European course that Belgium will advocate. Possibly the Netherlands will once more be in favour of a smaller European budget and call on the Union to concentrate on a few core issues, such as the expansion of the internal market. A more ambitious European course is probably not to be expected from the Netherlands in the near future.

Hendrik Vos
Translated by John Irons

The Belgian prime minister Elio Di Rupo.

A New Federal Government for Belgium after 541 Days

King Albert of Belgium was clearly enjoying it very much. On the 6th of December 2011 he finally gave a reception for his country's new government at Laken Castle, following 541 days of political negotiations and one deep crisis after another. Smiling and joking, he worked his way along the line of ministers and secretaries of state with raised hands who were swearing allegiance to himself, to the constitution and to the laws of the Belgian nation.

But if anyone still thought that at the end of the interminable process of forming a government nothing had changed in the country of King Albert, that view was no longer valid after the 6th of December. For who among those present took the oath, with self-assurance, in their own language alone? Almost all the Dutch-speaking

ministers and secretaries of state. And who did it all in both French and Dutch? The French-speakers, who, according to many Flemings, prefer to speak only their own language, and expect everyone else to adapt to this.

As a spectator you couldn't help thinking that the French-speaking members of government had been given a serious talking-to by the prime minister, the French-speaking socialist Elio Di Rupo. Di Rupo, whose Dutch is not very good either, was very aware how threatening the political crisis had become for the unity of the country. The differences of opinion between the Dutch-speaking north and the French-speaking south of the country seemed to be making Belgium ungovernable. The fact that it had now, nonetheless, been possible to form a government didn't mean that the danger had disappeared just like that. The new government had a majority in the Belgian Parliament, but not in Flanders.

And according to opinion polls, Belgium's largest party, the Flemish nationalist N-VA, who want independence for Flanders, had gained strength.

For more than a year the French-speaking politicians had been saying that the N-VA, who had won the elections in 2010, *must* be in the new government. The Flemish Christian-Democrats (CD&V) were also increasingly saying the same: without the N-VA leader, Bart De Wever, they would not participate. And De Wever himself was saying that he would very much like to see his party in the government. Not everyone believed that, but, according to the Flemish Socialist Johan Vande Lanotte, one of the 'royal intermediaries' in the formation of the government, he had very serious negotiations with De Wever.

It may never be completely clear why nothing came of all this. Who precisely didn't want to co-operate with whom? The N-VA says that they 'were forced out'. The other parties say the N-VA gave up. The breaking point was a memorandum in the summer from Di Rupo, the person charged with forming a government at the time. The N-VA rejected it, the others broke off negotiations.

There was relief among the French-speaking media: without the N-VA success was in sight at last. But De Wever's Flemish Nationalists were fierce fighters. In the discussions about a reformed state the Flemish Christian Democrats, in particular, felt threatened by them – if we're into 'Flemishness', N-VA is their chief rival. During the negotiations over a social and economic policy it was the Flemish Liberals (Open Vld) in the main who found them a nuisance: the N-VA is not only Flemish nationalist but also right-conservative.

But there was no way back – either by means of a new attempt at negotiation or fresh elections. Because that could only make the N-VA really important and powerful. In September there was an agreement over a new way of organizing the state of Belgium, with more powers for Flanders, Wallonia and Brussels, and a settlement was also reached on the fiercely disputed electoral district of Brussels-Halle-Vilvoorde, a symbol for decades of the tensions between Francophones and Flemings.

It was still months before the parties were also agreed on a social and economic policy, which needed to find savings of more than eleven billion euros. The Flemish Liberals and the French-speaking Socialists were diametrically opposed to each other. According to the Flemings, the Francophones were interested mainly in protecting their own unemployed and making no changes; according to the Francophones, the Flemings were only standing up for their own businesses.

Nonetheless an agreement was reached, under great pressure from the European Commission, which threatened to impose sanctions unless a budget was decided quickly, and from the financial markets – interest rates for loans to Belgium reached a record high. Di Rupo now heads a government with six parties: the Social-Democrats, Liberals and Christian Democrats from Flanders and those from French-speaking Belgium.

But he is not automatically the big winner and Bart De Wever the loser. From disclosures from after the formation of the government it appeared that Di Rupo, just like many other French-speaking politicians, is now taking serious account of the fact that Belgium may fall apart one day. They seem to have said that 'Plan B' is coming into operation. But Wallonia needs time to strengthen its position economically – the Francophones still can't do without the money from Flanders. The Francophone politicians must also have made clear to Di Rupo that they should grant their Flemish colleagues a lot of successes, otherwise at the next elections they'll stand no chance at all against the N-VA. And if that happens will it ever be possible to form a government again?

Petra de Koning
Translated by Sheila M. Dale

Land, Wind and Water
Eighty Years of the IJsselmeer Dam

This is a causeway that is visible from kilometres away. It shows up as just a strip on satellite photos. In reality this strip is more than thirty kilometres long and ninety metres wide. It is the *IJsselmeer Dam* between the *Waddenzee* and the *IJsselmeer*, the dam that separates the salt water from the fresh water. The road that connects the northern provinces of North Holland and Friesland. There is a pedestrian bridge over the road, so that people can cross from the *IJsselmeer* to the *Waddenzee*. Below, cars can now drive at a maximum of 130 kilometres per hour. The road along the *IJsselmeer Dam* was one of the first to have its speed limit raised by the cabinet under Mark Rutte, the Dutch Prime Minister, apparently so that the 32-kilometre stretch could be covered as quickly as possible. It's a dyke that is actually a dam. In fact a dyke is supposed to protect the land from the sea. But there is water on both sides, so it is more appropriate to call it the *IJsselmeer Dam*.

Plans to build the dam were already in existence at the end of the nineteenth century. At that time the *IJsselmeer* was called the *Zuiderzee* and it was often rough, so the dam was intended to offer greater safety. In 1916 there were serious floods, again caused by a storm. The idea was to prevent the same thing happening in the future. The Netherlands was also in urgent need of agricultural land, which could be acquired by impoldering part of the *Zuiderzee*. The engineer Cornelis Lely devised the plan. In 1927 work began on impoldering and then on building the dam. On 28 May 1932 the last gap was sealed up and the *Zuiderzee* was closed off from the *Waddenzee*. The *IJsselmeer Dam* was ready for use, and the *IJsselmeer* was born.

Impoldering continued. The Urk fishing area was first to be drained. This gave rise to the

North-East Polder, which was followed by East and South Flevoland. Plans to build more polders were put on hold. The town of Lelystad was named after the man who conceived the plan, and hundreds of thousands of people now live on this polder land, where the old and savage sea once raged.

The *Zuiderzee* has been tamed and agricultural land has appeared in its place. But after eighty years the *IJsselmeer Dam* is in need of repair. Studies show that the dam no longer conforms to the required safety standards. Officially it should be able to withstand storms that only occur on average once every ten thousand years. The changing climate means that because of rising sea levels this will no longer be the case. On the *Waddenzee* side, the water level is continually rising, which is why more and more water is flowing into the *IJsselmeer*. However, safety is not so serious a problem that millions need to be invested in the dam right away.

In the summer of 2011 a commission presented four different plans for making the *IJsselmeer Dam* safer. The government is now looking to see which is the most realistic. There is a fair chance that the dam will be raised using asphalt, and grass will be able to grow on top of it. The advantage of this new construction is that it can be implemented in two phases. If it appears to be safe enough after the first phase, the second phase can be cancelled. Security is precious in the Netherlands, but so apparently is finance.

The *IJsselmeer Dam* is clearly visible from the air, but is fairly discrete from the ground. Somehow it never really became a great tourist attraction. The Delta Works in Zeeland, built after the floods of 1953, attract hundreds of thousands of visitors every year. There is even a dedicated museum there called *Deltapark Neeltje Jans*, while at the *IJsselmeer Dam* there is only a look-out post and a small restaurant. But there are plans afoot to make the place more interesting for tourists. When the time comes to invest millions in making sure the dam complies with the required safety standards, it will also be time to look at how that money can be clawed back. The Dutch state is willing to contribute 600 million euro to the renovation of the *IJsselmeer Dam*, but the total costs are likely to exceed that by 300 to 400 million euro.

The dam also continues to have extraordinary potential for power generation. There is fresh water on one side and salt water on the other. Energy can be generated from the transition from salt to fresh water. Discussions have been going on for years about this and there are concrete plans, but the power plant has still not been built. There have also been years of discussion about constructing a gigantic wind farm on the *IJsselmeer Dam*. Because it's extremely windy there.

JORIS VAN DE KERKHOF
Translated by Gregory Ball

Animals More True to Life than Humans
Marten Toonder

2 May 2012 will see the centenary of Marten Toonder, the greatest of Dutch cartoonists, whose literary approach places him more fittingly alongside masters such as Jean de La Fontaine or Lewis Carroll than the strip cartoonist Walt Disney, but who nonetheless owed a lot to the latter indirectly.

It all started early. Toonder's father, who was also called Marten, was captain of the SS Alcyone and decided that his son really deserved an outing as a reward for passing his secondary school leaving examination in 1931. Why don't you come with me to South America, he asked, and Marten was over the moon at the idea.

In Montevideo he met Jim Davis, an American cartoonist who had been involved in working on *Felix the Cat* and who introduced him, in turn, to the Argentinian Dante Quinterno, a man with his own studio and a pupil of Walt Disney. "Drawing strips is a vocation", Quinterno confided to Toonder, "and you don't know if that is what you're cut out for until you've tried it." Father Toonder, who had introduced his son at the age

of five already to American cartoons featuring Mutt and Jeff and Barney Google in the newspapers he brought home from his travels, immediately had faith in his son and gave him a year to discover his talents.

After an unsuccessful passage through the art school in Rotterdam, where he became so disillusioned in three months that he gave up, Marten Toonder had no trouble in getting his first strips published, both in book and newspaper form. Two years later he began work as a draughtsman for existing cartoon series, while in his spare time also developing his own characters, such as Don Sombrero, who was successful in Argentina and Czechoslovakia at the end of the thirties, and Tom Puss, an adorable little white cat that was rejected by the Dutch public as too childish.

Nonetheless this clever cat made a comeback, and in 1941 at that, when the German occupation obliged the popular newspaper *De Telegraaf* to scrap Disney's Mickey Mouse. With his *Adventures of Tom Puss*, Marten Toonder provided a worthy alternative and his career took off. Tom Puss, who meanwhile had gained the company of the bear Sir Oliver B. Bumble at his side, became so popular that all kinds of spin-off products, such as calendars and jigsaws, came onto the market and Toonder had to take on a couple of assistants.

Eventually the German occupation confronted Toonder, like everyone else, with the choice between collaboration and resistance, and being both a convinced liberal and artistic individualist he opted resolutely for resistance. By mid-1943 more than a hundred people were employed by Toonder Studios, many of them in hiding and engaged in producing false papers. When the editorship-in-chief of *De Telegraaf* was taken over by the SS at the end of that year Toonder stopped his Tom Puss strip and had himself certified as manic-depressive, after which he began to draw secretly for the underground newssheet *Metro*.

Toonder did not really make a proper breakthrough until after the war. Sir Ollie and Tom

Puss were published in 22 languages and the work - and cartoon series - increased rapidly, to the point where in 1965 Toonder realised that he had become a business director and was no longer a cartoon artist. At that point he left the Netherlands and went to live in Greystones, in County Wicklow in Ireland, and devoted himself completely to his two most famous creatures, who seemed to live in a parallel, but also clearly recognisable, universe in *Rommeldam* (Rumbeldon).

After 47 years, 177 stories, 12,000 instalments, 35,000 pictures and 13 million words Marten Toonder drew a line under the adventures of Sir Ollie and Tom Puss on 20 January 1986. Toonder was then 73 and he lived for a further twenty years, just sufficient time to complete his three volume autobiography.

What made Toonder's work so unique, and particularly the adventures of *Bommel and co*, is that it not only provided a gentle criticism of society, based as much on popular phenomena such as astrology and fashion as on the cold war and the threat of the atomic bomb, but that in so doing he created animals so like people that, as with Jean de La Fontaine, they were even more true to life than human characters could ever have been. Moreover, Toonder also used highly original language that reminds us of the best work of Lewis Carroll.

MARNIX VERPLANCKE
Translated by Sheila M. Dale

Artistic Experience Knows No Bounds
Visual Arts Flanders 2012

In 2012, the year of the British cultural event Festiva - Finale of the Cultural Olympiad", on the occasion of the Olympic Games in London, and the year of dOKUMENTA 13 in the German town of Kassel, five interesting exhibitions are also being organized in Belgium. The people involved have joined forces for the publicity in Visual Arts Flanders 2012, a joint project with the Flemish Institute for Visual, Audiovisual and Media Art, the Arts and Heritage branch of the Flemish government and the participating institutions and organizations. It is the first time that a cluster of people like this has been formed in Flanders "to co-operate in strengthening their cultural impact abroad". At the invitation of Tate Modern, they put forward their plans in London at the end of 2010 and had a public discussion about a co-operative venture of this kind that would cross traditional boundaries and also have international implications.

In Flanders there are five sensational events to be seen, spread across all the provinces. At various locations along the Belgian coast, during the fourth edition of *Beaufort* (from 31 March to 9 September), there are exhibitions of works of contemporary artists from every member state of the European Union. In Ghent the tradition of the sensational exhibitions *Chambres d'Amis* (1986) and *Over the Edges* (2000) continues with *Track* (12 May to 16 September), in which more than thirty international artists are developing projects reflecting the social, cultural and economic context of the six districts of the inner city of Ghent. For its ninth edition *Manifesta* (2 June to 30 September), the European Biennale of Modern Art, is descending on a former mine site in Genk (in Belgian Limburg), with work from up-and-coming international artists. *Newtopia: the State of Human Rights* (1 September to 10 December), with works by fifty artists in various historical locations in Mechelen, is the first large in-

Jan Fabre, *Searching for Utopia*, first edition of Beaufort, 2003, Nieuwpoort.

ternational exhibition to look at the relationship between art and human rights. This year, too, the Middelheim sculpture park in Antwerp is undergoing a thorough metamorphosis with the opening of a half-open pavilion by the architect Paul Robbrecht, with an exhibition of Thomas Schütte and monumental creations by Ai Weiwei, among others, (from 26 May).

It is striking how in almost all the initiatives a lot of attention is paid to public space. In Mechelen it is about a sort of forum for human rights, in the former mining town of Genk about "the repositioning of a post-industrial community", along the North Sea about "the incorporation of art in the unique biotope of the dynamic coastal towns", in Antwerp about the art of sculpture in public spaces - including the city centre - and in Ghent about "the urban fabric and claiming a permanent place for modern art in the various districts of the inner city".

The first sentence of the *Track Manifesto*, which has been circulated in ten languages throughout the city by the Ghent Municipal Museum of Contemporary Art, emphasizes that a city has no boundaries. Director Philippe Van Cauteren and co-compiler Mirjam Varadinis say that the mu-

seum is aiming at interaction between the city and its inhabitants. For *Track* an imaginary line, a path for visitors, has been drawn between the two main railway stations in Ghent, a trajectory in a diagonal across the city centre, through six districts, six different realities and histories. The participating artists (who include the Dutchman Erik van Lieshout, the Fleming Michaël Borremans, Teresa Margolles from Mexico, the Swiss duo Fischli & Weiss, the Danish-Norwegian duo Elmgreen & Dragset and Ahmet Ögüt from Turkey) are interested in such variations, in the social context and in utopia. They are searching for the multi-faceted identity of a place and expose unexpected, surprising, forgotten and fresh approaches to, insights into and perspectives on art and the times in which we live.

The curator of *Manifesta* and *Newtopia*, the Greek Katerina Gregos, deals in a similar way with the history of a mining region or Belgium's wartime past, with genocide and human rights, and with the steadfast belief in Utopia. The work of the participating artists is embedded in society. Indeed, *Manifesta* is always closely connected to the political and social history of the region where the biennale takes place.

Paul Robbrecht, mentioned above, and Phillip Van Den Bossche, curator of Beaufort 2012, reflect on how images, installations and monumental works are given a place in public space, both in parks and along the Belgian coast. How these images are positioned and exhibited is also a history of how exhibitions are organized. It leaves a clear trail.

At the end of the day the people behind the five events want to leave such a trail behind, works of art as beacons, witnesses, monuments and inspirational resting places. After four editions of *Beaufort* a vast and lasting sculpture park is gradually being established; following city exhibitions such as *Chambres d'Amis*, *Over the Edge*s and now *Track*, the artistic intervention and the works of art themselves are forming "memory trails" in the image of the city. Track, as is stated in the exhibition manifesto, agitates, plays, reads, listens, looks, sees and provides an experience of art that is without boundaries.

PAUL DEPONDT
Translated by Sheila M. Dale

www.visualartsflanders2012.be

The Story of *De Stijl*.
From Mondrian to Van Doesburg

Two artists and an artistic movement belong to the canon of Dutch history: Rembrandt, Van Gogh and De Stijl. In order to raise the profile of De Stijl as a journal, an artistic movement and an idea in modern Dutch museums, the Gemeentemuseum Den Haag has decided to dedicate a wing of the museum to Mondrian and De Stijl in an exhibition lasting until 1 January 2014. The image that the museum is seeking to create of this group with the exhibition and the accompanying publication is one that is lively, joyful and free: "Although art historians, particularly in the 20th century, have described De Stijl above all as a coolly rational, structured, almost cold style, the intention of the De Stijl artists themselves was to make a work of art that was both dynamic and at the same time lively, free and joyful, just like the future itself. It is no coincidence that they were also involved with dance halls, advertising and fashion." The exhibition includes models, plans, paintings, sculptures, furniture, printed work, typography and fashion and presents them as an eclectic mix, with no hierarchy. The multitude of objects is not brought together to form a clear overall picture, but demands attention for the progressive, multidisciplinary character. Another aim of the exhibition is to reinforce a dynamic image of De Stijl. Starting from Mondrian's 1927 article on neo-plasticism 'in the home, on the streets and in the city' ('Neo-plasticisme: De Woning – De Straat – De Stad'), the exhibition builds on the theme of home/street/city: the presentation is staged "from the inside to the outside, from the small to the large". For the staging of the works, this implies among other things the inclusion of models of Mondrian's studio (which show an evolution from a traditional layout in 1909 to the experimental studio in New York in 1943). The artist Krijn de Koning and the architect Anne Holtrop have created an installation specially for the exhibition *(163 spaces for a work / 163 ruimten voor een werk)*, inspired by

Exhibition view of *Mondrian & De Stijl* © Gerrit Schreurs.

Mondrian's 1927 article Their design simultaneously forms the architecture of the exhibition space and is elaborately presented as a series of intimate domestic rooms which lead the visitor via a street-like route to another series of more open work rooms. The parallel is clear, if perhaps a little too literal, and has the effect of enclosing the exhibition within several relatively small rooms. Even the biggest rooms are themselves subdivisions of a museum wing which would only be able to convey a true impression of an urban space if it were presented as the open space that it really is.

By contrast, the publication accompanying the exhibition succeeds in its aim of projecting a lively image. After opening the cover which, with its detail of Mondrian's 1921 *Lozenge Composition with Yellow, Black, Blue, Red, and Gray* deliberately plays on the familiarity of rectangular relationships and primary colours, the reader is surprised by two photos which set the tone for the rest of the publication: 'Cheerful group near the shop selling artists' requisites in the alleyway behind Café du Dôme, after closing time. Mondrian second from the right, photographed in August 1926' and 'The germ of the Dada movement is released from a rubbish bin at the Conference of Constructivists and Dadaists in Wei

mar in September 1922. In the centre are Nelly van Doesburg, Cornelis van Eesteren (with stick) and Theo van Doesburg'. Yet this does not imply a naive idea of a jolly and cohesive group: from the start, the book does not shy away from the confrontations and the frictions which were partly responsible for the innovative power that characterised De Stijl. The book characterises De Stijl as a lively discussion between artists, architects and designers, and begins with the request by the collector Helene Kröller-Müller in 1916 to Bart van der Leck to suggest a colour design for the furnished 'art room' ('Kunstkamer') designed by the architect H.P. Berlage on her Groot Haesebroeck estate in Wassenaar. The collaboration failed because of differing views, but the conflict did result a year later in a manifesto published by Van der Leck in the first issue of the journal *De Stijl*. The publication is a concatenation of these kinds of events: the text is made up of fragmented storylines strung together on a series of meetings between 1916 and 1939, the latter being the year of the Dutch contribution to the World Exhibition in New York. In this article, De Stijl is described as a high point of Dutch art in the modern period and as an element of the reforming tradition of community art which has meaning for the future. At the same

Piet Mondrian, *Composition with Large Red Plane, Yellow, Black, Grey and Blue*, 1921, oil on canvas, 59.5 x 59.5 cm. Collection Gemeentemuseum Den Haag © 2007 Mondrian/ Holtzman Trust c/o HCR International, Warrenton (VA, USA).

time, the publication almost playfully contradicts the expectation of 'The story of De Stijl' which is evoked by the title, with its fragmentary structure reinforcing the affinity with Dadaism. The book enjoys this ambiguity and takes time to explore how Van Doesburg and Kurt Schwitters felt about the relationship between Dadaism and Neo-plasticism.

While the book and its fragmentary narrative come to an end in 1939, the exhibition also highlights the influence of De Stijl on later artists, architects and designers. The final rooms contain work by Wim Sinemus, Constant, Donald Judd, Imi Knoebel and Piet Hein Eek. This is a limited selection which could have been very different, and precisely because of that it is a selection which, like the book, holds out the promise of more.

LUT PIL
Translated by Julian Ross

- *Mondrian & De Stijl*, until January 1st, 2014, Gemeentemuseum Den Haag, www.gemeentemuseum.nl.
- HANS JANSSEN, MICHAEL WHITE, *The Story of De Stijl. Mondrian to Van Doesburg*, Gemeentemuseum Den Haag & Ludion, Antwerp, 2011, 267 p.

Closed yet Close By
The Royal Museum for Fine Arts in Antwerp

A number of large museums in the Low Countries are in scaffolding at present. In Amsterdam work has been going on for years on the *Rijksmuseum* and the *Stedelijk Museum*. Now the Royal Museum for Fine Arts in Antwerp has also closed its doors for extensive alterations. The three museums are housed in buildings that date from the end of the nineteenth century and urgently need to be modernised to the standards appropriate for a museum of the twenty-first century.

The renovation of the Museum for Fine Arts in Antwerp will take at least six years, and it is hoped that it will be able to reopen in 2017. That it will take so long is due, of course, to the far-reaching nature of the work needed, but also to the fact that the majority of the works of art will remain in storage in the museum, so that people will have to take care how they go about things.

However some six hundred works of art are being transferred to other locations. The museum management has devised a programme: "Closed yet close by", with which they wish to indicate that although the museum is closed at present, the collection is still accessible. The works of art are going to other locations where they will supplement other collections or where they will form part of temporary exhibitions.

A first batch of paintings left the museum as early as the end of 2009 to return to the place they were originally made for: Antwerp Cathedral. A great many altarpieces were taken from the cathedral during the period of the French Revolution and placed in various museums. Eight of these altarpieces, including work by Quinten Metsijs and Peter Paul Rubens, which currently form part of the collection of the Museum for Fine Arts, now hang again in the place where they hung until the end of the eighteenth century. The original intention was that the exhibition would be dismantled at the end of 2009, but because the museum was being closed anyway the canvasses will continue to hang there until 2017.

Important nineteenth and twentieth century works from the Royal Museum for Fine Arts are displayed in the exhibition "De Modernen. Topstukken uit het Koninklijk Museum" (The Moderns. Highlights from the Royal Museum). The museum has about 5,000 works from this period and some of them are exhibited in the restored Fabiolazaal in the centre of the city. Modigliani, Botero, Chagall, Degas, Magritte, these are just a few of the names the organizers can draw on for various exhibitions. A first exhibition closed its doors on 8 January this year, but there are still partial exhibitions to come dealing with art in the Netherlands, abstract art, Constant Permeke and further trends in contemporary art.

The Museum aan de Stroom (MAS), which is housed in a striking new building, opened its doors in Antwerp on 17 May 2011. Such a short time ago, yet already it has become the most visited museum in Belgium. For the opening exhibition MAS drew on key works from three important museums in Antwerp, including the Royal Museum for Fine Arts. Through the works the exhibition sketches the evolution of the culture of images from the Middle Ages to the present day. The Royal Museum for Fine Arts provided masterpieces by the Flemish Primitives, as well as genre paintings and works of art by Rubens and his contemporaries. This exhibition is open for visits until the end of 2012.

In Lier, a small town some twenty kilometres from Antwerp, the "Bruegelland" exhibition will be on show throughout the period that the Royal Museum is closed. Its main theme is the folk tradition in Flemish and Dutch art from the time of the sons of Pieter Bruegel the Elder. Painters such as Adriaen van Ostade, David Teniers and Jan Steen interpreted the Bruegel-like fair and ale-house scenes in their own manner. In the 18th and 19th centuries artists such as Ferdinand De Braekeleer and Jan Josef Horemans followed in Bruegel's footsteps with folksy subjects, and at the beginning of the twentieth century the Flemish Expressionists in their turn discovered Bruegel all over again. Artists such as Constant

Anthony van Dyck, *Portrait of a Man*, around 1619, oil on canvas, 119 x 126 cm. This painting is going on long loan to the Worcester Art Museum in Massachusetts, USA. © Royal Museum for Fine Arts, Antwerp.

Permeke, Gustave De Smet and Gustave Van de Woestyne breathed new life into his rustic scenes. The Royal Museum for Fine Arts lent the City Museum of Lier a hundred or so works for this purpose. The focus of the exhibition changes every six months so that visitors can keep finding new emphases. "Bruegelland" will run to the end of 2017.

Thanks to a gift from a collector in Antwerp in 1989 the Royal Museum for Fine Arts came into possession of 13 paintings, 36 drawings and watercolours and 8 sculptures by Rik Wouters. The Antwerp Museum now has a total of 109 works by this talented painter and sculptor, who died in 1916 at the age of thirty three. During the alterations to the Royal Museum for Fine Arts this rich collection is going to Mechelen, where Rik Wouters was born. Until the end of 2017 the Schepenhuis Museum there is being transformed into a veritable Wouters museum, where the

Rik Wouters, *Rik with a Black Eye-Patch*, 1915, oil on canvas, 102 x 85 cm. This painting is part of the Wouters collection that is temporarily going to Mechelen, where the painter was born. © Lukas – Art in Flanders vzw / Sabam Belgium 2012.

under the best conditions. The old nineteenth-century building will have been restored to its full glory by then, but the interior will have been extended and adapted to suit the needs of a museum in the 21st century. It will be a new magnet to draw people to Antwerp.

DIRK VAN ASSCHE
Translated by Sheila M. Dale

http://www.kmska.be/en/

collection from the Royal Museum will be supplemented by works from the Mechelen City Museums. The intention is to put the spotlight on a different aspect of Wouters' work every year.

In addition to these lengthy exhibition projects some works are being lent by the museum for a specific period to museums both at home and abroad. For example, Anthony van Dyck's "Portrait of a Man" is going on long loan to the famous Worcester Art Museum in the American state of Massachusetts, where it will also undergo restoration. Works are going to Zürich and Mexico City too. Work by James Ensor, of which the Royal Museum for fine Arts has the largest collection in the world, is travelling to Silkeborg, in Denmark, among other places, but especially to Japan, where the exhibition "Ensor in Context", which was shown in Brussels in 2010, will be on display in five different museums from April 2012 to March 2013.

If everything goes according to plan, all of these works will come back in the course of 2017 to a fully renovated and enlarged museum, where they will be exhibited to the public at large

A Twenty-Year Long Success Story
Museum De Pont in Tilburg

Whereas the city, regional and national museums in the Netherlands are going through hard times now that the government is carrying out large cuts to culture, the situation is different for museums that have resources of their own. Independent museums such as Beelden aan Zee in Scheveningen, De Buitenplaats in Eelde, in the province of Groningen, Singer in Laren (Noord-Holland), Panorama Mesdag in The Hague or Beeldengalerij Het Depot in Wageningen have been proving for years that they can put on an attractive show for their benefactor (often the person who founded the collection or provided the basis for it) with relatively small means.

To the examples named above can be added the De Pont Museum in Tilburg. The museum is named after Jan de Pont, an entrepreneur who originally came from Brabant, who left part of his fortune to three worthy causes, one of which had to be art. De Pont has a small jubilee to celebrate: in 2012 it will have existed for twenty years. In itself a twentieth anniversary is not so exceptional, of course, especially as there are other much older private museums that have remained independent from the government. But De Pont is definitely a maverick in other ways. With its consistent choice of contemporary art, which until the 1980s was exhibited almost exclusively in the famous national museums (the Stedelijk Museum in Amsterdam, Boijmans van Beuningen in Rotterdam and Van Abbe in Eindhoven), De Pont scores surprisingly well. The 65,000 or so visitors come not only from Tilburg and the surrounding area, but equally often from elsewhere in the country. Moreover, the museum also attracts visitors from abroad. These are nice figures, but the museum is even more pleased with the fact that its consistent acquisitions and exhibition policy stands it in good stead with internationally renowned artists; such good stead that they are more than willing to have their work displayed there.

Those who criticise that the museum is treading "well-worn paths" are overlooking the fact that in the 90s De Pont was the first Dutch museum to exhibit a number of names that have since become well-known. De Pont got in early with Luc Tuymans, for example, in 1995 – and not by Dutch standards alone. In the previous year the Belgian painter had been preceded by Jeff Wall and Roni Horn. The Tilburg museum was also the only place in the

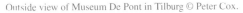

Outside view of Museum De Pont in Tilburg © Peter Cox.

Exhibition view of Giuseppe Penone at De Pont © Peter Cox

Netherlands to manage to devote a large exhibition to Rosemarie Trockel. Moreover, it quickly established one of the largest museum collections of work by Thomas Schütte. Those are names with a reputation that is directly linked to shows like Documenta in Kassel and the international biennales.

De Pont's selection policy has been consistent now for twenty years and that is mainly down to its director, Hendrik Driessen. He was already director of the museum when the decision had to be made about premises, a former wool-spinning mill built on the edge of the city centre of Tilburg just before the Second World War. Over the years, when making his selection, Driessen has taken into account where the works of art would be hung. Although the location has been radically changed by Benthem Crouwel Architects (who are also renovating the Stedelijk Museum and the Rijksmuseum in Amsterdam) to bring it into line with all the requirements of a modern museum, the industrial character of the former textile factory has not been obliterated. Large installations do well here because they have space in the vast rooms, as was already evidenced in 2011 at the Mark Wallinger exhibition. At the opposite end of the scale, work by Thierry De Cordier, Richard Serra and Marien Schouten, is shown to advantage in the cabinet-like wool stores.

Yet the industrial setting was not the deciding factor in going for these names. From the beginning Driessen sought his strength in limitations: no more than three large exhibitions in a year. The museum works with a permanent group of artists

that is slowly growing. The group of artists whose work is included in the collection consists of sixty or so names at present. Among these are artists such as Sigmar Polke and Marlene Dumas, whose earlier purchased works would now be unaffordable for the museum. So De Pont seems to collect with an eye to the future. Moreover, Driessen focuses on three different types of artist. There are those who continue the tradition, the artists who present themselves as anarchists and those who operate primarily as soloists, who cannot readily be assigned to a style or trend or be placed within a movement. In this way a varied permanent collection is being built up in which, above all, there is plenty of room for contrasts. This means you can confront the cerebral approach of Gerhard Merz with the "romantic" Richard Long, who looks for the controlling factor in nature in his landscape art. But also the work of a soloist such as Thierry De Cordier is thrown into relief by the anarchist Luc Tuymans (who, one must admit, can also be included in the two other categories). "Contrariness", an attitude that can sometimes cause an uneasy feeling, may well be the guideline to the De Pont policy. There are not many museums like this.

CEES STRAUS
Translated by Sheila M. Dale

www.depont.nl. In 2012 there are exhibitions of Ai Weiwei and Berlinde De Bruyckere, among others.

Contributors

Dirk Van Assche
Deputy Editor *Ons Erfdeel vzw*
dirkvanassche@onserfdeel.be

Martino Bidotti
Fashion Journalist
martino.bidotti@gmail.com

Derek Blyth
Journalist
derekblyth@lycos.com

Raf De Bont
Historian at the University of Leuven
Raf.DeBont@arts.kuleuven.be

Marja Bosma
Curator Central Museum Utrecht
mbosma@centraalmuseum.nl

Jos Bouveroux
Former Journalist
jos.bouveroux@telenet.be

Robin Briggs
Historian/Emeritus Fellow All Souls
College, Oxford
robin.briggs@all-souls.ox.ac.uk

Patrick Cornillie
Author
patrick.cornillie@skynet.be

Pieter Coupé
Secretary *Ons Erfdeel. Vlaams-
Nederlands cultureel tijdschrift*
onserfdeel@onserfdeel.be

Evelyne Coussens
Theatre Critic
evelynecoussens@gmail.com

Anneleen De Coux
Literary Critic
anneleendecoux@hotmail.com

Paul Depondt
Art Critic
paul.depondt@skynet.be

Luc Devoldere
Chief Editor *Ons Erfdeel vzw*
luc.devoldere@onserfdeel.be

Jeroen Dewulf
Professor of Dutch Studies at the
University of California, Berkeley
jdewulf@berkeley.edu

Lieve Dierckx
Dance Critic
lieve.dierckx@skynet.be

Max Dohle
Author
maxdohle@casema.nl

Stefanie van Gemert
PhD Candidate Comparative Literature,
University College London
svangemert@gmail.com

Amy Golahny
Professor of Art History at Lycoming
College Williamsport, Pennsylvania
golahny@lycoming.edu

Jaap Harskamp
Former Curator of the Dutch and Flemish
Collections in the British Library
jaapharskamp@btinternet.com

Arnold Heumakers
Author/Critic
heumakers@planet.nl

Tom Van Imschoot
Literary Critic/Editor
tom.vanimschoot@telenet.be

Joris van de Kerkhof
Journalist
Joris.van.de.Kerkhof@nos.nl→

Petra de Koning
Journalist
P.dekoning@nrc.nl

Anton Korteweg
Poet
antonkorteweg@planet.nl

Petri Leijdekkers
Art Critic
p.g.j.leijdekkers@gmail.com

Nop Maas
Literary Historian/Biographer
nop.maas@planet.nl

Erik Martens
Film Critic
eiae@telenet.be

Lutgard Mutsaers
Music Critic
lut@ision.nl

Jos Nijhof
Theatre Critic
nijhof@xs4all.nl

Willem Otterspeer
Professor of University History at Leiden
University
W.Otterspeer@BB.LeidenUniv.nl

Lut Pil
Art Historian at the University of Leuven
lut.pil@arts.kuleuven.be

Ewald Pironet
Journalist
ewald.pironet@gmail.com

Karel Porteman

Emeritus Professor of Dutch Literature
at the University of Leuven
karel.porteman@arts.kuleuven.be

Gert Jan Pos

Comic Critic
GPos@fondsbkvb.nl

Eric Rinckhout

Journalist/Art Critic
ericrinc@antwerpen.be

Marieke van Rooy

Architecture Historian
mvrooy@zonnet.nl

Reinier Salverda

Director Fryske Akademy
rsalverda@fryske-akademy.nl

Ruben Schalk

Historian at the University of Utrecht
r.schalk@uu.nl

Walter Simons

Professor of History, Dartmouth College,
Hanover, New Hampshire
Walter.P.Simons@Dartmouth.EDU

Cees Straus

Art Critic
cfstraus@hotmail.com

David Stroband

Art Critic
davidstroband1@versatel.nl

Hans Vanacker

Secretary *Septentrion. Arts, lettres et
culture de Flandre et des Pays-Bas*
septentrion@onserfdeel.be

Johan Vandenbroucke

Literary Critic/Bookseller
boeken@dezondvloed.be

Hans Vandeweghe

Journalist
hansvdw@telenet.be

Tomas Vanheste

Journalist
t.vanheste@kpnmail.nl

Marnix Verplancke

Critic
marnixverplancke@skynet.be

Hendrik Vos

Professor at the Centre of EU Studies,
Ghent University
hendrik.vos@ugent.be

David Winner

Author/Journalist
dswinn@yahoo.com

Karin Wolfs

Film Critic
mail@karinwolfs.nl

Translators

Gregory Ball
Pleuke Boyce
Sheila M. Dale
Lindsay Edwards
Chris Emery
Peter Flynn
Nancy Forest-Flier
Donald Gardner
Tanis Guest
John Irons
Yvette Mead
Julian Ross
Paul Vincent
Laura Watkinson

ADVISORS ON ENGLISH USAGE

Tanis Guest (United Kingdom)
Lindsay Edwards (Belgium)

Colophon

Association

This twentieth yearbook is published by the Flemish-Netherlands Association 'Ons Erfdeel vzw', with the support of the Dutch Ministry of Education, Culture and Science (The Hague), the Flemish Authorities (Brussels) and the Provinces of West and East Flanders.
The Association 'Ons Erfdeel vzw' also publishes the Dutch-language periodical *Ons Erfdeel* and the French-language periodical *Septentrion. Arts, lettres et culture de Flandre et des Pays-Bas,* the bilingual yearbook *De Franse Nederlanden – Les Pays-Bas Français* and a series of books in several languages covering various aspects of the culture of the Low Countries.

The Board of Directors of 'Ons Erfdeel vzw'

President:
Herman Balthazar

Managing Director:
Luc Devoldere

Directors:
Bert De Graeve
Mark Leysen
Marita Mathijsen
Frits van Oostrom
Danny De Raymaeker
Paul Schnabel
Adriaan van der Staay
Ludo Verhoeven

Honorary President:
Philip Houben

Address of the Editorial Board and the Administration

'Ons Erfdeel vzw', Murissonstraat 260,
8930 Rekkem, Flanders, Belgium
T +32 56 41 12 01, F +32 56 41 47 07
www.onserfdeel.be, www.onserfdeel.nl
thelowcountriesblog.onserfdeel.be
VAT BE 0410.723.635

Kevin Vandenbussche *Head of Administration*
Adinda Houttekier *Administrative Secretary*

Aims

With *The Low Countries,* a yearbook founded by Jozef Deleu (Chief Editor from 1993 until 2002), the editors and publisher aim to present to the world the culture and society of the Dutch-speaking area which embraces both the Netherlands and also Flanders, the northern part of Belgium.

The articles in this yearbook survey the living, contemporary culture of the Low Countries as well as their cultural heritage. In its words and pictures *The Low Countries* provides information about literature and the arts, but also about broad social and historical developments in Flanders and the Netherlands.

The culture of Flanders and the Netherlands is not an isolated phenomenon; its development over the centuries has been one of continuous interaction with the outside world. In consequence the yearbook also pays due attention to the centuries-old continuing cultural interplay between the Low Countries and the world beyond their borders.

By drawing attention to the diversity, vitality and international dimension of the culture of Flanders and the Netherlands, *The Low Countries* hopes to contribute to a lively dialogue between differing cultures.

ISSN 0779-5815
ISBN 978-90-79705-115
Statutory deposit no. D/2012/3006/3
NUR 612

Copyright © 2012 'Ons Erfdeel vzw' and SABAM Belgium 2012
Printed by Die Keure, Bruges, Flanders, Belgium
Design by Luc De Meyer and Henk Linskens (Die Keure)

All rights reserved. No-part-of this publication may be reproduced in any form without the prior permission of the copyright holder.

Prices for the yearbook 2012, no. 20

Belgium € 37, The Netherlands € 39, Europe € 39

Other Countries: € 45
All prices inclusive of shipping costs

**As well as the yearbook
The Low Countries,
the Flemish Netherlands
Association 'Ons Erfdeel vzw'
publishes a number of books
covering various aspects of
the culture of Flanders and
the Netherlands.**

Wim Daniëls
Talking Dutch.
Illustrated; 80 pp.

J.A. Kossmann-Putto &
E.H. Kossmann
*The Low Countries.
History of the Northern
and Southern Netherlands.*
Illustrated; 64 pp.

Isabella Lanz &
Katie Verstockt,
*Contemporary Dance
in the Low Countries.*
Illustrated; 128 pp.

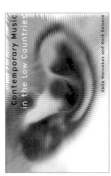

Mark Delaere &
Emile Wennekes,
*Contemporary Music in
the Low Countries.*
Illustrated; 128 pp.

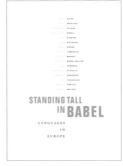

*Standing Tall in Babel.
Languages in Europe.*
Sixteen European writers
about their mother tongues.
Hardcover; 144 pp.

Between 1993 and 2011
the first nineteen issues
of the yearbook *The Low
Countries* were published.

20 years **TLC**

Politics
Language
Literature
Fashion
Film and theatre

Visual arts
Science
Music
Society
History

EUROPE

NORTH
SEA

GRONINGEN
• Groningen
Leeuwarden •
FRIESLAND
Assen •
DRENTHE

**NORTH
HOLLAND**

FLEVOLAND
Lelystad •
Haarlem •
• Zwolle
AMSTERDAM
OVERIJSSEL
Utrecht •
The Hague •
UTRECHT
GELDERLAND
**SOUTH
HOLLAND**
Arnhem •

's-Hertogenbosch •
ZEELAND
Middelburg •
NORTH BRABANT
LIMBURG

Antwerp •
ANTWERP
Bruges •
LIMBURG
**WEST
FLANDERS**
• Ghent
FLEMISH BRABANT •
Hasselt •
GERMANY
**EAST
FLANDERS**
BRUSSELS ◉
• Leuven
Maastricht •

• Wavre
WALLOON BRABANT
• Liège
HAINAUT
Namur •
LIÈGE
Mons •
NAMUR
FRANCE

LUXEMBOURG

LUX.
Arlon •

0   km   50

© Carto

▨	DUTCH LANGUAGE-AREA
☐	FRENCH LANGUAGE-AREA IN BELGIUM
▥	BRUSSELS BILINGUAL AREA :
▧	DUTCH AND FRENCH GERMAN LANGUAGE AREA : IN BELGIUM
▨	BILINGUAL AREA : DUTCH AND FRISIAN
◉	CAPITAL CITY
•	PROVINCIAL CAPITAL
—	NATIONAL FRONTIER
⋯⋯	PROVINCIAL BOUNDARY